The Dog ENCYCLOPEDIA

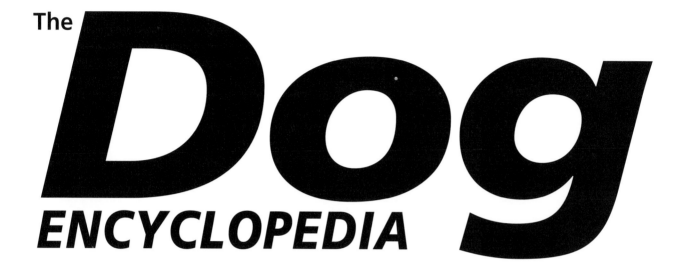

The Dog ENCYCLOPEDIA

Tome 1

ANIWA PUBLISHING

ROYAL CANIN

Adaptations:

German :
   Translations   K. Ayche, C. Belakhdar, B. Janka, A. Lucke, V. Matyssek, E. Moser, M. Neumann, B. Sallegger, S. Schmidt-Wussow, U. Wapler,
                    P. Warnier-Kofler, R. Xanthopoulos.
   Layout   Magali Barrailler, Vania Soraru, Nathalie Courdent, Irina Azvedo-Tadieu, Joël Chapuis, Sabrina Monchi
   Rewriting   Kathrin Busch-Kschiewan, Nadja Hultsch, Sonja Zabel, Ursula Zabel
English :
   Translations   Diane Dinsmore, Julie Plounick, Chart Voss, Andrene Everson.
   Layout   Catherine Naas
   Rewriting   Roy Herridge, Emmanuel Pacitto, Anne Karpoff
Brazilian :
   Translations   S. Artamonoff, B. Delevallee, M. D'Orey de Faria, L. Goncalves, B. Magne, E. Rio Branco, M. Rosemberg, Madame Antunes.
   Layout   Florbela Lourenço Pires, Joël Chapuis, Irina Azvedo-Tadieu, Nathalie Courdent, Sabrina Monchi
   Rewriting   Claude Mouette, Yves Micelli, Valeria Cardoso de Melo Carvalho
Chinese :   Royal Canin Chine / François Gergaud
Spanish :
   Translations   Maria-Claudia Filgueira, Carles Sanchez
   Layout   Isabelle Riener
   Rewriting   Marie-Pierre Ellie, Maria-Claudia Filgueira
Italian :
   Translations   B. Baldi, D. Benigni, G. Conollo, D. De Leo, L. De Berardinis, L. Desotgiu, V. Fucci, C. Galimberti, S. Guazzoni, R. Kohn,
                    P. Mequin, A.-M. Negrerte, A. Sudano, C. Torossi Bovo.
   Layout   Sabrina Monchi, Vania Soraru, Irina Azvedo-Tadieu, Nathalie Courdent, Joël Chapuis
   Rewriting   Franco Rapetti, Luca Bussolati
Netherlands :
   Translations   C. Boerhigter, K. Desmarsevers, A. Detelder, C. Dijkman, A. Frehen-Asures, B. Raemaekers, A. Scherpbier, P. Smift, M. Van Den
                    Berg, B. Van Oosterhout, M. Van Zanten.
   Layout   Nathalie Courdent.
   Rewriting   Muriel Jacqmin, Cécile Devroy, Bastiaan Rohrer & The team Royal Canin Nederland b.v.
Swedish :
   Translations   A. Brantley, H. Hellberg, M. Jarvelin, R. Johansson, S. Jonsson, H. Karlson, J. Lindberg, U. Lundquist, M. Persson, S. Petersson,
                    B. Sandstrom, C. Wallen, M. Vikberg.
   Layout   Joël Chapuis, Irina Azvedo-Tadieu.
   Rewriting   Bo Edoff, Anne-Catherine Edoff, Susanne Hellman, Ronan Mage, Hanna Edoff, Maud Dickson, Elisabeth Raab-Alvarson, Carin
                    Lyrholm, Leg. Vet. Katarina Bewig, Wilhelm Dufwa, Ninni Hjortvall, Siw & Charles de Windle, Leg. Vet. Monica Stavenborn

This book is also available in French.

Coordination Royal Canin: Catherine Legros
Project Editors: Diffomédia / Paris
Art Director: Guy Rolland
Coordination: Béatrice Fortamps, Marie-Édith Baret
Illustrations: Agnès Pezon
Cover: Teckel, Épagneul breton, Berger allemand - © F. Nicaise & Dogue Allemand - © Ch. Renner

© 2000 First edition in French

© 2001 Aniwa SA

Publisher Aniwa Publishing
10, rue du Colisée - F.-75008 - Paris
Tél. : + 33 (0) 1 44 95 02 20 Fax : + 33 (0) 1 44 95 02 22
www.aniwa.com

ISBN : 2-7476-0003-3

Printed in EEC by Italia Media Industries / G. Parmigiani

Contributors

SCIENTIFIC DIRECTION

PROFESSOR DOMINIQUE GRANDJEAN
Department of Breeding and Sport Medicine (UMES)
Alfort National School of Veterinary Medicine
Main author and scientific coordinator

JOSÉE AND JEAN-PIERRE VAISSAIRE,
Doctors of Veterinary Medicine, France

AND IN ALPHABETICAL ORDER

Karine Alves, veterinarian, Department of Breeding and Sport Medicine, Alfort National School of Veterinary Medicine, France
Hélène Bacqué, Digest of Veterinary Medicine, France
René Bailly, Doctor of Veterinary Medicine, President of the National Union of Free Exercise Veterinarians
Vincent Biourge, Doctor of Veterinary Medicine, Royal Canin Research Center, France
Mark Bloomerg (†), Doctor of Veterinary Medicine, Professor at the University of Florida, Gainesville, USA
Monique Bourdin, Doctor of Veterinary Medicine, Behavior Consultant, Alfort National School of Veterinary Medicine, France
Brigitte Bullard-Cordeau, animal journalist, Editor-in-Chief of *Animal Junior*, France
Eliane Chatelain, Doctor of Veterinary Medicine, Professor at the School of Veterinary Medicine of Lyon, Department of Anatomy
Jean-François Courreau, Doctor of Veterinary Medicine, Professor of Zootechnology, Alfort National School of Veterinary Medicine, France
Fabrice Crépin, Doctor of Veterinary Medicine, Royal Canin
Fathi Driss, Doctor of Sciencs, Professor of Nutrition, Université René-Descartes, Paris V, France
Milette Dujardin, Royal Canin, France
Catherine Escriou, Doctor of Veterinary Medicine, Researcher at the Neurological Laboratory, Alfort National School of Veterinary Medicine, France
Jean-Louis Esquivié, Commanding General, National Gendarmerie School, France
Vanessa Fuks, Doctor of Veterinary Medicine, Department of Breeding and Sport Medicine, Alfort National School of Veterinary Medicine, France
Aude-Gaëlle Heitzman-Béné, Doctor of Veterinary Medicine, Dept of Breeding and Sport Medicine, Alfort National School of Veterinary Medicine, France
Petra Horvatic-Peer, Doctor of Veterinary Medicine, University of Vienna, Austria
Ann Hudson, Royal Canin, USA
Elen Kienzle, Doctor of Veterinary Medicine, Professor of Nutrition, University of Munich, Germany
David Kronfeld, Doctor of Veterinary Medicine, Professor of Physiology, Virginia Tech, Blacksburg, USA
Henri Lagarde, CEO, Royal Canin, France
Dominique Lebrun, Royal Canin, France
Nathalie Moquet, Veterinarian, Department of Breeding and Sport Medicine, Alfort National School of Veterinary Medicine, France
Robert Moraillon, Doctor of Veterinary Medicine, Alfort National School of Veterinary Medicine, France
Nicolas Nudelmann, Doctor of Veterinary Medicine, Professor of Reproductive Pathology, Alfort National School of Veterinary Medicine, France
Bernard Paragon, Doctor of Veterinary Medicine, Professor of Nutrition, Alfort National School of Veterinary Medicine, France
Sandrine Pawlowiecz, Veterinarian, Department of Breeding and Sport Medicine, Alfort National School of Veterinary Medicine, France
Jacques Philip, Fairbanks, Alaska, USA
Pascale Pibot, Doctor of Veterinary Medicine, Royal Canin Research Center, France
Jacques Pidoux, Royal Canin, U.K.
Philippe Pierson, Doctor of Veterinary Medicine, Royal Canin
Bruno Polack, Doctor of Veterinary Medicine, Professor of Parasitology, Alfort National School of Veterinary Medicine, France
Jean-Marc Poupard, Researcher at the Laboratoire de biosociologie animale et comparée, University of Paris-Sorbonne, France
Jean-Pierre Samaille, Doctor of Veterinary Medicine, Editor-in-Chief of L'Action vétérinaire, France
Renaud Sergheraert, Director of the Royal Canin Research Center, France
Adolfo Spektor, Doctor of Veterinary Medicine, international judge
Helena Spektor, international judge, Royal Canin, Argentina
Florence Tessier, Royal Canin, France
Anne-Karen Tourtebatte, Veterinarian, Department of Breeding and Sport Medicine, Alfort National School of Veterinary Medicine, France
Jérôme Vanek, Doctor of Veterinary Medicine, University of Minnesota, St. Paul, Minnesota, USA
Pierre Wagner, Royal Canin, USA

Publishing Managment

BERNARDO GALLITELLI
Chairman and Chief Executive Officer
Aniwa S.A.

GUY ROLLAND
Aniwa Publishing

MARIE-PIERRE ELLIE
Aniwa Translating

FROM KNOWLEDGE COMES PRECISION...
...FROM PASSION COMES KNOWLEDGE

"Mankind's real moral test,
a test so radical and so deep that it escapes our gaze,
is probably the one of its relations with those that are the most at its mercy: the animals".
MILAN KUNDERA

MAN IS SUCH that he can't help bringing everything back to himself, comparing everything with himself, with his own condition, sometimes ending up treating his dog like a human being, or even a child.
And yet, true respect for the dog, like for any human being, does not lie there!

It has to do with each of us becoming aware of the real identity of the canine species. A morphological, biological identity and, of course, a psychological and behavioral identity, highly complex thanks to an animality that has adapted to man over the centuries.

Therefore, respecting the dog means respecting both the original prehistoric animal, and the modern animal, the fruit of a zoological evolution that has been wanted and conducted by man.

The prehistoric animal was above all a pack animal, obeying a precise hierarchy, both instinctive and imposed upon, within this pack, a source of efficiency in its struggle for survival.

The modern animal has retained, in the depth of its true nature, the same need for hierarchical integration, and it has indeed integrated, with a fantastic adaptability, into all forms of human societies and civilizations.

The dog is a social and hierarchical animal; it expects from its master the coherence, the consistency and the same respect that its ancestors found in the hierarchy of the pack.

Respecting the animal means first respecting its true biological and psychological needs.

Such an approach is possible only if it is based on the understanding, analysis and synthesis of our knowledge of the canine species.

And from knowledge comes competence, precision.

A specialist in canine high nutrition, Royal Canin pioneered the taking into account of the exceptional diversity of the canine species, and of the consequences of this diversity as regards nutrition, as early as in 1980 with the large-breed puppy food (AGR), and in a comprehensive and global manner in 1997 with Size.

Indeed, of all the animal species to be found on earth, the dog is undoubtedly one of the most diversified ones. Not only may its adult size vary from 1 to over 90 kg, but also one now knows that small, medium and large breeds have neither the same life expectancy (8/9 years in large breeds, 14/15 in small breeds), nor the same length of growth, nor the same number of puppies per litter (1 to 3 in small breeds, 8 or even 12 in large breeds). Moreover, one knows now that there are fundamental physiological differences, depending on the breeds' size and format. Thus, for instance, the digestive tract of a large breed dog accounts for only 2.8% of its total weight, as against 7% in a small-sized dog, which explains many digestive, bone, biological problems left unsolved for a long time.

This consideration led us to propose from now on, for example for Maxi Giant Breed (between 45 kg and 90 kg) (99.5-198.5 lb)a totally specific diet;
- Giant kibbles to encourage the dog to chew, salivate and slowly ingest to favour a better digestion.
- A kibble with maximum digestibility enriched with Vit. E, chondroitine, …

At the same time, the scientific advances of the last few years have led us to go beyond the two traditional roles of nutrition (on the one hand, build and maintain the body, and on the other hand, supply energy), in order to integrate a third dimension: prevention.

It's the birth of nutrition-health, which will be the nutrition of the 21st century, combining pleasure with health.

Nurtured on the considerable passion, knowledge and scientific precision of the teams at Royal Canin and at the Alfort National School of Veterinary Medecine, the edition of this encyclopedia represents a decisive step in and a radical upgrading of the approach to knowledge of the canine species: from now on, the evolution of the nutritional approach is dependent on the dog's size considered as a fundamental element.

This encyclopedia is also the expression of all the contributors' commitment to a rational and not exclusively emotional vision of the relations that must prevail between man and this fascinating animal.

It is no accident that it has been carried out under the supervision of Professor Dominique Grandjean: this is the fruit of a long and productive scientific collaboration between the Research Center of the Royal Canin company and the teams of the State Veterinary School of Alfort, especially that of the Breeding and Sports Medicine Unit (UMES).

This is also the result of a tradition of intense scientific partnership with researchers and institutes all over the world, in Europe, in the United States and in South America.

May they all be thanked.

HENRI LAGARDE
Chairman and Chief Executive Officer
Royal Canin Group

Notice

Even if excuses may be found, assimilating the dog to a small human being is a biological mistake, which can be dangerous for the animal.

Respecting the dog in what he it brings us and represents for us, should not consist in developing an anthropomorphic approach, aiming at turning him into "a child who cannot talk", as you can often hear it. Biology created the diversity of the living beings, making of each species the complement of the others, thus reaching a frail and unsteady balance, which Man must alter in no way.

Therefore, this anthropomorphic reflex, although it can be understood considering the strong feelings we bear to our dogs, should be banned. It does not respect the biological and physiological functioning of the dog, and is consequently dangerous for it.

The best examples of this reality can be found in the field of alimentation:

- Man can change his alimentation at each meal without any problem... but if his digestive tract were identical to that of the dog, this permanently changing alimentation would cause him to suffer from constant diarrhoea!
- Man needs cooking, salt, sugar, aromas, the appearance of his plate to enjoy is meal, but if his senses were those of the dog, he would only need the odours to fully enjoy it...
- Man has been able to take his time to have his lunch without the fear of being the prey of some predators, but if he were a dog, he would have kept the reflex of eating quickly. Indeed, any animal, which is likely to have its food stolen by another, or to be attacked, will eat quickly...

Dogs are dogs, no matter what some may think, and it must be appreciated, treated and respected as such. Science and knowledge back up these facts, if you refer to the above-mentioned examples.

Digestion is a typical example of reactions and mechanisms specific to each species. Making an amalgam could be dangerous for the dog (or the man), as the differences are very obvious, and the behaviours opposed.

Following the food inside the organism enables to better understand these essential notions.

Thus, in a general way, the digetive apparatus of Man represents 10% of his body weight, against 2.7 from 7% in dogs, according to their size. You can already understand why it is easier for Man to digest more varied food.

Enjoying the food: the sense of smell and taste do not have the same roles

Dog, unlike Man, mostly enjoys his food through his sense of smell. The surface of its olfactory mucous is, according to the breed, from 10 to 100 more spread than that of Man. A German Shepherd's nose, for instance, contains 200 million olfactory captors, whereas a Man's nose will contain no more than 20 millions.

Unlike what most people think, taste plays a very little part in the choice of the food by dogs. While Man claims 9000 "gustative buds", dogs have from 6 to 8 times less. Besides, once the food is in a dog's mouth, it does not linger in it and rushes towards the stomach.

Predigestion of food: from the mouth to the stomach

Dogs do not chew their food, they swallow it, whereas Man prepares his for digestion by prolonged mastication - thus liberating aromas and causing pleasure – which squashes the food and, by mixing them with saliva, is the beginning of the digestion process via the enzymes contained in the latter. On the contrary, for dogs, it is in the stomach that the digestive process really begins.

The scientific truth is here to demonstrate it yet again: the stomach represents 2/3 of the total weight of the digestive apparatus in dogs, against only 1/10 in humans.

The very high acid rate of the stomach's pH, related to the great amount of hydrochloric acid (6 times more than in humans), gives a very good idea of the purifying role held by the stomach in dogs. It gives them an extraordinary efficient natural barrier against digestive infections.

DIFFERENCES BETWENN DOGS AND MEN

	DOGS		MEN
	Mini	Giant	
Adult Average Weight	1 to 10	45 to 100	60 to 80
Relative Weight digestive tract/ body weight	**7%**	**2.7%**	**10 to 11%**
Life expectancy	16 years	8 years	75 years
Number of young per litter	1 to 4	6 to 10	-
Length of gestation	58 to 63 days		9 months

ODOUR

	DOGS		MEN
Surface of olfactory mucosa	25 to 250 cm^2		2 to 3 cm^2
Number of olfactory cells (receptors)	67 millions (Cocker) to 200 millions (German Shepherd)		5 to 20 millions

TASTE

	DOGS		MEN
Number of gustatory receptors	1706 buds		9000 buds
Dentition	42 teeth, very reduced mastication phase		32 teeth, long mastication

STOMACH

	DOGS		MEN
Weight of stomach/ weight of digestive tract	62%		10 to 15%
Hydrochloric acid in stomach	6 times more than in Men		1
Gastric pH in a faste state	1 to 2		2 to 4
Presence of digestive enzymes in saliva	no		yes

INTESTINE

	Mini	Giant	MEN
Length intestine/body	X7	X6	X10
Length of small intestine	1.6 to 6 m		6 to 6.5m
Intestinal flora	Targeted		wider specter
Bacteria per gram of content inside the colon	10.000		100.000
Gastric enzyme digestion (volume of pancreatic juice secreted)	2.4g/kg of weight/d		11.4g/kg of weight/d
Length of total digestive transit	12 to 30 hours		30 to 48 hours

DIVERSE

	Mini	Giant	MEN
Length of growth	10 months	18 to 24 months	16 years
Ratio adult weight/ birth weight	X20	X100	X20
Length of meal	3 min to - 1 min for 100 gr of dry food ingested		1 hour
Daily energy requirement (kcal/j	130 to 750	2300 to 4000	200 to 2500 kcal/j
Range of vibrations perceived by the ear	2.5 X more than Men		1
Life expectancy of hairs	1 year		2 to 7 years

Digestive performance: inherited from genes

Long ago, dogs used to live in packs, and it was of prime importance to them to be able to digest their prey rapidly and be able to get as much nutritive elements from it as possible. That explains why the digestive transit is very rapid in dogs comparatively to humans (12 to 24 hours against 30 to 48 hours).
The intestinal flora in dogs is very close-targeted, contrary to what it is in a total omnivore such as a human. Indeed, humans must be able to adapt to a wide variety of meats, vegetable, fruit…thus, they have an intestinal bacterial flora 1000 times more dense than dogs do!

To understand such elements, which can be looked at from other levels in biological functions, is to understand and accept that dogs are very different from humans, not just in their appearance or because of the fact that they cannot "talk". The sometimes extreme anthropomorphism, the kind of which can be publicised in films for instance, is not only scientifically unacceptable, but is also highly detrimental, and can even reduce the animal's life expectancy.

Summary

List of breeds

NB:
Many countries have forbidden ear-cropping and/or tail-cutting in dogs.

Photo Credits

All photos in this Encyclopedia are from the Cogis photo archives:

Francais, Garguil, Gauzargues, Gehlmar, Gelhar, Gengoux, Grissey, Hermeline, Ingeborg, Labat, Lanceau, Lepage, Lili, Nicaise, Potier, Remy, Rocher, Schwartz, Seitre, Varin, Vedie, Vidal, Willy's, Zizola.
Except:
- *Photos by Yann Arthus-Bertrand appear on the following pages:*
37, 40, 43, 47, 48, 49, 57, 59, 60, 65, 68, 70, 71, 72, 80, 81, 85, 87, 88, 95, 97, 98, 99, 101, 106, 108, 111, 112, 114, 115, 118.
- *Photos from the Royal Canin archives: Philippe Psaïla, Jean-Pierre Lenfant et Yves Renner*
- *Illustrations provided by museums and private institutes specializing in art or historical*
photos are clearly referenced in the captions of the illustrations.
- *UMES : 144, 146, 147, 148, 149, 152, 153, 154, 155, 162.*
- *Agence Giraudon, Paris: 11, 122, 123, 127, 129.*
- *Photographie Selva, Paris: 17, 124, 126, 128, 132, 133, 135, 137, 141, 142, 166*
- *Kharbine-Tababor, Paris: 24, 25, 134, 135, 140, 145, 161, 165.*

*Diana
The Huntress.
School of
Fontainbleau
(France). Paris,
Musée du Louvre.
Giraudon coll.*

Part 1

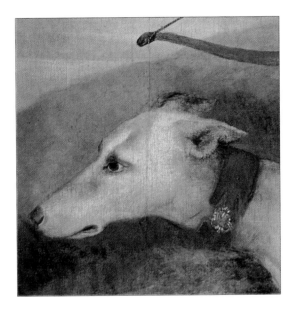

Yesterday to Today

Dog Breeds

Origin and Evolution of the Dog

When we consider that Earth is approximately 4.5 billion years old, and that the first mammals appeared one hundred million years ago, and the first dogs fifty million years ago, the appearance of early man a mere three million years ago seems quite recent. If the history of Earth were recorded on a kilometer measure, mammals would appear only on the last few meters and dogs the last few centimeters!

Origin of Canids

Canids are mammals characterized by pointed canines (developed for an omnivorous diet) and a skeleton built for a mode of walking or running called digitigrade (walking on the toes without the heels touching the ground).

They belong to the Carnivora order, which developed in the early Tertiary Era in ecological niches abandoned by large reptiles that disappeared at the end of the Mesozoic Era.

At that time, they began to spread throughout North America and diversify with the appearance of a Carnivora family—Miacidae—which resembled the modern-day weasel. Miacids (a family which included forty-two different genera) flourished forty million years ago; today, only sixteen genera remain. The modern Canid family includes three sub-families: Cuoninae (Lycaon), Otocyoninae (South African Otocyon), and Caninae (dog, wolf, fox, jackal, coyote).

Evolution of Canids

Canids gradually replaced Miacids, giving rise to the *Hesperocyon* genus, which was very common approximately thirty-five million years ago. Their skull and toes showed skeletal and dental features similar to those of modern-day wolves, dogs, and foxes, indicating a direct link to these early carnivores.

During the Miocene, the *Phlaocyon* genus appeared. It is thought to have resembled a raccoon. The teeth of the *Mesocyon* genus, which also developed at that time, were similar to those of modern dogs.

The body profile of Canids evolved through the *Cynodesmus* (which looked like a coyote), the *Tomarctus*, and the *Leptocyon*, gradually taking on the appearance of today's wolf or even Spitz-type dogs with the loosening of the curl of the tail, the lengthening of the legs and extremities, and the diminution of the fifth toe (dewclaw), which allowed the animal to run more quickly.

Rise of the Canis genus

Canis Canids did not appear until the end of the Tertiary Era. They crossed the Bering Strait and reached Europe during the late Eocene, but seemed to disappear during the early Oligocene as Ursids (bears) grew in numbers. In the late Miocene, *Canis lepophagus* migrated to Europe from North America. This new arrival looked much like modern dog, though was closer to the size of a coyote. During the Pliocene, these Canids spread toward Asia then Africa. Ironically, they apparently did not move into South America until much later, during the early Pleistocene.

Finally, humans introduced the genus to Australia around 500,000 years ago, during the late Pleistocene. However, there is no proof that these early Canids gave rise to the Dingo—modern-day wild dogs that were brought to Australia a mere 15,000 to 20,000 years ago.

Ancestor of the wolf, jackal, and coyote

Canis etruscus (Etruscan dog) appeared approximately one to two million years ago. Despite its smaller size, it is thought to be the ancestor of European wolves. *Canis cypio*, which lived in the Pyrenees eight million years ago, seems to be the ancestor of modern jackals and coyotes.

Importance of archeological sites in Europe and China

Several varieties of dogs have been found at European archeological sites. The largest are thought to be descended from the large northern wolves which stood as tall as the withers of today's Great Dane. They probably gave rise to Nordic dogs and large herders. The smaller dogs, morphologically similar to modern-day wild Dingos, are likely descended from smaller wolves from India or the Middle East.

Is the Wolf the Ancestor of the Dog?

The oldest dogs'skeletons ever found are approximately 30,000 years old, and therefore lived after Cro-Magnon (*Homo sapiens sapiens*) was already walking the earth. These ancient remains have always been found near human skeletons; this is why they were given the name Canis familiaris (- 10,000 years). It only seems logical that domestic dogs are descended from early wild Canids. Other possible ancestors include the wolf (*Canis lupus*), the jackal (*Canis aureus*), and the coyote (*Canis latrans*).

In addition, the oldest dog remains have been found in China, where it is believed jackals and coyotes never lived. It was also in China that the first authenticated association (dating to 150,000 years ago) between man and a small wolf variety (Canis lupus variabilis) took place. The coexistence of these two species during a period prior to their evolution, seems to corroborate the theory that the wolf is the ancestor of the domestic dog.

This hypothesis was recently reinforced following several discoveries, including the finding that some Nordic breeds are directly descended from the wolf. In addition, studies that compared the mitochondrial DNA of these species revealed similarity greater than 99.8% between the dog and the wolf, compared to only 96% between the dog and the coyote. Moreover, more than forty-five wolf sub-species have been classified; the diversity of the wolf species could explain the diversity of dog breeds. Finally, body and vocal languages are very similar and commonly understood between the two species.

Similarities between the dog and the wolf: a difficult analysis

The similarities between dogs and wolves make it difficult for paleozoologists to accurately determine whether remains are that of a wolf or a dog when remains are incomplete or the archeological context suggests that cohabitation is unlikely. Only a few minor, and highly unreliable, differences existed between primitive dogs and their ancestors. These included the length of the nose bridge, the angle of the stop, and the distance between the carnassial tooth and the upper tubercles. In addition, there were certainly fewer Canids than the animals that they preyed upon, and

BATTLE OF THE THEORIES

Numerous (conflicting) theories have been formed based on comparisons of skeletal and dental structures of wolves, jackals, and coyotes. Each, in turn, is credited as being the ancestor of the modern dog. Some experts even hypothesize that various breeds as different as the Chow Chow or the Grayhound may be descended from different species of the Canis genus.

In 1968, Fiennes suggested that four distinct sub-species of wolf—the European Wolf, the Chinese Wolf, the Indian Wolf and the North American Wolf—gave rise to the four main groups of modern-day dogs.

Others hold that crosses between the individual species resulted in the development of the canine species. They base their arguments on the fact that wolf/coyote, wolf/jackal, or even jackal/coyote matings can produce fertile hybrids, each with thirty-nine chromosome pairs. This hybrid theory is now thought to be invalid given the ecological barriers that separated the various species at the time that domestic dogs appeared, which would have made it impossible for coyotes and jackals in particular to mate.

Wolves were present throughout the world, but given the differences in size and behavior compared to the jackal and the coyote, it seems highly improbable that interspecies mating took place. This, of course, refutes one of many theories that argue that the hybridization of the jackal (canis aureus) and the Grey Wolf (Canis lupus) gave rise to the modern dog.

13

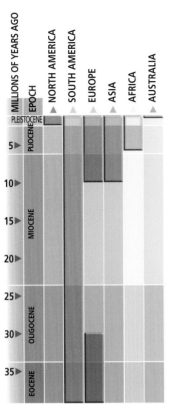

GEOGRAPHIC DISTRIBUTION OF CANIDS OVER TIME
(by F. Duranthon, SFC, 1994).

According to recent research in the United States and Sweden, the dog appeared approximately 135,000 years ago, 100,000 years earlier than previously believed. Canid remains morphologically similar to wolves that were found with human skeletal remains at sites dated at 100,000 years old.

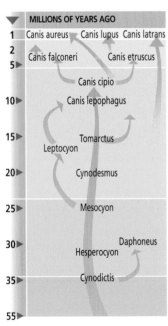

GENUS CANIS FOSSILS
(by M. Thérin).

therefore, it is less likely that Canid remains will be uncovered. These difficulties and the possibility of dog-wolf hybridization explain why many links are missing in the chain of events that led to the development of modern dog. Perhaps one day we will discover the link between *Canis lupus variabilis* and *Canis familiaris*, and the battle of the theories will come to an end.

It is worth noting that the diffusionist theory, which suggests primitive dogs adapted to their new environs as humans migrated, does not exclude the evolutionist theory, which states that dog varieties came from different areas where the wolf was domesticated.

Domestication of the Wolf

Wolf prints and skeletal remains as much as 40,000 years old have been discovered in territories occupied by humans in Europe, though the use of dogs by *Homo sapiens* has not been validated by prehistoric cave drawings.

At that time in history, humans had not yet settled into a sedentary existence. They followed the animal that they hunted for food. Climatic changes (end of an ice age and sudden atmospheric warming) that took place approximately 10,000 years ago between the Holocene and Pleistocene Epochs changed the landscape; forests replaced tundra, and as a result, mammoths and bison became rare as deer and boar flourished. When the game they hunted became smaller, humans developed new weapons and hunting techniques. Suddenly, man was competing with wolves for the same food and using the same "pack" hunting methods using "beaters".

It is only natural that early humans felt the need to find a way to use the wolf for hunting. For the first time, they attempted to tame an animal, long before humans had settled into a sedentary life style and began raising livestock.

Therefore, primitive dogs were without a doubt hunting dogs, not herders.

Taming the wolf and domestication

Wolves were domesticated when humans passed from "predation" to "production". A few individual wolves would have been tamed in early attempts. Each time a tamed wolf died, work had to begin again to tame another; but this early work marked a first, vital step toward domesticating a species. The second step was controlled breeding.

Domestication of wolves probably began in several locations in Asia. It did not happen overnight based on the number of domestication centers discovered at archeological sites.

Several attempts were made around the world with young wolf pups from various groups. These pups irreversibly imprinted to man during their first months of life. When they rejected their wild relatives, domestication was successful. The fact that wolf pups naturally submit to the hierarchical rules of the pack undoubtedly made domestication easier. Though, occasionally, some domesticated bitches were impregnated by wild wolves, the pups were raised in proximity with humans, and therefore were far less likely to return to the wild.

From the wolf to the dog

As is always the case with any animal, the domestication of wolves led to several morphological and behavioral changes, following the evolution of humans. By studying skeletal remains, scientists have found there was a juvenile regression, called pedomorphosis, as if over the generations, the adult ani-

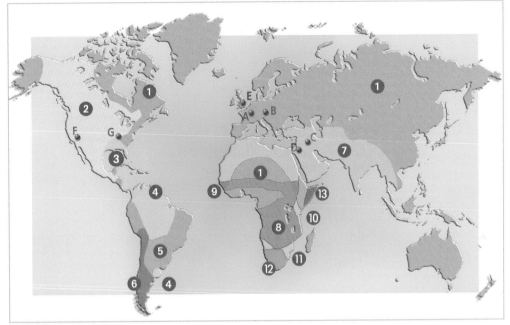

GEOGRAPHIC RANGE OF CANIS, SOUTH AMERICAN FOXES, AND REMAINS OF FIRST DOGS.

(by Y. Lignereux, I. Carrière, SFC, 1994, La Recherche, 1996.)

1	Canis lupus	6	Dusicyon (psedalopex)	10 Canis mesomelas / C. adustus / C. avreus
2	Canis latrans	7	Canis avreus	11 Canis mesomelas / Canis adustus
3	Canis rufus	8	Canis adustus	12 Canis mesomelas
4	Cerdocyon	9	Canis adustus / Canis avreus	13 Canis mesomelas / Canis aureus
5	Dusicyon (psedalopex) Cerdocyon			

REMAINS OF FIRST DOGS

A Bonn-Oberkassel: -14 000
B Dobritzgniegrotte: -13 000
C Palagawra Cave: -12 000
D Matlaha (and several others): -11 000 / -12 000
E Starr car / Seamen car: -9 000 / -10 000
F Danger Cave: -9 000 / -10 000
G Koster: -8 500

mals retained certain immature characteristics and behaviors, including decreased size, shortened nose bridge, deepened stop, barking, whining, playful disposition, etc. This led some archeozoologists to believe that the dog is still undergoing speciation, that it has become stuck at adolescence and must depend on humans for survival.

Paradoxically, the phenomenon is accompanied by a shortening of the growth stage, meaning puppies reach puberty early, and therefore, are capable of reproducing at an early age. This explains why small breeds reach puberty earlier than large breeds, and why all domestic dogs reach puberty earlier than wolves, which do not mature sexually until approximately two years of age. In addition, the teeth of domestic dogs have adapted to an omnivorous diet rather than a primarily carnivorous diet, since domestic dogs could make do with table scraps rather than hunting for survival.

This type of degeneration as a result of domestication is seen in most species. Other examples are the pig (shortening of the snout) and foxes, which can take on puppylike behavior after only twenty generations of breeding. So it seems that domestication modifies natural evolution (unless humans are considered an integral part of nature's equation) and becomes a new method of selection.

Results of Selective Breeding

Though described as the greyhound in Egyptian paleontology or the Molossus in Assyrian history, different breeds are simply varieties, types of dogs, sub-species of *Canis familiaris*. Dating from antiquity, the development of individual breeds is much more recent than domestication of wild dogs.

Apart from a few breeds such as the Maltese Bichon, whose bloodline was maintained in a limited

Man's attempts to domesticate animals failed regularly. Ancient Egyptians tried to domesticate hyenas, gazelles, wild cats, and foxes, but they only managed to tame a few individuals at best. More recently, attempts to domesticate wild Dingos also failed. Some would say domestication of cats is still a work in progress.

territory, most dog breeds were produced through selective breeding carried out by humans. Selective breeding only became possible after dogs were domesticated and mating could be controlled.

Adaptation of the canine species over time

Unlike undomesticated species such as crocodiles, which have hardly evolved in two hundred million years (twenty meters on our kilometer scale), the canine species adapted (or was adapted) in record time to a wide range of climates, civilizations, and geographic areas. The Siberian Husky, Mexican Hairless, Pekinese, Great Dane, Boxer and Dachshund, just a few of the four hundred breeds currently standardized by the Fédération Cynologique Internationale (FCI) which, despite their diversity, all belong to the genus *Canis familiaris*. It is interesting to note that the shape of the head, legs and spine have evolved independently from breed to breed throughout the evolution of domestic dogs.

This diversification began as humans moved from a nomadic to sedentary lifestyle, from "consumer" to "producer", in the late Stone Age. At that time in history, dogs were most likely of medium size and looked like the "Tourbières Loulou" (similar to the modern-day Spitz type) described by von den Driesch in England.

Appearance of different types

Two large types appeared in the third millenium in Mesopotamia—the Molosser dogs that protected livestock against predators (bears and ironically, its own ancestor, the wolf) and the greyhound type which was adapted for running and desert regions and which became an indispensable hunting tool for man.

In addition to these two basic types, there undoubtedly were already types that correspond to the

When humans set their minds and efforts to selective breeding, results can be achieved in a remarkably short time. For example, it took only one hundred years in Argentina to produce miniature horses, measuring only forty centimeters at the withers, from standard horses. Comparable results can be achieved in even shorter periods with dogs since they are quite fertile and gestation is much shorter.

primary groups as defined by Kennel Clubs around the world.

Growing ties between dogs and humans

From antiquity, dogs have filled numerous roles and have been used in a wide variety of activities, including fighting, meat production, sled pulling in polar regions, and sacrificial rites in mythology. Later in history, the Roman Empire became the pioneer in dog breeding and was proud to call itself the "fatherland of a thousand dogs", foreshadowing the diversity of dog varieties whose primary uses would be to provide companionship, to guard farms and herds, and to help with the hunt.

It is easy to imagine how diversification increased over the centuries as human populations crossed paths through genetic mutation (probably the origin of chondrodystrophic dwarfism in modern Bassets), selective breeding, and natural or voluntary thinning. Some extreme results were achieved, such as the Bulldog originally bred for bull-baiting or the Pekinese that provided companionship to Chinese empresses.

Hunting dogs and the first standard

In the Middle Ages, different dog varieties were bred according to their aptitude for various hunting techniques. Bloodhounds and pointers were used to locate game without hunting, scent and sighthounds were used to tire deer, and bird dogs were used to flush feathered game. Barking dogs were also described as being used to pursue prey. The use of bassets for underground hunting was even mentioned. Though it is impossible to positively identify a skeleton as being that of a specific breed, some breeds are no doubt now extinct.

"Fixing" of characteristics, inextricably linked to the concept of standard, did not truly begin until the sixteenth century for hunting dogs. In the seventeenth and eighteenth centuries, an attempt was made to establish a family tree for Buffon's breeds. In the nineteenth century, interest in breeding soared after the first dog shows in London in 1861 and in Paris in 1863.

Thereafter, fanciers strove to create new morphological types from existing breeds. Each breed club has recorded the precise date of the show that officially recognized a breed which, until that point, had been classified only as a variety.

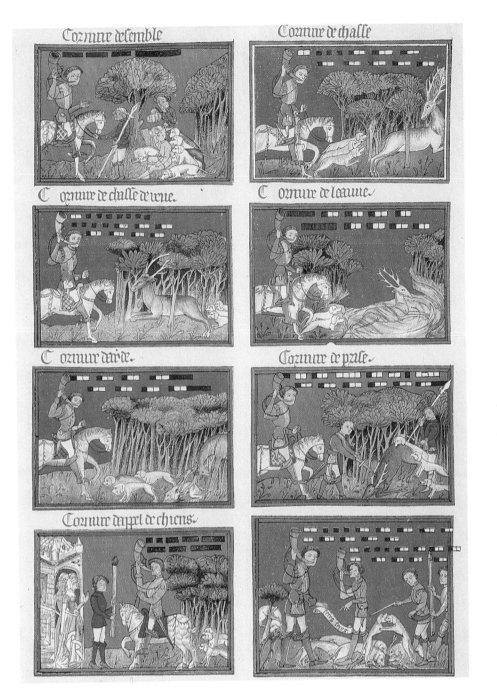

Hunting scenes. Miniature from the Treasury of Hunting, after the manuscript from Harduin de Fontaines-Garin. Selva, Paris.

Modern Dog

From Roman antiquity, dogs have been classified according to their skills. Originally, they were divided into herders, hunting dogs and house dogs. Aristotle recorded seven separate dog breeds, but made no reference to greyhounds, which had long lived in Egypt. In the eighteenth century, Buffon attempted to classify dogs by ear shape, separating them into thirty straight-eared breeds, drop or semiprick, whereas Cuvier proposed dividing the canines into hounds, mastiffs, and spaniels based on the shape of the dog's skull. In 1885, the Livre des Origines Français (French Stud Book) divided canines into twenty-nine separate sections. These sections were narrowed to eleven groups in the early twentieth century, then in 1950, reduced to the ten groups that are recognized today.

Concept of Breed, Variety and Standard

In 1984, the FCI formally approved Professor R. Triquet's proposal to establish a technical zoological definition of the concepts of dog group, breed and variety.

Species and Breed

According to Prof. Triquet, breed is "a group of individuals with common characteristics that distinguish them from other members of their species and that can be genetically passed on to the next generation". He held that, "species is determined by nature while breed is determined by the culture or fashions of the show ring". Indeed, selective breeding may produce a new breed, but will never result in the creation of a new species.

For example, Jack Russell Terriers (a breed) were created when Parson Jack Russell crossed various terriers in an attempt to create a better hunting dog. However, some dogs, such as Languedoc Sheepdogs, have never been officially recognized as separate breeds. Others, such as the Chambray, the Lévesque, or the Normand-Poitevin, slowly disappeared because of lack of numbers of interest and were permanently removed from the FCI registry. Currently, the Belgian Shorthaired Pointer and the Ardennes Cattle Dog are under consideration for removal, whereas the Saint-Usuge Spaniel and the American Bulldog have been submitted to the FCI for approval. Over the past fifty years, the number of breeds recognized by the FCI has practically tripled in response to increased precision in breeding, sometimes simply in an effort to create something original.

Group, breed, variety

Group is defined as "a group of breeds have certain distinguishing characteristics in common that can be transmitted genetically". For example, Group 1 (sheepdogs) dogs have different morphology, but all instinctively strive to guard livestock.

Variety, according to Raymond Triquet, is "a subdivision within a breed wherein all specimens have a common, genetically transmittable characteristic that distinguishes them from other specimens of that breed".

For example, the Longhaired German Shepherd is a variety of the German Shepherd breed, though it is possible that the offspring of a Longhaired variety may not have long hair (the long hair characteristic being passed on by a recessive gene).

Many breeds include a number of varieties, including color and texture of the coat or ear carriage. There are three Dachshund varieties—smooth, wire and long.

Breed and standard

Standard is defined as "the group of characteristics that defines a breed". It serves as a reference point when a specimen is examined to judge its conformation to the behavioral and morphological characteristics of the breed.

Each breed has a standard which is established by the breed association of its country of origin. Only the original association may modify the standard. The standard established in the country of origin is the only one recognized by the FCI, despite the fact that some countries try to impose their own varieties. For example, English, American, and Canadian Akita varieties have been proposed to the FCI for recognition, but without success. Others are recognized only through national genealogical proceedings.

Some varieties, such as Toy and Apricot Poodles, have eventually been accepted by the country of origin as officially belonging to the Poodle breed.

Some breeds are no longer used for their original purpose. For example, few Yorkshire Terriers are used as earth dogs; most are now kept as house pets. The same is true of Labrador Retrievers, which were used for hunting with pointers. Today it is rare that they are bred for their working abilities.

Standard of beauty and sporting body-type

Some dog breeds are difficult to classify within the existing groups because they may no longer be used for their original purpose. To maintain the purity of breeds, some breed associations require natural aptitude tests, or working trials, such as field trials for pointers. This allows the dog to be judged on his skills, not just physical appearance and phenotype.

Usefulness of breeding across varieties

Dog shows, competitions, and championships allow judges and conformation experts to promote breeding of dogs that will "improve" a breed, since it has been judged to display desired working or appearance traits. This practice of judging dogs keeps selection in line with breed club goals. As a result, however, there is a risk that specimens of exaggerated type will be created which do not reflect the original standard for the breed. Different varieties could even gradually appear if working qualities are incompatible with appearance standards. In order to avoid this trend to create new varieties, which threatens the integrity and standard of a breed, the best specimens of each variety of the breed must be crossed regularly to preserve working and appearance qualities unique to that breed.

An excellent example is that of the Belgian Sheepdog, which has four distinct varieties. Inter-variety mating between

Groenendaels and Tervuerens is done regularly, maintaining a degree of homogeneity, while Malinois and other breeds are crossed to improve working abilities (bite, indifference to gunfire), which could threaten the integrity of this variety.

Intra-breed selection aimed only at developing working abilities may then result in the creation of a specimen that does not conform to standard, as is true for the English Setter. In addition, morphological characteristics are lost much more rapidly than working abilities are acquired.

Rootstock, Line, Family

Each breed has its own rootstock which gives rise to different lines with each litter.

Even if the genetic input of the sire and the dam to the first generation of puppies is the same, we refer to maternal rootstock and paternal rootstock when several generations of the pedigree are studied.

There are always more descendants of an elite stud than of a champion brood bitch, which is physiologically limited to fewer than two litters per year.

Confirmation and recommendation of a stud is therefore always given considerable weight since the male has a much greater impact on the breed than the female.

Family and inbreeding

A dog's origin is revealed by examining its pedigree. The pedigree will also indicate the degree of inbreeding in a particular line (or strain). Parallel breeding of several related lines ("blood relatives") is the most common method used for dog breeding. The breeder ends the line several generations later after fixing the sought-after characteristics. This line then constitutes a family that can be recognized by an expert fancier. A family is a group of related individuals that have similar characteristics and come from the same breeding lines. Each line is identified by name.

The need to introduce new blood

However, excessive inbreeding within the same family can result in a decrease of occurrence and variation of genetic traits. In this case, the breeder may choose to introduce new blood. With modern technology, it is even possible to preserve semen and therefore the hereditary material of certain family lines possessing qualities worth reintroducing at a later date.

What About Mutts?

Unlike mixed breed dogs that are the product of a cross between two dogs of different breed or a purebred dog and one of undetermined heritage, mutts are impossible to classify accurately since there is no rhyme or reason to their bloodlines. Mutts are the result of a cross between two dogs of unknown breed. Experts estimate that as much as 60% of all dogs in France are mutts or mixed breeds, though it is difficult to determine precisely how many exist.

Working abilities and rusticity

Though far from beautiful, mutts are greatly respected by their owners for their working abilities and rusticity.

Mutts typically have "wild dog" coloration (the dominant colors of the coat are gray or fawn) and are generally of medium size. Instinctively self-reliant, they are excellent hunting dogs, and their natural coloration acts as camouflage so they blend in with their surroundings. Only ten percent of hunting dogs in France have a pedigree.

Thanks to their colorful backgrounds, mutts have an extremely rich genetic heritage. Undesirable genes (often recessive) are likely to be dominated by desirable genes.

Unknowns of genetic diversity

The unfortunate side effect of this genetic diversity is that there is no guarantee that desirable characteristics will be passed on to the next generations. It is also very difficult to anticipate the morphological and psychological characteristics of puppies born to mutt parents, even if both parents present the desired characteristics.

Though it is often said that mutts are lively, intelligent, hardy and game, it is, in fact, impossible to make this broad statement since only the most lucky and skilled products of this genetic roulette find a place in society. The truth is, mutts account for the vast majority of dogs in shelters and pounds.

We have seen that quantitative characteristics such as working ability, that depend on the action of numerous genes, are less inheritable than morphological characteristics such as color or coat texture, that are passed on through a more limited number of genes. Mutt devotees are often hunters and will admit that it is difficult to raise mutts in the hopes of fixing their traits. However, since they have no market value and they are so numerous, hunters often have no qualms about starting over with their stock.

Do Wild Dogs Still Exist?

Even today it is still difficult to classify some Canids such as the Abyssinian Wolf *Canis simensis* (500 still exist in Ethiopia) among wolves, foxes or wild dogs.

Whatever the case, if we exclude wolves from the wild dog group, there are still some wild dogs, including the singing dogs of New Guinea, Indian and African Pariah dogs, the Congo Basenji (many have been domesticated and recognized by the FCI), Carolina dogs, and Australian Dingos. All wild dogs have similar morphology.

We know that dogs are descended from wolves. So if dogs were left in the wild, would they revert to wolves?

Starting from the principal that evolution never backtracks, researchers at the University of Rome studied colonies of wild dogs living in the Abruzzes in central Italy. They noticed that these dogs of the forest lived like wolves, in packs with clearly defined territories, unlike stray village dogs that generally looked out only for their own interests. However, wild dogs do not look like wolves. They are smaller and of an amber-brown color, indicating that they have permanently lost some alleles, undoubtedly as the result of a period of domestication in their history.

Dogs of the Future

By studying the annual statistics gathered by the French Kennel Club, we can identify current breeding trends and, from this information, try to determine what dogs will look like in the future. Registered births by breed indicate a trend away from the most well known breeds in favor of increasingly more original breeds.

Exaggerated type

This quest for originality and extreme types is a selection technology that has been developed primarily in the United States and England. The result is the creation of specimens with exaggerated type, such as Bull Dogs, whose faces are now so pushed in that they must be born by cesarean and can breathe only if their mouth is open. Labradors are predisposed to obesity. Dachshunds are getting longer. Shar-Pei's have more natural folds in the

Dingo: Scientists know that the Australian Dingo reached Australia 15,000 to 20,000 years ago when crossing to the continent on land was still possible. However, they do not know if the Dingo was a domesticated dog that returned to the wild or a distinct species. If it was a domesticated dog, it should be called Canis familiaris dingo, but if it was a separate wild species, it would be called Canis dingo. Until its origins can be clarified, the dingo will not have a scientific name.

skin. German Shepherds have increasingly sloped croups. Small breeds are getting smaller and are now referred to as Toys and Miniatures. On the other hand, large breeds are growing increasingly large. These trends seem to leave only mutts in the medium size category. We see a tendency to push the extremes and ignore those that fall in the middle.

Genetic influence for custom dogs

Morphing is a computer technique that could perhaps serve as an analogy to demonstrate how we can predict these trends, taking into account changes in lifestyles and progress in genetic manipulation. Lifestyle changes follow urban development. A decrease in the number of farm dogs can be anticipated with a corresponding increase in the number of pets, as a result of telecommuting becoming more commonplace and improved connectivity. However, it is difficult to predict what dogs will look like since people's preferences change as fashion evolves.

If current trends continue, we can expect an increase in the number of breeds. Future dogs will be anything but average! Coat color and texture genetics are advancing by leaps and bounds; therefore it will likely be possible to "genetically color" dogs. The mechanics of genetics will be more fully understood. In fact, we estimate a canine genome map will be achieved within twenty years. As a result, it will be possible to eliminate genetic faults and reduce chance in breeding, meeting demand for increasingly original breeds.

The development of artificial insemination, using refrigerated or frozen sperm, will eliminate the need to bring animals together. Borders and quarantine will disappear as two animals selected from a catalog on the Internet are "virtually" mated. The semen of a prime stud dog could even be preserved to impregnate a brood bitch after the death of the stud. However, these techniques will never be as successful in dogs as they have been in cattle since the concentration of sperm in canine ejaculate is much lower than in that of steers.

It is possible fewer dogs will be abandoned in the future. But these "made-to-order" dogs of the future will look less and less like wild dogs. Future dogs may look so different that their wild cousins may no longer even recognize them!

Fédération Cynologique Internationale (FCI)

Though the FCI stemmed from the French SCC and the Belgian Société Royale Saint-Hubert, it is no longer officially linked to either organization. The FCI is an international organization based in Thuin, Belgium. It is responsible for:

• Establishing the criteria for recognition of stud books of member countries (more than fifty are currently members, including most European countries and many Asian, Latin American, and African countries);

• Standardizing international dog show rules (organization, judging, international working or beauty championship titles);

• Promoting the sharing of breed standards established by the country of origin. These standards are regularly published in the French Official Dog Fancier's Review;

• Monitoring member countries to ensure that each country holds a minimum of four international championships each year.

Dog Fancy around the World

Three independent organizations work closely with the FCI, without being subordinated to it —the Kennel Club (KC) of the United Kingdom, the American Kennel Club (AKC) of the USA, and the Canadian Kennel Club (CKC) of Canada. Several other kennel clubs promote dog fancy throughout the world as well. They include:

The Kennel Club

Created in 1873, earlier than the French SCC, the Kennel Club is the oldest organization devoted to purebred dogs. For the first one hundred years of its existence, only men could be members of the Kennel Club. It was not until 1979 that women were admitted.

Poster E.E. Doisneau (1902)
Coll. Kharbine-Tapabor, Paris

The function of the Kennel Club is similar to that of the French SCC. The KC organizes approximately 6,000 dog shows each year. The most prestigious on the international stage is undoubtedly Crufts, which assembles more than 26,000 dogs over four days of competition.

The American Kennel Club

Formed in 1884, the AKC was created around the same time as the French SCC. The AKC is made up of breed clubs and associations, but also admits multi-breed clubs. The AKC's staff works in offices in North Carolina and New York. The AKC organizes more than 13,000 dog shows each year and also contributes in several other fields, such as the creation of a training institute for judges and a foundation for research in the field of dog health.

The Bermuda Kennel Club

The youngest of all the federations, the BKC was founded in 1955 and is still affiliated with the FCI. The BKC organizes two annual shows, one in fall and one in spring.

Australian National Kennel Council (ANKC)

The ANKC was founded in 1911 as an affiliate of the FCI. It maintains the same standards, but judging of the 153 breeds it recognizes differs slightly. The ANKC's committee is made up of two delegates from each of eight Member States. The committee meets two times per year for four days.

Judges are chosen by the General Council of each Member State from candidates who must have at least ten years of experience. There are currently 876 judges recognized in Australia, 233 of which are approved to judge all breeds.

The Canadian Kennel Club

Based in Toronto, the CKC was formed in 1888. The CKC has approximately 25,000 individual active members represented by twelve delegates elected by the different regions. In 1995, the CKC organized 1,961 dog shows, with a seemingly higher registration than in previous years.

Dog Breeds

Each international registering body has established different groupings to classify the breeds that it recognizes: the Société Centrale Canine of France – 10; the FCI (Fédération Cynologique Internationale) – 10; the Kennel Club of England – 6; the American Kennel Club – 7; the Canadian Kennel Club – 7; the Svenska Fennel Klubben of Sweden – 8; the Real Sociedad Canina of Spain – 5; the Australian National Kennel Council – 6; and the Bermuda Kennel Club – 6. The breed names listed in this encyclopedia are those proposed by the FCI and approved by the FCI General Assembly held in Jerusalem from June 23-34, 1987, and updated in March 1999.

Groups

For the reader's convenience, the dog breeds in this book have been presented by group and by section. Dogs within the same group and section are listed in alphabetical order, not by country of origin.

The groups and sections are the following:

Group 1:
Sheepdogs (Section 1) and Cattledogs (Section 2), except Swiss Cattledogs.

Group 2:
Pinschers and Schnauzers (Section 1), Molossians (Section 2), and Swiss Cattledogs (Section 2).

Group 3:
Terriers.

Group 4:
Dachshunds.

Group 5:
Spitz and primitive types: Nordic breeds (Section 1); European Spitz (Section 2); Asian Spitz and related breeds (Section 3); primitive types (Section 4); primitive hunting dogs (Section 5).

Group 6:
Scenthounds (section 1); Leash (scent) Hounds (section 2) and related breeds (section 3)

Group 7:
Continental pointing dogs (Section 1) and British and Irish Pointers and Setters (Section 2).

Group 8:
Flushing dogs (Section 1), Retrievers (Section 2), and Water Dogs (Section 3).

Group 9:
Companion and toy dogs, divided into twelve sections: Bichons and related breeds (Section 1); Poodles (Section 2); small Belgian dogs (Section 3); hairless dogs (Section 4); Tibetan breeds (Section 5); Chihuahuas (Section 6); Dalmatians (Section 7); English toy spaniels (Section 8); Japanese Chin and Pekingese (Section 9); Continental toy spaniels (Section 10); Kromfohrländer (Section 11); small Molossian type dogs (Section 12).

Group 10:
Sighthounds and related breeds.

Miscellaneous rare breeds are mentioned at the end of the chapter.

Standards

The FCI classification, original name, other common names, and varieties (if applicable) are listed for each breed. Information regarding behavior, personality, training, use and standard is also provided.

The standard covers the origin of the breed, accepted varieties, general appearance, and a description of the head, neck, body, legs and tail, followed by disqualifying faults. When such faults are present, the dog is not considered a desirable candidate for breeding to carry on or improve the breed, since it is presumed that such a dog would pass on a hereditary fault. If a dog is descended from two purebred parents, he can be registered as a purebred. Dogs with particularly impressive bloodlines can be pedigreed and will be in high demand to be mated with the best of their breed.

Standards are modified over the years. Some standards established at the turn of the century have been updated as the breed has evolved.

Vocabulary

A highly specialized vocabulary has evolved to describe dog breeds and their standards. The reader will find the key terms defined in the following glossary useful (from M. Luquet and R. Triquet).

Small Breeds under 10 kg (20 lb)

Medium Breeds between 10 and 25 kg (20-55 lb)

Large Breeds between 25 and 45 kg (55-100 lb)

Giant Breeds over 45 kg (over 100 lb)

The outlines at right are used to indicate the size category of a given breed. This outline is used throughout the book and is particularly relevant in the chapters on health and nutrition.

SMALL BREEDS
MEDIUM BREEDS
LARGE BREEDS
GIANT BREEDS

The weight and height of domestic dogs vary dramatically from one breed to the next, perhaps more than any other species in the animal kingdom. The Chihuahua weighs only one kilogram, yet the Great Dane can weigh more than one hundred kilograms. Compare this to humans or domestic cats, whose largest members are only 2 to 2-1/2 times the size of the smallest. These great variations in size result in differing morphology, physiology, metabolism, behavior and interaction with humans. A dog also has different health and nutritional needs depending on its size. Based on their weight and height at full maturity, dogs are divided into four general categories: small breeds, medium breeds, large breeds and giant breeds.

Active: Describes a dog that is always alert, in action, on the lookout, moving, hunting.

Aggressive: The tendency to attack without being provoked. This behavior is unacceptable in all standards.

Albino: Describes a white coat caused by lack of pigment in the hairs.

Aquiline: Having a curved shape.

Arched loin: Arched curvature of the back.

Balanced: Said of a well-proportioned dog whose individual parts appear in correct ratio to one another.

Bare patch: An area lacking pigment.

Barrel: Describes a round thoracic region, or well-arched in cobby breeds.

Basset: A type of dog having the body of a larger dog from which it is descended, supported by short legs. These are low-stationed dogs.

Bay: The sound a hunting hound makes when it barks; good voice.

Beagle: A medium-sized hound bred with excellent results from a larger breed. Smaller than the breed from which it is descended, larger than the Basset.

Belton: A white coat with ticking or roaning (orange, lemon).

Bi-color: Said of a coat composed of two distinct colors.

Bichon: An abbreviation for the Barbichon descended from the Barbet. Toy breed with a long or short, silky, stand-off coat.

Black and Tan: Refers to a black dog with tan or sable markings.

Blaze: A narrow white band running up the center of the face.

Blood: Breed. To inject new blood, to cross a dog with a bitch of another breed.

Bloodhound: A dog specialized in searching out large wounded game—a practice called "blood hunting" because the dog follows the blood trail. (Group VI dog breeds)

Blotch: Color covering a large area on a white background.

Blue: The dilution of black coat color.

Blunt muzzle: A short, flat muzzle.

Bobtail: A dog with a naturally short tail.

Brachet: A short-haired, medium-sized hound from the Middle Ages.

Pointer

Close-coupled type

Dish-faced

Domed

Brachycephalic skull: A short, wide, round skull (Bulldog, Pug).

Breast: The chest.

Brick-shaped: Describes a dog whose shape resembles a rectangle, the longest side of the rectangle generally being the length of the dog.

Brindle: Refers to a coat with more or less vertical dark streaking on a lighter color.

Brisket: The chest, thoracic cavity.

Broad: Said of a wide, powerful chest.

Brown: Chocolate and liver are shades of brown. tan and beige are obtained by the dilution of brown.

Brush: A tail that resembles that of a fox.

Cape: The long, thick hair covering the neck and shoulders.

Cat foot: Round.

Chestnut: Fawn with a red or orange cast.

Chippendale Front: A dog with a Chippendale front has forelegs out at the elbows, pasterns close and feet turned out.

Chiseled: Clean-cut head and muzzle. Well-defined, precise lines.

Chocolate: A dark, reddish brown. A chocolate or liver coat is brown.

Cloddy: Said of a dog that is short, compact and thickset.

Close-coupled: Describes a dog that is comparatively short from the last rib to the commencement of the hindquarters.

Close-lying: Said of straight hair that falls flat against the skin.

Coat: Refers to the hair and its color; sometimes refers simply to the color of the hair.

Cobby: Said of a thick-set, compact dog with relatively short, strong, bowed legs. The Pug is cobby.

Coin-sized: The size and shape of a coin, like the spots on Dalmatians.

Collar: White markings around the neck. Hairs around the neck.

Collarette: A ruff formation around the neck.

Corky: Said of a lively, active dog that is constantly in motion.

Cropped: Refers to very short hair close against the body. Some cropped hair is called short in official standards.

Crossbreeding: The mating of a dog of one breed with a bitch of another for one generation to avoid inbreeding. Crossing of dogs of the same breed, but from different lineage or parentage.

Croup: The region of the pelvic girdle formed by the sacrum and surrounding tissue. When the croup is very sloped, it is referred to as goose rump.

Breeching: Long, thick hairs covering the thighs. Sometimes a fringe on the back of the upper thighs.

Dense: Describes very thick hair.

Dewlap: The fold of skin under the neck at the throat; can extend down to the chest.

Dish-faced: Said of a dog with a concave profile having slightly depressed frontal bones. Example: Bulldog, Boxer, Pug.

Dolichocephalic: Having a long, narrow skull, as in that of the Greyhound.

Domed: Describes the skull of a dog with a convex profile, having arched frontal bones. Example: Bedlington Terrier.

Dwarfism: A balanced decrease in size of all body parts of a normal-sized specimen.

Ear: Depending on the breed, ears can be erect or pricked, pendulous, drop, semi-prick. The rose ear is a small drop ear that folds over and back, revealing the burr. In the button ear, the ear flap folds forward, barely away from the head, with the tip lying close to the skull.

Eye: Spaniels have oval eyes; Bulldogs have round eyes; Greyhounds have almond eyes.

Fallow: The result of the dilution of brown, a variation of tan.

Fawn: A color ranging from tan to red. Tan markings are fawn. The dilution of the fawn color produces a tawny color.

Fawn: Fawn red; fawn coat ranging from red to rust.

Fearlessness: The quality of a dog that fears nothing and may bite.

Feathering: Long hairs forming a fringe on the external ear, back of the legs, the tail and the chest.

Filled-up: Refers to a filled-up face: finely chiseled, smooth skin over the bones, flat muscles.

Flare: A white stripe on the forehead that often continues along the head.

Flashings: Irregular white markings on the face and chest.

Flecked: Said of a variegated coat with spotted markings (small dark spots on a white background).

Flushing Dog: A dog, such as the spaniel, that flushes game, that is, forces the game out in the open without pursuing it like hounds and without indicating its presence like pointers.

Forehead: The portion of the head above the muzzle.

Forequarters: The region from the shoulder blades down to the feet.

Gait: The pattern of the footsteps. Natural gaits—walk, trot, gallop. Free gait—easy, untiring movement. Frictionless gait—made with no apparent effort. Balanced gait—uniform speed and stride.

Griffon: A medium- or long-haired pointer or hound with tousled, wiry or shaggy hair.

Hare foot: Long and narrow.

Harlequin: Refers to a multicolored coat with patched or pied coloration on gray or blue; spots of black on white (patches of black on white, as in Great Danes).

Harsh: Describes hard, coarse, weather-resistant hair.

Hedge hunter: A dog that hunts in the brush. A dog that flushes game, but does not point or retrieve. (Synonym of springer)

Height: The height of the body measured by a vertical line running from the withers to the ground when the animal is in a relaxed standing position. Size can range from 0.2 to 1 meter.

Herder: A dog used to herd stock.

High-Standing: Said of a tall dog with plenty of leg, like the Greyhound.

Hindquarters: The region including the croup and hind legs.

Hollow: Said of an area of the body with a convex profile.

Hound: A dog with drop ears that takes to the trail and tracks while giving tongue, eventually running down the animal being hunted. (Group VI dog breeds).

Interbreeding: The mating of two dogs of different breeds.

Isabella: A fawn or light bay color.

Kissing spot: A round spot of color on the head of the King Charles and the Cavalier King Charles Spaniels. A tan or fawn mark above and between the eyes on black and tan dogs.

Large: Said of dogs that are larger than average (such as the Great Dane).

Leashhound: A hunting dog with a refined sense of smell that tracks silently on a leash.

Leggy: Describes a dog with long legs and giving the impression of being high off the ground.

Line: All the descendants of a common ancestor.

Liver: Brown.

Loin: The lumbar region posterior to the ribs and anterior to the croup.

Long back: Describes the back when the distance from the withers to the rump exceeds the height at the withers.

Low to ground: Said of dogs with relatively short legs and well let down chest. (Dachshund).

Mantle: A dark portion of the coat on the back that differs in color from the rest of the coat.

Marking: A white or other color marking on different colored background.

Mask: A dark shading on the face.

Mastiff: A large-headed, thick-set guard dog with strong jaws. Short-haired Molossian types are mastiffs.

Medium: Describes an average-sized dog.

Merle: A coat with dark, irregular blotches against a lighter, often gray, background. French dogs with this coat are called harlequin; British dogs are called blue merle.

Mesomorph: A dog having a well-proportioned, muscular body. Example: setters, pointers, French Shepherd, Belgian Shepherd.

Mismarks: Self color with any area of white hairs.

Molossian type: A large thick-muscled guard dog with a large head and powerful body. Mastiffs are Molossian types.

Morphology: P. Megnin (1932) classified dog breeds into four main morphological groups:

Braccoids: Fairly long muzzle. Marked stop. Hanging ears. Pointers, Spaniels, Setters and Dalmatians belong to this group.

Graioids: Long-bodied dogs with an elongated conical head. Straight skull. Small ears. Long muzzle. Indistinct stop. Tight-lipped. Slender body, thin legs, abdomen well tucked up. The Greyhound belongs to this group.

Lupoids: Wolf-like. Prick ears, long muzzle, short, tight lips. Example: Belgian shepherds.

Molossoids: Massive, round head. Pronounced stop. Short, powerful muzzle. Drop ears. Thick lips. Massive body low to ground. Loose skin. Heavy-boned.

Mottled: Describes a coat with blotches of dark hairs on a lighter background of the same color. Example: Australian Cattle Dog.

Multi-color: A coat of several colors. The juxtaposition of colored spots or patches.

Mute: Refers to a dog that does not bark or bay while trailing.

Muzzle: The facial region comprising the stop, the nose, and the jaws. Only the dorsal portion of the stop is included in the muzzle.

Griffon

Long-limbed type

Mesomorph

Molossian

Pips

Foot shape :

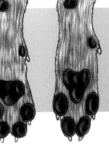

Normal foot   Cat foot   Hare foot

Note: In the almond-shaped eye, the tissue surrounding the eye is longer than the eye. The eye itself, of course, is round.

Nuance: A variation in the intensity of a color.

Pace: A gait in which the left foreleg and left hind leg advance together, followed by the right foreleg and right hind leg.

Pack: An organized group of hounds that hunt larger animals.

Pad: The foot's shock-absorber located under and behind the toes. The pads are covered by calloused, hard, rough, irregularly patterned, highly pigmented skin.

Parti-color: Describes a variegated coat with two or more colors.

Patch: A limited area of color or white in the coat.

Pear-shaped: Having the shape of a pear.

Pendulous: A long, hanging ear.

Pied: Refers to a coat with large patches of white and another color. Example: Pied-Black (white is dominant); Black-Pied (black is dominant).

Pig Dog: A dog used for hunting boar.

Pigmented: Colored by pigments.

Pips: The tan (fawn) spots above each eye giving the impression that the dog has four eyes. This is the typical pattern in black and tan breeds.

Plume: A long fringe of hair on the tail.

Point: The action or position of a dog that has found game. The dog freezes to indicate the presence of game.

Pointer: A dog that assumes an immovable stance when it scents a bird nearby. It "points out" the bird. (Group 7 dog breeds)

Pointer: A short-haired hunter that indicates the presence of game by pointing in the direction of the game with its nose.

Primitive: Related to the most ancient breeds closest to the ancestral wolf (Nordic breeds).

Proportions: The body parts in relation to each other. Each part considered separate as compared to the whole. There are many terms to describe a dog's proportions: close-coupled, low-stationed, off-square, etc.

Puce: Dark brown, brown.

Red-Roan: Describes a coat with a uniform mixture of white and orange or fawn hairs.

Red: One extreme of fawn (from fallow to red).

Retriever: A hunting dog trained to find and bring wounded or killed game back to the handler.

Roan: A coat in which white blotches have a fine mixture of white and fawn hairs or a mixture of three colors (white, red, black or brown).

Robust: Describes a strong, hardy, heavy-boned dog.

Rolling: A transversal movement of the body with each step. A dog can have a "rolling gait".

Ruby: Bright red.

Rustic: A dog adapted to living outdoors in all kinds of weather without special care.

Sable: Describes a coat having black-tipped hairs on a background of fawn.

Saddle: A small blanket.

Sedge: A color between fallow and red in the range of fawn shades.

Self-Color: A one-color coat (except for lighter shadings), without white spots or hairs.

Self-Marked: Refers to a coat with white markings on a whole colored dog.

Setter: A bird dog trained for net hunting in which the net is dropped over both the crouched dog and the bird.

Setter: A pointer from the British Isles. Like the ancient "crouchers", he sets by crouching or half crouching.

Shaded: A light coat with dark areas.

Skeleton: The bones of the body and legs.

Skewbald: Describes a white coat with brindle markings (French Bulldog).

Smoky: A fairly light-colored coat (fawn, sable) tipped with black, brown or blue.

Socks: White markings on the feet.

Sole: An improper term used to describe the surface of the paw pads.

Spaniel: A hunting dog with long- or medium-length (often silky) hair, rectangular body outline, medium size. A mesomorph. Continental Spaniels are pointers. British Spaniels are called spaniels or hedge hunters.

Spaniel: From the French word espaigneul designating spaniels of British, Irish or American origin.

Speck: A small light spot (fawn) on white background.

Speckled: Refers to a coat with small flecks or dapple.

Splashed: Refers to a white coat with patches of color or a colored coat with patches of white.

Spot: Any area of color that differs from that of the background. The spot can be white or colored. Spots have different names depending on size: fleck (small spot), patch (large spot), blotch (very large spot). If a coat has several juxtaposed colored spots, it is a multi-color coat.

Spotted: Describes a coat covered with small spots, including dappled and mottled.

Square body outline: Describes a dog whose height at the withers is equal to the length from the point of the shoulder to the point of the rump.

Standard: A description of the ideal dog. The first dog standard, written in 1876, was that of the Bulldog. Standards are often imprecise.

Stop: The facial indentation between the forehead and the muzzle where the nasal bones and cranium meet. Bulldogs have distinct stops; Greyhounds have almost no stop; Pointers have moderate stops.

Straight: Describes the lines of the body. Example: straight back, straight front, straight in pastern.

Strain: The ancestor from which a family descends. A group of animals breeding amongst themselves for several generations without the introduction of new blood.

Svelte: Thin, supple, slender.

Tail: The guide mark for tail length is the hock. The tail is of medium length if it reaches the hock, short if it does not reach the hock, and long if it extends beyond the hock. The tail carriage can be described in many ways: horizontal, saber, gay, sickle, scimitar, tightly curled (Shar-Pei), double curl (Pug), snap (Akita), docked (German Short-Haired Pointer), etc.

Tan: The fawn or tawny markings on black and tan dogs.

Tawny: Light fawn color resulting from the dilution of fawn.

Terrier: From the French word terre (earth). A hunting dog that roots animals from burrows, that "hunts underground".

Thick: Said of an abundant coat.

Thorax: The length of the thorax is measured horizontally from the chest at the last rib. It is well let down when the brisket reaches slightly below the knees. (Depth and length of – example, a long, deep chest.)

Tight-lipped: Having thin, firm lips.

Tongue: The baying of hounds on the trail. Hounds "give tongue", they do not bark.

Toy: A very small companion dog (Toy Poodle).

Track: A succession of footfalls, footprints (the imprint left by the foot as it strikes the ground).

Track: Action of a dog hunting for game.

Trail: The route followed by an animal; the print or scent left along its path.

Trousers: Long hair on the thighs, longer than the culotte. For Poodles, the hair left on the legs during grooming – English Saddle clip (also called the Lion Clip).

Tufted tail: A tail with a tuft of hair at the end.

Turn-up: Describes a short, uplifted muzzle.

Undercoat: The fine, soft, dense hair under the outer coat.

Undershot Jaw: This term usually applies only when the lower jaw projects beyond the upper jaw. This can be a fault or a characteristic of a breed.

Variety: A subdivision of breed; dogs possessing the distinctive characteristics of the breed, yet having at least one common hereditary trait that distinguishes them from other varieties (size, length and texture of coat, coat color, ear carriage).

Walleye: An eye that lacks pigment. The unpigmented portion of the eye appears to be a light gray-blue, sometimes whitish (Pearl Eye). Can affect one or both eyes. Acceptable in some breeds. Note: Not to be confused with heterochromatic eyes, where each eye is of a different color.

Washed out: Said of a very light color appearing as though it has been highly diluted with water.

Waterdog: A dog that hunts in marshy areas for waterfowl; particularly a retriever. (Group 8 dog breeds)

Wedge-shaped: In the form of a wedge, v-shaped, tapering.

Well-knit: Describes body sections that are firmly joined by well-developed (but not over-developed) muscles.

Well-muscled thighs: Thighs that are well-developed with rounded musculature.

Wheaten: A pale fallow or fawn color.

Whip tail: A tail carried stiffly at back level, like that of hunting dogs.

Wire-haired: A very hard coat, rough to the touch.

Wire-haired: Describes a dog with hard, wiry hair.

Wise: Describes a dog that is calm, docile and even-tempered, but that will not be intimidated.

Withers: A point between the neck and the back. Height at the withers determines the size of the dog.

Wolf gray: A smoky fawn or sable coat.

Jack Russell Terrier

Poitevin Hound

St. Bernard

English Cocker Spaniel

Guidelines for Understanding

Dog Profile (1)

Background and Discussion of the Breed

Complete Name of the Breed

Group Color (2)

Group Number (3)

Section Number (4)

Section Color (5)

Extract from FCI Standard

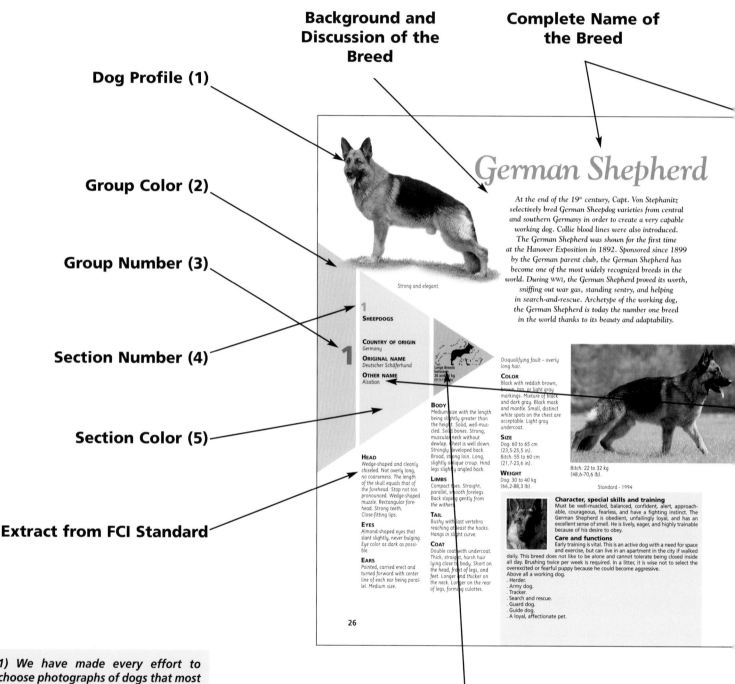

German Shepherd

Strong and elegant.

At the end of the 19th century, Capt. Von Stephanitz selectively bred German Sheepdog varieties from central and southern Germany in order to create a very capable working dog. Collie blood lines were also introduced. The German Shepherd was shown for the first time at the Hanover Exposition in 1892. Sponsored since 1899 by the German parent club, the German Shepherd has become one of the most widely recognized breeds in the world. During WWI, the German Shepherd proved its worth, sniffing out war gas, standing sentry, and helping in search-and-rescue. Archetype of the working dog, the German Shepherd is today the number one breed in the world thanks to its beauty and adaptability.

1

SHEEPDOGS

1

COUNTRY OF ORIGIN
Germany

ORIGINAL NAME
Deutscher Schäferhund

OTHER NAME
Alsatian

Large Breeds between 26 and 40 kg (57,3-88,2 lb)

Disqualifying fault – overly long hair.

COLOR
Black with reddish brown, brown, tan, or light gray markings. Mixture of black and dark gray. Black mask and mantle. Small, distinct white spots on the chest are acceptable. Light gray undercoat.

SIZE
Dog: 60 to 65 cm (23,5-25,5 in).
Bitch: 55 to 60 cm (21,7-23,6 in).

WEIGHT
Dog: 30 to 40 kg (66,2-88,3 lb).

Bitch: 22 to 32 kg (48,6-70,6 lb).

Standard - 1994

BODY
Medium size with the length being slightly greater than the height. Solid, well-muscled. Solid bones. Strong, muscular neck without dewlap. Chest is well down. Strongly developed back. Broad, strong loin. Long, slightly oblique croup. Hind legs slightly angled back.

HEAD
Wedge-shaped and cleanly chiseled. Not overly long, no coarseness. The length of the skull equals that of the forehead. Stop not too pronounced. Wedge-shaped muzzle. Rectangular forehead. Strong teeth. Close-fitting lips.

LIMBS
Compact toes. Straight, parallel, smooth forelegs. Back sloping gently from the withers.

EYES
Almond-shaped eyes that slant slightly, never bulging. Eye color as dark as possible.

TAIL
Bushy with last vertebra reaching at least the hocks. Hangs in slight curve.

EARS
Pointed, carried erect and turned forward with center line of each ear being parallel. Medium size.

COAT
Double coat with undercoat. Thick, straight, harsh hair lying close to body. Short on the head, front of legs, and feet. Longer and thicker on the neck. Longer on the rear of legs, forming culottes.

Character, special skills and training
Must be well-muscled, balanced, confident, alert, approachable, courageous, fearless, and have a fighting instinct. The German Shepherd is obedient, unfailingly loyal, and has an excellent sense of smell. He is lively, eager, and highly trainable because of his desire to obey.

Care and functions
Early training is vital. This is an active dog with a need for space and exercise, but can live in an apartment in the city if walked daily. This breed does not like to be alone and cannot tolerate being closed inside all day. Brushing twice per week is required. In a litter, it is wise not to select the overexcited or fearful puppy because he could become aggressive. Above all a working dog.
. Herder.
. Army dog.
. Tracker.
. Search and rescue.
. Guard dog.
. Guide dog.
. A loyal, affectionate pet.

26

1) We have made every effort to choose photographs of dogs that most closely match the breed standard.

(2) (3) The 10 FCI groups are easy to locate because they are presented in a different color (background and lettering).

(4) (5) FCI sections have also been presented in a different color (background and lettering).

Silhouettes on colored background indicating weight/size: Small, medium, large and giants breeds (see page 17)

the Breed Descriptions

General Appearance of the Breed

Name of Breed Section

Official Country of Origin

Original Name

Other Names

Practical Information and Suggestions

Snapshot of Dog's Face

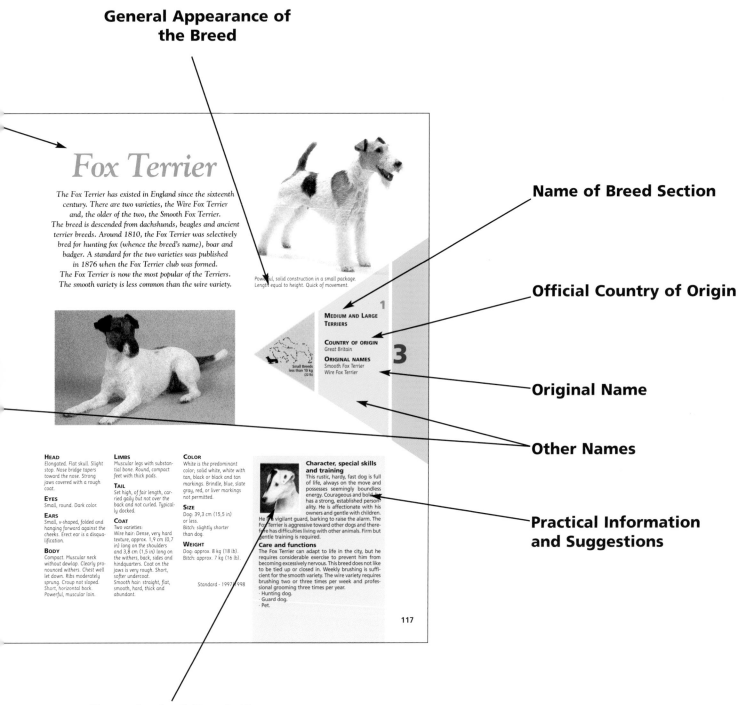

Fox Terrier

The Fox Terrier has existed in England since the sixteenth century. There are two varieties, the Wire Fox Terrier and, the older of the two, the Smooth Fox Terrier. The breed is descended from dachshunds, beagles and ancient terrier breeds. Around 1810, the Fox Terrier was selectively bred for hunting fox (whence the breed's name), boar and badger. A standard for the two varieties was published in 1876 when the Fox Terrier club was formed. The Fox Terrier is now the most popular of the Terriers. The smooth variety is less common than the wire variety.

Powerful, solid construction in a small package. Length equal to height. Quick of movement.

MEDIUM AND LARGE TERRIERS

1

COUNTRY OF ORIGIN
Great Britain

3

ORIGINAL NAMES
Smooth Fox Terrier
Wire Fox Terrier

Small Breeds less than 10 kg (22 lb)

HEAD
Elongated. Flat skull. Slight stop. Nose bridge tapers toward the nose. Strong jaws covered with a rough coat.

EYES
Small, round. Dark color.

EARS
Small, v-shaped, folded and hanging forward against the cheeks. Erect ear is a disqualification.

BODY
Compact. Muscular neck without dewlap. Clearly pronounced withers. Chest well let down. Ribs moderately sprung. Croup not sloped. Short, horizontal back. Powerful, muscular loin.

LIMBS
Muscular legs with substantial bone. Round, compact feet with thick pads.

TAIL
Set high, of fair length, carried gaily but not over the back and not curled. Typically docked.

COAT
Two varieties:
Wire hair: Dense, very hard texture, approx. 1,9 cm (0,7 in) long on the shoulders and 3,8 cm (1,5 in) long on the withers, back, sides and hindquarters. Coat on the jaws is very rough. Short, softer undercoat.
Smooth hair: straight, flat, smooth, hard, thick and abundant.

COLOR
White is the predominant color; solid white, white with tan, black or black and tan markings. Brindle, blue, slate gray, red, or liver markings not permitted.

SIZE
Dog: 39,3 cm (15,5 in) or less.
Bitch: slightly shorter than dog.

WEIGHT
Dog: approx. 8 kg (18 lb)
Bitch: approx. 7 kg (16 lb).

Standard - 1997/1998

Character, special skills and training
This rustic, hardy, fast dog is full of life, always on the move and possesses seemingly boundless energy. Courageous and bold, he has a strong, established personality. He is affectionate with his owners and gentle with children. He is a vigilant guard, barking to raise the alarm. The Fox Terrier is aggressive toward other dogs and therefore has difficulties living with other animals. Firm but gentle training is required.

Care and functions
The Fox Terrier can adapt to life in the city, but he requires considerable exercise to prevent him from becoming excessively nervous. This breed does not like to be tied up or closed in. Weekly brushing is sufficient for the smooth variety. The wire variety requires brushing two or three times per week and professional grooming three times per year.
· Hunting dog.
· Guard dog.
· Pet.

117

Group 1

SECTION 1

SECTION 2

Belgian Sheepdog Malinois

German Shepherd

At the end of the 19th century, Capt. Von Stephanitz selectively bred German Sheepdog varieties from central and southern Germany in order to create a very capable working dog. Collie blood lines were also introduced. The German Shepherd was shown for the first time at the Hanover Exposition in 1892. Sponsored since 1899 by the German parent club, the German Shepherd has become one of the most widely recognized breeds in the world. During WWI, the German Shepherd proved its worth, sniffing out war gas, standing sentry, and helping in search-and-rescue. Archetype of the working dog, the German Shepherd is today the number one breed in the world thanks to its beauty and adaptability.

Strong and elegant.

1

SHEEPDOGS

1

COUNTRY OF ORIGIN
Germany

ORIGINAL NAME
Deutscher Schäferhund

OTHER NAME
Alsatian

Large Breeds between 25 and 45 kg (55-100 lb)

HEAD
Wedge-shaped and cleanly chiseled. Not overly long, no coarseness. The length of the skull equals that of the forehead. Stop not too pronounced. Wedge-shaped muzzle. Rectangular forehead. Strong teeth. Close-fitting lips.

EYES
Almond-shaped eyes that slant slightly, never bulging. Eye color as dark as possible.

EARS
Pointed, carried erect and turned forward with center line of each ear being parallel. Medium size.

BODY
Medium size with the length being slightly greater than the height. Solid, well-muscled. Solid bones. Strong, muscular neck without dewlap. Chest is well down. Strongly developed back. Broad, strong loin. Long, slightly oblique croup. Hind legs slightly angled back.

LIMBS
Compact toes. Straight, parallel, smooth forelegs. Back sloping gently from the withers.

TAIL
Bushy with last vertebra reaching at least the hocks. Hangs in slight curve.

COAT
Double coat with undercoat. Thick, straight, harsh hair lying close to body. Short on the head, front of legs, and feet. Longer and thicker on the neck. Longer on the rear of legs, forming culottes.

Disqualifying fault – overly long hair.

COLOR
Black with reddish brown, brown, tan, or light gray markings. Mixture of black and dark gray. Black mask and mantle. Small, distinct white spots on the chest are acceptable. Light gray undercoat.

SIZE
Dog: 60 to 65 cm (23.5-25.5 in).
Bitch: 55 to 60 cm (22-23.5 in).

WEIGHT
Dog: 30 to 40 kg (66.2-88.3 lb).

Bitch: 22 to 32 kg (48.6-70.6 lb).

Character, special skills and training
Must be well-muscled, balanced, confident, alert, approachable, courageous, fearless, and have a fighting instinct. The German Shepherd is obedient, unfailingly loyal, and has an excellent sense of smell. He is lively, eager, and highly trainable because of his desire to obey.

Care and functions
Early training is vital. This is an active dog with a need for space and exercise, but can live in an apartment in the city if walked daily. This breed does not like to be alone and cannot tolerate being closed inside all day. Brushing twice per week is required. In a litter, it is wise not to select the overexcited or fearful puppy because he could become aggressive.
Above all a working dog.
. Herder.
. Army dog.
. Tracker.
. Search and rescue.
. Guard dog.
. Guide dog.
. A loyal, affectionate pet.

Australian Shepherd

In the twentieth century,
the Australian Shepherd was developed in California
from Australian sheepdogs. Californian farmers
and ranchers used the breed as a working dog.

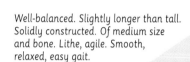

Well-balanced. Slightly longer than tall.
Solidly constructed. Of medium size
and bone. Lithe, agile. Smooth,
relaxed, easy gait.

SHEEPDOGS

COUNTRY OF ORIGIN
United States

ORIGINAL NAME
Australian Shepherd

Medium Breeds
between
10 and 25 kg
(20-55 lb)

1

HEAD
Clean-cut, strong, and dry.
Length equal to width. Moderate, well-defined stop.
Black or brown nose in harmony with coat color.

EYES
Almond shape. Brown, blue,
amber, or any variation or
combination thereof.

EARS
Set on high. Triangular. Moderate size. Break forward or
to the side when dog is alert.
Prick or hanging ears are
severe faults.

BODY
Strong neck. Straight, strong
topline. Deep chest. Ribs well
sprung. Moderately sloped
croup.

LIMBS
Legs strong of bone. Oval,
compact feet.

TAIL
Straight, naturally short or
docked (may not exceed
10 cm (4 in).

COAT
Of medium length and texture. Straight and wavy.
Moderate mane, frill, and
breeching.

COLOR
Blue merle, black, red merle.
All of these colors with or
without white markings,
with or without tan (copper). White color must not
extend beyond the withers.
White permitted at the neck,
on the chest, legs, and muzzle underparts, with a blaze
on the head. Eyes must be
fully surrounded by color.

SIZE
Dog: 51 to 58 cm
(20-23 in).
Bitch: 46 to 53 cm
(18-21 in).

WEIGHT
20 to 25 kg (44-55 lb).

Character, special skills, and training:
The Australian Shepherd is extremely active, hardy, and
fast. This intelligent dog can cover up to 60 km per day
while tending large herds. This exceptional herder also
guards the farm. Affectionate, gentle, good-natured, and
very loyal, the Australian Shepherd makes a good pet.

Care and fonctions
This dog of almost unlimited energy is made for wide-
open spaces. He should not be kept in enclosed spaces
and is not made for life indoors. Regular brushing is sufficient to maintain the coat.
· Herder.
· Guard dog.
· Pet.

Berger de Beauce

The Berger de Beauce is descended from the "Plains Dogs" that guarded the flocks near Paris. At the end of the 19th century, the short-haired "Plains Dogs" were named Beaucerons; long-haired varieties were named Briards. E. Boulet (best known for his Griffons) introduced the breed and helped set up the French Shepherd club in 1896. In 1911, the Friends of the Beauceron Club was founded. The name "Bas Rouge" was given to the Beauceron because of the tan markings on its legs, that look like socks (bas). Breed selection has vacillated between working dogs, show dogs and dogs bred to compete in guard and defense events. Nevertheless, the Berger de Beauce is, above all, a herder. Very popular in France, this breed is almost unknown in other countries, except Belgium.

Well-balanced. Wolf-like. Well-built. Free, relaxed gait (stretched out trot).

1

SHEEPDOGS

COUNTRY OF ORIGIN
France

OTHER NAMES
Beauceron,
Bas rouge,
French Shorthaired Shepherd

Large Breeds between 25 and 45 kg (55-100 lb)

HEAD
Long (2/5 of height), chiseled, with a flat skull. Stop not pronounced. Slightly convex forehead. Muzzle neither straight nor pointed.

EYES
Round, dark color. Frank regard.

EARS
Set on high. Naturally drop, short and flat, but not close against the head. Carried erect if cropped.

BODY
Solid, powerful, well-developed and muscled, but not heavy. Muscular neck. Broad, deep chest. Straight back. Croup barely sloped Broad loin

LIMBS
Two dewclaws on the inside of each hind leg, close to the foot. Leg held slightly back. Round, strong feet

TAIL
Carried straight down reaching the hocks and forming a slight J-hook. Slightly bushy.

COAT
Flat on the head. Heavy and dense, lying close to the body (3 to 4 cm (1.5 in) long). Slight fringing on thighs and along underline. Very short, fine, dense, soft undercoat preferably of slate color.

COLOR
Black and tan (bi-color), bas rouge (most common). Glossy black. Tan is squirrel red. Tan markings: spots above the eyes, on sides of muzzle, throat, and under the tail. Tan extends down legs to feet and wrists (coloration pattern forms a "sock", whence the name Bas Rouge, or Red Socks). Harlequin: gray, black and tan (tri-color): even amounts of gray and black in spots with the same characteristic tan spots.

SIZE
Dog: 65 to 70 cm (25.5-27.5 in).
Bitch: 61 to 68 cm (24-27 in).

WEIGHT
27 to 37 kg (60-80 lb).

Character, special skills and training
This breed is forthright, courageous, fast, hardy and alert, and has amazing dissuasive powers. He is wary with strangers and not easily won over.
This dog is loyal to his owner and gentle with children. He bonds to the entire family, but is guarded when strangers are present. Owners are warned that this breed openly exerts its dominance over other male dogs. His well-developed sense of smell is used to sniff out truffles. A wise breed, he is forthright, dynamic and courageous when working, yet is obedient and easy to handle.

Care and functions
This hardy "country gentleman" needs space to run and is not suited to apartment living. Do not leave him leashed; he cannot tolerate being closed in. This dog needs firm training, discipline, and lots of exercise to burn off energy. He matures late. Two to three brushings per month are sufficient. Dewclaws must be trimmed regularly.
· Herder (Sheep and Cattle), guard dog, defense dog, army dog, tracker, search and rescue.
· Pet.

Bergamasco

This ancient Sheepdog spread throughout the Alps region of Italy, but was most concentrated in the Bergamo area where sheep farming was particularly developed. Some believe the Bergamasco is descended from the Briard. Others hypothesize that the Bergamasco came to Italy from Asia, stating that sheepdogs of this type arrived in Western Europe during the Mongol invasions.

Medium size. Well proportioned. Solid skeleton. Muscular. Fast, easy gait.

HEAD
Large appearance. Capacious skull. Pronounced superciliary arches. Marked stop. Fairly short, blunt muzzle. Large nose.

EYES
Large and oval. Brown color. Darkness of shade varies with color of coat. Black rims. Long fall covering the eyes.

EARS
Soft, triangular drop ears. Thin leather.

BODY
Square body outline. No dewlap on the neck. Full brisket. Short, powerful loin. Straight, well-muscled back. Broad, sloping, solid, well-muscled croup

TAIL
Thick and strong at the base tapering toward the tip. Covered in slightly wavy, shaggy hair. Hangs in the shape of a saber when relaxed.

COAT
Very long and wiry (goat hair) on the front portion of the body. Corded over the rest of the body. Short, dense, soft undercoat.

LIMBS
Forelegs: oval, compact feet. Strong, oval hare feet. Compact, arched toes. Solid-boned, well-muscled hind legs

COLOR
Gray flecked with black, tan, or white. Uniform black coat is acceptable, though uniform white is not. White spots covering no more than 1/5 of the body are permitted.

SIZE
Dog: 58 to 62 cm (23-24.5 in).
Bitch: 54 to 58 cm (21-23 in).

WEIGHT
Dog: 32 to 38 kg (70-84 lb).
Bitch: 26 to 32 (57.5-70 lb).

Large Breeds between 25 and 45 kg (55-100 lb)

SHEEPDOGS

COUNTRY OF ORIGIN
Italy

ORIGINAL NAME
Cane de Pastore Bergamasco

OTHER NAME
Bergamese Shepherd

1

1

Character, special skills and training
Alert, keen and well-balanced, this dog has an ideal personality for flock guarding. This breed's friendly disposition, gentleness and patience also make him an excellent pet. His impressive size makes him a good guard dog. This often stubborn dog requires early, firm training.

Care and functions
This is not a city dweller. He needs space and a lot of exercise. Groom the coat by running your fingers through the hairs to separate the cords.
· Sheepdog.
· Guard dog, search-and-rescue (avalanches, natural disasters).
· Pet.

Briard

Like the Berger de Beauce, the Briard descended from "Plains Dogs" from the region around Paris. The name Chien de berger de Brie describing long-haired sheepdogs was first used in 1809 at the Agriculture Show at the Rozier Abby. In 1863 at the first dog show in Paris, a bitch resembling a Briard placed Best in Show. In 1888, P. Mégnin wrote in L'Eleveur (Breeder), "The Briard is a cross of the Barbet with the Berger de Beauce, the Briard's distinguishing trait being his long, wooly coat." The Briard was registered for the first time in 1885 with the LOF. The first standard was written by the French Shepherd dog club in 1897, describing a variety with wooly hair and another with goat hair. The goat hair variety won out and is the breed described in the current 1988 FCI standard.

During WWI, the Briard was used as a guard dog. Cropping this breed's ears is an old practice. Originally, the ears were cropped so there would be fewer exposed areas where other dogs or wolves attempting to attack the flock could get a grip.

1

Slightly longer than tall.
Well-proportioned.
Lively, bright gait.

SHEEPDOGS

COUNTRY OF ORIGIN
France

ORIGINAL NAME
Berger de Brie

Large Breeds
between
25 and 45 kg
(55-100 lb)

HEAD
Strong and long. Pronounced stop. Rectangular forehead. Squarish nose. Head covered in hairs forming a beard and mustache with fall shading the eyes.

EYES
Set horizontally. Large and of dark color. Long fall covering the eyes.

EARS
Set on high. Preferably cropped and carried erect.

BODY
Solid, muscular, well constructed and of good length. Broad, deep chest. Muscular loin. Slightly sloped croup. Straight back

LIMBS
Two dewclaws close to ground Strong, round feet. Compact toes. Muscular legs strong in bone

TAIL
Not docked. Well-feathered, forming a hook at the tip. Carried low, not falling to the right or left.

COAT
Coarse, dry (goat hair), light undercoat no more than 7 cm (3 in) long.

COLOR
All uniform colors (except white), brown, mahogany and bi-color. Dark colors are preferred.

SIZE
Dog: 62 to 68 cm (24.5-27 in).
Bitch: 56 to 64 cm (22-25 in).

WEIGHT
30 to 40 kg (66-88 lb).

Character, special skills and training
Though he looks a bit like a teddy bear, this dog is a proud, powerful athlete. He is agile, well-balanced, courageous, wise and vigorous. Underneath his hard exterior lies a heart of gold. The Briard is very affectionate, loyal and playful. He is very attached to his owner and plays well with children. He is reserved with strangers. The male is dominant. Strict training from a very young age is required for this somewhat stubborn, independent dog. He does not reach full maturity until the age of two or three.

Care and functions
This robust, active, powerful dog needs lots of space and exercise. He is not a city-dweller. His coat should be brushed and combed regularly to keep it mat-free: two to three times per week if he is an outdoor dog; once per week if he is an indoor dog.
· Sheepdog.
· Handsome pet.

Maremma Sheepdog

It is believed that the Maremma Sheepdog is an ancient breed. The Roman agronomist Varro mentions a breed of white dogs in his writings as early as 100 BC. Like most European Molossian types, this breed's roots can be traced to the Shepherd dogs of central Asia that arrived in Western Europe with the Mongols. Until 1950/1960, the Maremma Sheepdog (short-haired) was distinguished from the longer-haired Abruzzes Sheepdog. It was determined that this distinction had been made only because of the fact that this dog worked from June to October in the Abruzzes and from October to June in the region of Maremma. Approximately twenty-five years ago, Prof. G. Solaro wrote one standard for the breed and the names were joined.

Large, majestic breed. Powerfully built. Rustic appearance. Fairly thick skin. Gaits: extended walk and trot.

SHEEPDOGS

Large Breeds between 25 and 45 kg (55-100 lb)

COUNTRY OF ORIGIN
Italy

ORIGINAL NAME
Cane da Pastore Maremmano-Abruzzese

OTHER NAME
Pastore Abruzzese

1

1

HEAD
Large, flat, wedge-shaped; similar to that of the polar bear. Stop not pronounced.

EYES
Almond-shaped, relatively small in relation to the rest of the body. Ocher or dark brown color.

EARS
Set on high. Relatively small, drop, triangular (V-shaped). Cropped ears acceptable for working dogs.

BODY
Length greater than height. Large, strong neck. Deep chest is well open. Well-sprung ribs. Powerful, muscular, slightly sloped croup. Rectangular back

LIMBS
Large feet, almost round. Toes covered with thick, short hair.

TAIL
Covered with thick hair. Set on low. Carried down when relaxed; when alert, carried at the level of the back with the tip curved up.

COAT
Thick, long (8 cm (3 in) on the body), harsh to the touch. Short on the head. Collarette and fringes on the back of the legs. Heavy undercoat in winter.

COLOR
Solid white. Ivory, pale orange or lemon nuances are permitted.

SIZE
Dog: 65 to 73 cm (25.6-28.7 in).
Bitch: 60 to 68 cm (23.6-26.8 in).

WEIGHT
Dog: 35 to 45 kg (77-99 lb).
Bitch: 30 to 40 kg (66-88 lb).

Character, special skills and training
Calm, reflective, proud, and not likely to be submissive, this dog needs firm training. He is devoted to his owner, is good with children, and makes a good companion. Very distrustful of strangers, he is a reliable, dedicated guardian.

Care and functions
This breed is not suited for apartment living. He needs space and a lot of exercise. This robust dog does not handle heat well. Regular brushing is required.
· Sheepdog.
· Guard dog.
· Pet.

41

Picardy Sheepdog

The Picardy Sheepdog is probably one of the oldest Shepherd breeds. Paintings and etchings from the Middle Ages depict this hardy breed. Its ancestors were possibly of Celtic origin and introduced to France during the invasions of the 9th century. The Picardy Sheepdog, which looks somewhat like a Griffon, accompanied Shepherds that watched over the flocks in the 18th century. At the end of the 19th century, the breed was selectively bred. But this newly emerging breed almost disappeared during WWI. Officially recognized in 1923, breeders reestablished the breed in 1948. The FCI approved a standard for the Berger de Picardie in 1964.

Average size. Rustic, yet elegant, appearance.

1

SHEEPDOGS

COUNTRY OF ORIGIN
France

ORIGINAL NAMES
Berger de Picardie,
Berger Picard

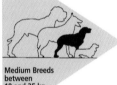

Medium Breeds
between
10 and 25 kg
(20-55 lb)

HEAD
Good proportion to overall size. Hair 4 in long. Prominent brow. Slight stop. Strong muzzle, but not overly long. Mustache and beard.

EYES
Dark color, medium size. Light colors or walleyes are objectionable.

EARS
Medium size, wide at the base with points slightly rounded. Carried erect.

BODY
Muscular and well-construct-
ed. Strong, muscular neck. Deep chest. Long through the shoulders and thighs. Chest slightly up. Straight back. Strong loin.

LIMBS
Strong, sound legs. Arched, short, compact feet. Dark nails. No dewclaw.

TAIL
Hangs straight down, reaching the hocks and forming a slight hook at the tip.

COAT
Wiry, of medium length (5 to 6 cm (2-2.4 in), neither curly
nor flat. Rough and crisp to the touch.

COLOR
Gray, gray-black, gray-blue, rusty gray, light or dark fawn. Large white markings are undesirable.

SIZE
Dog: 60 to 65 cm
(23.5-25.5 in)
Bitch: 55 to 60 cm
(22-24 in).

WEIGHT
19 to 23 kg (42-51 lb).

Character, special skills and training
This quicksilver, courageous dog is well-balanced and stable. Adapted to life in the country, he is very hard and has a penchant for hard work. The Picardy Sheepdog thrives in a family setting and is gentle with children.

Care and functions
This dog is not a city-dweller. He needs space and room to run. Regular, vigorous brushing is required.
· Sheepdog.
· Guard dog.
· Pet.

Pyrenean Shepherd Dog

The history of the smallest French Sheepdog traces back many years. It is thought that he descended from local breeds and never left the high valleys of the Pyrenees mountains until the late 19th century. During WWI, the Pyrenean Shepherd Dog was used as a lookout and messenger dog and to search for wounded. The breed was standardized in 1936. This breed was called by various names, which reflected its region of origin, such as the Labrit, the Landes Shepherd, the Bagnères Shepherd, the Auzun Shepherd, the Arbazzi Shepherd, etc. The Labrit, the largest and most rustic looking, measuring 50 to 55 in at the withers, was almost recognized as a separate breed in 1935. Today, the Labrit no longer exists; it is considered a Pyrenean Shepherd dog. There are two varieties of this breed, the very common long-haired variety and the rarer smooth-muzzled variety, which has short hair on the head and has a shorter body than the long-haired variety.

Bushy coat. Elegant gait. Smallest of the french Sheepdogs.

1

SHEEPDOGS

Up to 25 kg (55 lb)

COUNTRY OF ORIGIN
France

ORIGINAL NAME
Berger des Pyrénées

1

HEAD
Wedge-shaped, like that of the brown bear. Stop not accentuated. Long-haired variety has a fairly short muzzle. Smooth-muzzled variety has a longer muzzle.

EYES
Dark brown color. Black rims. Walleyes are permitted in dogs with harlequin or slate-gray coat.

EARS
Short, generally cropped. Carried three-fourths erect with tips breaking forward or to the side.

BODY
The body of the smooth-muzzled variety is slightly shorter than that of the long-haired variety. Strong neck. Deep, broad chest. Oblique croup. Long back.

LIMBS
Two dewclaws on hind legs.

Well-knit hind legs. The feet of the smooth-muzzled variety are more compact and arched than those of the long-haired variety.

TAIL
Long-haired variety: not too long, full fringe, attached low and forming a hook at the tip; often docked. Smooth-muzzled variety: fairly long, thick hair forming a flag, carried low; hook at the tip; tail circles over the back making a wheel when dog is alerted.

COAT
Long-haired variety: long- or medium-length, thick, almost flat or slightly wavy; more wooly on the croup and thighs; hair on muzzle and cheeks falls forward. Smooth-muzzled variety: thick, flat, fairly long and flexible; longer on the tail

and around the neck; head covered with short, fine hair; short hair on legs and breeching on the thighs.

COLOR
Long-haired variety: dark fawn with or without a mixture of black hairs, occasionally with white spots on the chest and feet; light gray with white on the head, chest and legs; shades of harlequin. White coat is a disqualification. Smooth-muzzled variety: white or white with gray (badger), pale yellow, wolf gray or tan spots on the head, ears and base of the tail. Badger coat preferred.

SIZE
Long-haired variety
Dog: 40 to 48 cm (16-19 in).
Bitch: 38 to 46 (15-18 in).
Smooth-muzzled variety
Dog: 40 to 54 cm (16-21 in).
Bitch: 40 to 52 cm (16-20.5 in).

WEIGHT
Both varieties: 8 to 15 Kg (17.5-33 lb).

Character, special skills and training
The smooth-muzzled pyrenean Shepherd dog is a less nervous, more trainable dog than the long-haired variety. Hyperactive and energetic, with an excessively nervous disposition, this dog needs constant exercise. This is not an easy breed. This courageous dog is rather vocal, is wary of anything unknown, and is constantly on guard. He needs a strong-minded owner.

Care and functions
This dog is not suited to apartment living. If left alone, he will destroy everything within reach. If not given enough exercise, he will become aggressive. Weekly brushing is adequate.
· Sheepdog.
· Guard dog.
· Pet.
· Utility dog: search-and-rescue (in wreckage), drug and explosives dog.

Southern Russian Sheepdog

This breed is descended from Asian Molossian types and was later crossed with Borzois to give it a more streamlined silhouette. The breed was officially recognized in the USSR in 1952 and was the first Russian breed to be recognized by the FCI. The red army used this dog as a sentry. This breed is still rare outside of its country of origin.

1

SHEEPDOGS

COUNTRY OF ORIGIN
Russia

ORIGINAL NAME
Yuznarusskaya Ovtcharka

OTHER NAMES
Southern Russian Owtcharka
Ovtcharka de Russie
Meridionale

Robust constitution. Muscular.
Natural gaits: lumbering
trot and gallop.

Medium Breeds
between
10 and 25 kg
(20-55 lb)

HEAD
Elongated, with a moderately wide forehead. Slight stop. Large nose.

EYES
Dark color, oval. Set horizontally in the skull.

EARS
Fairly small, drop, triangular.

BODY
Very muscular. No dewlap. Fairly deep, broad chest, slightly flattened on the sides. Belly moderately tucked up. Strong, straight back. Short, broad, rounded loin.

LIMBS
Legs with plenty of bone. Strong, oval feet with well-arched toes.

TAIL
Long.

COAT
Long (10 to 15 cm) (4-6 in), rough, thick, bushy, slightly wavy. Heavy undercoat.

COLOR
White, white and yellow, straw, gray, dark gray. White with small gray markings or flecked with gray.

SIZE
Dog: less than 65 cm (25.6 in).
Bitch: less than 62 cm (24.5 in).

WEIGHT
Approx. 25 kg (55 lb).

Character, special skills and training
This active dog is robust, strong and well-balanced. He is well-known for his courage and is distrustful of strangers. This dominant dog is very protective of his owner. Though he can be aggressive, he can be a good companion with proper training.

Care and functions
This dog needs a lot of exercise. Regular brushing is required.
· Sheepdog.
· Guard and defense dog.
· Pet.

Shetland Sheepdog

The Shetland Sheepdog's name indicates where this breed originated – the Shetland Islands off the northern coast of Scotland. He is thought to have been the result of crosses between Scottish collies, the "Yakki" dogs of Greenland whalers, and the Spitz that accompanied Scandinavian fishers. Others believe the Shetland Sheepdog is descended from the King Charles Spaniel. Called "Sheltie" for short, this breed looks like a miniature, long-haired collie. A Shetland Sheepdog club was formed in the Shetlands in 1908. The breed was introduced in England in the late 19th century but was not officially recognized until 1914.

Miniature version of the collie.
Balanced body.
Free action.

SHEEPDOGS

COUNTRY OF ORIGIN
United Kingdom

OTHER NAME
Sheltie

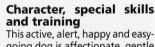

WEIGHT
5 to 10 kg
(11-22 lb).

Small Breeds under 10 kg (under 20 lb)

1

HEAD
Long and wedge-shaped. Flat, straight skull. Slight stop.

EYES
Set obliquely in skull, almond-shaped. Dark brown color, though blue or merle eyes are permitted for some merle varieties.

EARS
Small, carried three-fourths erect breaking forward at the tip.

BODY
Length slightly greater than height. Muscular and well-balanced. Deep chest with well-sprung ribs. Straight back.

LIMBS
Oval feet. Thick pads. Compact, knuckled-up toes. Strong-boned legs.

TAIL
Carried low. Abundantly feathered. Raised when dog is alert, but never carried above the level of the back.

COAT
Long, straight, harsh. Abundant, short, soft undercoat. Very full mane and frill giving the dog a majestic air. Hind legs are heavily feathered.

COLOR
Shades of sable – from golden through mahogany; tricolor – jet black with tan and white markings; blue merle – silvery blue, mottling, merled with black; black and white; black and tan.

SIZE
Dog: 36 to 40 cm (14-16 in).
Bitch: 34 to 38 cm (13-15 in).

Character, special skills and training
This active, alert, happy and easy-going dog is affectionate, gentle and easy to train. He is reserved toward strangers, but never fearful. This dog is vocal.

Care and functions
Brushing two times per week is required, more often during periods of seasonal shedding. Do not bathe this breed more than once per month. Daily walks are necessary.
· Sheepdog.
· Pet.

Old English Sheepdog

The ancestry of the Bobtail is disputed. Some believe this breed descended long ago from Sheepdogs, including the Italian Mastiff (extinct), introduced by the Romans. Others believe the Bobtail is the result of crossing continental and English Sheepdogs, such as the Puli and the Briard. Wherever he came from, the Bobtail has been around for centuries. A 1771 Gainsborough painting depicts this breed. The Old English Sheepdog was shown for the first time at the 1873 dog show in Birmingham. Officially recognized in the United Kingdom in 1888, the first Old English Sheepdog club was formed in the United States in 1900.

Cobby, muscular and short-bodied. Body high on the legs. Square body outline. Characteristic rolling, elastic gallop.

1

SHEEPDOGS

COUNTRY OF ORIGIN
United Kingdom

OTHER NAME
Bobtail

Large Breeds between 25 and 45 kg (55-100 lb)

HEAD
Strong and blocky. Capacious skull. Well-defined stop. Square, strong, truncated muzzle. Large nose.

EYES
Wide-set. Dark color or walleye. Blue eyes are acceptable.

EARS
Small, carried flat against the head.

BODY
Short and compact. Deep, full chest with well-sprung ribs. Shoulders well laid back. Legs with plenty of bone. Gently arched, stout loin. Withers lower than the loin. Long neck.

LIMBS
Small, round feet with well-arched toes. Thick, hard pads.

TAIL
Bobtailed or docked.

COAT
Profuse, hard texture, shaggy, free from curl. Thicker on the hindquarters than on the rest of the body. Soft, dense undercoat.

COLOR
Any shade of gray, grizzle, or blue. The body and hindquarters are of uniform color, with or without small white markings on the feet (socks). The head, neck, legs and underbody must be white. Any brown markings are faults.

SIZE
Dog: minimum of 61 cm (24 in). Bitch: minimum of 56 cm (22 in).

WEIGHT
25 to 30 kg (55-66 lb).

Character, special skills and training
The old english Sheepdog is a vigorous, playful animal. He is neither fearful nor aggressive. This affectionate breed is calm and even-tempered. Nicknamed the "nanny dog", he always looks out for the children. Though he has the heart of a guardian, he is not aggressive and will not bite. Besides, with his teddy bear appearance and "broken" bark, he does not look particularly threatening.

Care and functions
The old english Sheepdog can adapt to city life in an apartment if he is always with his owner and can have time to run each day. He does not bear the heat well. This intelligent dog has a mind of his own, and therefore needs firm training. Daily brushing is very important to keep his profuse, shaggy coat from knotting.
. Sheepdog (now rarely used as a Sheepdog).
. Pet.

Border Collie

It is thought that the Border Collie's ancestors are Nordic breeds that guarded reindeer herds. When they arrived on the British Isles with the Vikings, they were crossed with local sheepdogs. The Border Collie was named after the region where the breed was developed, the hilly border country between England and Scotland. The most common of the Collies, the Border Collie still has the same duties today as he did in the eighteenth century—guarding the herd.
The breed was not standardized until the nineteenth century. It was recognized by the Kennel Club of England in 1976 and by the Canadian Kennel Club in 1985.

Agile and elegant. Moves with minimal lift of the feet.

SHEEPDOGS

1

COUNTRY OF ORIGIN
Great Britain

Medium Breeds between 10 and 25 kg (20-55 lb)

HEAD
Moderately long skull. Strong, relatively short muzzle. Distinct stop. Black, brown, or dark gray nose, according to coat color.

EYES
Oval, set well apart. Brown color except for merles, which may have blue eyes.

EARS
Medium size, set well apart, and carried erect or semi-erect.

BODY
Well-balanced and athletic. Strong neck. Ribs well sprung. Muscular loin. Moderately broad chest, well let down.

LIMBS
Oval feet. Compact, arched toes.

TAIL
Moderately long. Set low, curving up slightly at the tip.

COAT
There are two varieties, the rough coat, which has a mane, culottes and fox tail (brush), and the smooth coat. In both varieties, the coat is dense and of medium texture; dense, soft undercoat.

COLOR
Generally pied, with white collar, blaze and socks, with the remainder of the coat being black. All colors permissible, but white must not be the dominant color.

SIZE
Dog: 50 to 55 cm (20-22 in).
Bitch: 47 to 52 cm (18.5-20.5 in).

WEIGHT
15 to 20 kg (33-44 lb).

Character, special skills and training
This energetic, eager dog is very gentle by nature, though is a tenacious worker. He is exceptionally devoted to his owner and is easy to train because he is alert and highly intelligent. The Border Collie is reserved toward strangers, but is not shy or aggressive. This breed has a keen sense of smell, but it is best known for its ability to "eye", a skill that he uses to will sheep to move and turn. While working with his owner, the dog crouches a short distance from a sheep and stares intently into its eyes, seeming to hypnotize it; he then slowly creeps up like a hunting dog. The Border Collie is the best represented breed at herding trials.

Care and functions
This dog is a sheepdog through and through and must remain as such. His training begins around the age of six months and can last one or two years. He does not adapt well to urban living, though can adapt rather easily to life as a family pet. This tireless sheepdog requires daily exercise. No special grooming or other care is required.
. Sheepdog. This dog's inborn skills and breeding make it the ideal herder, which it should remain.

BELGIAN SHEEPDOG, MALINOIS

Belgian

The four varieties of the large Belgian Sheepdog are thought to be descended from herders from central Europe or from interbreeding of local breeds of Mastiff and Deerhound brought over from England in the 13ᵗʰ century. In the 19ᵗʰ century, there were many Sheepdog-looking native dogs of varied coloration and hair type. The first breeds were recognized around 1885. The Belgian Shepherd Club was formed in 1891 after A. Reul, a professor of animal breeding, cataloged four distinct varieties.

1

SHEEPDOGS

1

COUNTRY OF ORIGIN
Belgium

ORIGINAL NAMES
Groenendael, Groenendaler, Lakense, Mechelaar, Tervurense, Tervuren

OTHER NAMES
Groenendael, Laekense, Malinois, Tervuren

Balanced proportions. Square body.
Wolf-like. Well-balanced.
Elegant solidity without bulkiness.

Large Breeds
between
25 and 45 kg
(55-100 lb)

BELGIAN SHEEPDOG, TERVUREN
The second most popular of the Belgian
Sheepdogs (following the Malinois).

Sheepdog

In 1898, the long-haired black Belgian Sheepdog was given the name Groenendael. At the same time, at the Royal Castle of Laeken, the wire-haired, fawn Belgian Sheepdog was named the Laekenois. This last variety is now very rare. Most short-haired Belgian Sheepdogs from the area of Malines were named Malinois. A brewer near Tervuren bred long-haired, fawn Belgian Sheepdogs and produced what came to be called the Tervuren.

BELGIAN SHEEPDOG, GROENENDAEL
Named after the castle of the variety's primary breeder, N. Rose.

BELGIAN SHEEPDOG, LAEKENOIS
The rarest of the Belgian Sheepdogs.

HEAD
Long, filled-up, and finely chiseled. The muzzle tapers gradually. Straight forehead. Moderate, though marked, stop. Lips well closed. Smooth, flat cheeks.

EYES
Medium size, almondlike. Browncolor. Black rims.

EARS
Set on high, straight, rigid, triangular.

BODY
Powerful without being bulky. Long neck. The chest is not broad. Tight, strong musculature. Proud carriage of the head. Straight, broad, powerful back. Slight sloping of the croup

LIMBS
Round, compact toes. Powerful hind legs, not bulky

TAIL
Medium length, strong at the base. Carried down when relaxed; does not form a hook or curve.

COAT
Always abundant and dense. Wooly undercoat. Collarette, culottes on the thighs. Long-haired (short on the head) – Groenendael and Tervuren. Short-haired (flat on the head) – Malinois. Wire-haired (harsh, dry, shaggy, 6 cm (2,4 in) long – Laekenois.

COLOR
the mask must cover the face with a solid area of black. Tervuren: warm fawn well-filled with black (preferred). Malinois: only fawn tinged with black, with black mask. Groenendael: only solid black. Laekenois: fawn with flecks of black on the muzzle and tail.

SIZE
Dog: 60 to 66 cm (23,5-26 in).
Bitch: 56 to 62 cm (22-24,5 in).

WEIGHT
28 to 35 kg (61,5-77 lb).

Character, special skills and training
Nervous, sensitive and impulsive, this breed is extremely lively in his response to stimuli. Watchful, attentive, with a strong personality, he is remarkably devoted to his owner and is occasionally aggressive toward strangers. He is very energetic, active and dynamic, and needs a lot of exercise. The Belgian Sheepdog will not accept a leash. The Malinois, which was chosen for guard dog and sporting activities at the end of the 19th century, is more assertive and has a stronger personality than the other calmer varieties because of its true sheepdog origins. These very sensitive dogs cannot tolerate harsh treatment. Training must be firm, but gentle, and undertaken with the greatest patience.

Care and functions
This breed needs peaceful surroundings and regular exercise to blossom. Long-haired varieties require weekly brushing.
. Sheepdog.
. Guard dog, police dog, good trackers, search-and-rescue, customs.
. Pet (very attached to his owner and environment).

Catalan Sheepdog

This breed came from Catalonia, Spain.
It is presumed that he is descended from the ancient
Pyrenees Sheepdogs. During the Spanish Civil War,
the Catalan Sheepdog served as messenger and sentry.

Medium breed. Slightly longer than tall. Dark, thick skin. Normal gait: short trot.

1

SHEEPDOGS

COUNTRY OF ORIGIN
Spain

ORIGINAL NAMES
Gos d'Atura Catala
Perro de Pastor Catalan

OTHER NAME
Catalonian Shepherd

Medium Breeds
between
10 and 25 kg
(20-55 lb)

HEAD
Strong, slightly convex. Pronounced stop. Straight, short forehead. Cone-shaped muzzle.

EYES
Round. Dark amber eyes. Black rims.

EARS
Set on high. Fine leather. Drop, triangular ending in a point. Cropped ears are acceptable for working dogs.

BODY
Strong with length being slightly greater than height. Deep chest. Ribs well sprung. Straight back Powerful, slightly sloped croup

LIMBS
Oval feet. Black nails and pads. Strong legs. Two dewclaws on hind legs

TAIL
Attached low. Long or short (maximum length 10 cm (4 in). Some varieties are naturally tailless. Docked tail is permitted for working dogs. Hangs in a hook when relaxed. Richly clad with hair.

COAT
Long, flat and rough. Thick undercoat. Full beard, mustache, forelock and fall. Seasonal shedding occurs in two stages, beginning with the front half of the body, followed by the back half of the body.

COLOR
Color created by a mixture of hairs of various shades – fawn, reddish-brown, gray, black and white. The base colors are fawn, gray and sable.

SIZE
Dog: 47 to 55 cm (18.5-22 in).

Bitch: 45 to 53 cm (18-21 in).

WEIGHT
Dog: approx. 18 kg (40 lb). Bitch: approx. 16 kg (35 lb).

Character, special skills and training
The Catalan Sheepdog is courageous, intelligent and energetic. His greatest traits shine through when herding; not only is he obedient to the commands of his handler, but he often takes the initiative, directing the sheep with remarkable ease. This brave, alert breed also makes an excellent guard dog. As a pet, he is loyal and gentle with children. This breed is well adapted to living outdoors.

Care and functions
While this dog can live indoors, he needs a lot of exercise. Daily brushing is required.
. Sheepdog (guard and herder)·
. Guard dog, police dog.
. Pet.

Croatian Sheepdog

This dog of eastern origin is almost unknown outside his home country, where he has guarded farms and herds for centuries. The breed is thought to be descended from northern Croatian sheepdogs.

Rectangular body outline. Fine-boned.
Preferred gait: Trot.

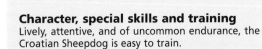

SHEEPDOGS

COUNTRY OF ORIGIN
Croat Republic

ORIGINAL NAME
Hrvatski Ovcar

Medium Breeds
between
10 and 25 kg
(20-55 lb)

1

HEAD
Fine, wedge-shaped (approx. 20 cm (7,9 in) long), dry overall. Eyebrows not pronounced. Cheeks filled out. Stop not pronounced. Straight nose bridge.

EYES
Chestnut to black color. Medium size. Almond shape. Dark rims.

EARS
Triangular, erect or semi-erect. Moderate length. Attached toward the sides of the head. Erect ears are preferred and must not be cropped.

BODY
Slightly longer than tall. Short, muscular back is very muscular in the short lumbar region. Chest not prominent. Ribs well sprung. Solid, well-filled out flanks. Croup slightly sloped.

LIMBS
Muscular legs. Small, slightly oval feet.

TAIL
Set on moderately high. Long, bushy hair. Carried below the line of the back at rest, above when alert.

COAT
Relatively soft. Wavy or curly. Never wooly. Short on the face. Long (7 to 14 cm) (2.8-5.5 in) on the back. Feathering and culottes on the legs. Bushy undercoat.

COLOR
Black background. Some white markings on the throat, forechest, and chest are permissible. White markings on the feet and toes are tolerated, but not desirable.

SIZE
Approx. 40 to 50 cm (16-20 in).

WEIGHT
15 to 20 kg (33-44 lb).

Character, special skills and training
Lively, attentive, and of uncommon endurance, the Croatian Sheepdog is easy to train.

Care and functions
This dog requires exercise and room to run.
· Herder.
· Guard dog.

Dutch Shepherd

This breed, developed in the Netherlands in the 19th century, is a cross between local Sheepdogs and the Belgian Malinois. The varieties (short-, long- and rough-haired) have been introduced over the years at dog shows.

Medium size. Lupoid. Powerfully built. Free, relaxed gait.

1

SHEEPDOGS

COUNTRY OF ORIGIN
Netherlands

ORIGINAL NAMES
Hollandse Herder
Hollandse Herdershond

Large Breeds between 25 and 45 kg (55-100 lb)

HEAD
Clean, long, not massive. The rough-haired variety has a slightly more blocky head. Straight forehead. Stop barely perceptible. The muzzle is slightly longer than the skull.

EYES
Almond-shaped, of medium size. Dark color.

EARS
Small, erect, held forward. Rounded ears are not permitted.

BODY
Solid and well-balanced. No dewlap. Deep chest. Ribs are slightly sprung. Solid loin. Straight, short, powerful back.

LIMBS
Well-muscled, strong legs with solid bones. Round feet with compact, arched toes. Black nails and pads.

TAIL
Attached low, hanging in a slight curve. Reaches the hocks when relaxed; carried high when in motion.

COAT
The most common variety has short hair over all of the body, with a wooly undercoat. Collarette, culottes and flag tail. Long-haired variety has long hair over all of the body lying close to the body. Straight, harsh, not wavy or curly, with a wooly undercoat. Tail is covered with long, thick hair. The rough-haired variety has thick, wiry hair over all of the body, held away from the body by a thick, wooly undercoat. Dense, long hair on tail and long breeching.

COLOR
Short- and long-haired varieties: shades of brindle on a brown or gray background. Black mask preferred. Rough-haired variety: blue-gray, salt and pepper, gold or silver brindle.

SIZE
Dog: 57 to 62 cm (22.5-24.5 in).
Bitch: 55 to 60 cm (22-24 in).

WEIGHT
Approx. 30 kg (66 lb).

. Sheepdog.
. Guard dog.
. Pet.

Character, special skills and training
This lively, rustic breed has great endurance and is an excellent jumper. He is affectionate, calm, loyal, gentle with children and very attached to his owner. The Dutch Shepherd is fairly aggressive toward other dogs. A guard dog to the core, he makes an excellent army or police dog.

Care and functions
This dog needs heavy physical activity on a daily basis. The three hair-types require weekly brushing.

Perro de Pastor Mallorquin

This ancient breed originating on the Balearic Islands is used as a guard dog and herder for flocks of sheep and goats.

Solid, rustic appearance. Well-balanced. Light gray skin. Swift, elegant, confident gallop.

SHEEPDOGS

Large Breeds between 25 and 45 kg (55-100 lb)

COUNTRY OF ORIGIN
Spain

ORIGINAL NAMES
Perro de Pastor Mallorquin
Ca de Bestiar

1

1

HEAD
Massive. Gently sloped stop. Broad muzzle. Black lips.

EYES
Slightly almond-shaped, set obliquely. Light or dark color. Black rims.

EARS
Drop, triangular, set on high. Thick.

BODY
Large, sturdy and well-proportioned. Solid neck. Full chest with well-sprung ribs. Broad, powerful loin. Broad, square croup. Horizontal back.

LIMBS
Hare-like feet. Sound legs.

TAIL
Fairly long, curves up in the shape of a saber when dog is alert.

COAT
Short-haired (most common) variety – 1.5 to 3 cm (0.6-1.2 in) on the back. Very fine undercoat. Long-haired variety – slightly wavy on the back (approx. 7 cm) (2.8 in). Fairly light undercoat. Both varieties have soft, fine, weather-resistant hair.

COLOR
Black, white markings acceptable only on the breast and the feet. Jet black is preferred.

SIZE
Dog: 66 to 73 cm (26-29 in). Bitch: 62 to 68 cm (24-26.8 in).

WEIGHT
Approx. 40 kg (88 lb).

Character, special skills and training
This fleet-footed, robust breed is agile, brave and extremely territorial. The Perro de Pastor Mallorquin is calm, affectionate and loyal. He bonds only to his owner and is wary by instinct around strangers.

Care and functions
This breed needs to be brushed occasionally and requires room to run and exercise.
. Herder.
. Guard and defense dog.
. Pet.

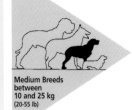

Polish Lowland Sheepdog

The Polish Lowland Sheepdog was bred from the Hungarian Puli and other Asian Sheepdogs, such as the Tibetan Terrier. This relative of the Old English Sheepdog (and possibly the Bearded Collie) is a good guardian of the flock. The breed almost disappeared after WWII, but in 1971, it was recognized by the FCI.

Medium breed. Rectangular silhouette. Relaxed, extended gait (pace).

1

SHEEPDOGS

COUNTRY OF ORIGIN
Poland

ORIGINAL NAME
Polski Owczarek Nizinny

OTHER NAME
Valee Sheepdog

Medium Breeds between 10 and 25 kg (20-55 lb)

HEAD
Medium size. Domed skull. Distinct stop. Large nose. Long, tousled hair on the forehead, cheeks and chin, giving the face a soft look.

EYES
Oval, hazel color, with dark rims.

EARS
Medium size, drop, set on fairly high.

BODY
Stocky, strong and muscular. Strong neck. Deep chest. Broad loin. Very muscular back. Short croup.

LIMBS
Oval, compact feet.

TAIL
Naturally short; docked if necessary.

COAT
Coarse, dense, thick and abundant. Soft undercoat. Long fall over the eyes is characteristic of the breed.

COLOR
All colors acceptable, including piebald.

SIZE
Dog: 45 to 50 cm (17.5-20 in).
Bitch: 42 to 47 cm (16.5-18.5 in).

WEIGHT
15 to 20 kg (33-44 lb).

Character, special skills and training
This is an alert, courageous, rustic breed that is well-adapted to living outdoors in harsh weather conditions. The Polish Lowland Sheepdog is intelligent, dominant, vocal and strong-willed. This dog requires firm training. Very distrustful of strangers, he is an excellent guard dog. Unfailingly loyal, this happy dog adores his owner and children, making him a good pet.

Care and functions
This sheepdog can adjust to city living if he is given a lot of exercise. Brushing once or twice per week is required.
· Sheepdog.
· Guard dog.
· Pet.

Portuguese Sheepdog

Some experts believe today's Portuguese Sheepdog is descended from a pair of Briards imported by the Conde de Castro Cuimaraes in the early 20th century. But today's breed has its own distinct characteristics. It is very similar to the Pyrenean Shepherd Dog, which leads us to believe a branch of this breed already existed and breeders tried to improve the breed by crossing it with the Briard.

Medium size. Monkey-like appearance and behavior.

1

SHEEPDOGS

COUNTRY OF ORIGIN
Portugal

ORIGINAL NAME
Cao da Serra de Aires

OTHER NAME
"Monkey Dog"

Medium Breeds
between
10 and 25 kg
(20-55 lb)

1

HEAD
Strong and broad. Domed skull. Occipital protuberance is visible. Marked stop. Rectangular, slightly hollow forehead. Well set off, slightly turned up nose.

EYES
Dark color, round, set horizontally, full of life. Black rims.

EARS
Set on high, drop (without folds). Cropped: carried erect, triangular, medium length, finely textured and smooth.

BODY
Length greater than height.

No dewlap. Broad, prominent chest. Muscular thighs. Deep chest is well let down. Long back. Short, arched loin.

LIMBS
Round feet, not flat. Long toes covered with hair that is darker in color than the rest of the coat. Thick, tough pads. Strong legs.

TAIL
Set on high. Pointed. Reaches the hocks curving at tip when relaxed, curling up slightly when the dog is in motion.

COAT
Long, straight or slightly

wavy, forming a long beard and mustache.

COLOR
Shades of yellow, brown, gray, fawn, wolf gray and black, marked with tan, with or without a mixture of white hairs.

SIZE
Dog: 45 to 55 cm (17.5-21.5 in).
Bitch: 42 to 52 cm (16.5-20.5 in).

WEIGHT
12 to 18 kg (26.5-39.8 lb).

This dog needs space and

Character, special skills and training
Rustic, serious and very active, the portuguese Sheepdog is extremely devoted to his owner and the animals that he guards. He is always hostile toward strangers.

Care and functions
This is not a city-dweller. exercise. Weekly brushing is adequate.
· Sheepdog.
· Guard dog.
· Pet.

Polish Mountain Dog

Like many European Molossian types, the Polish Mountain Dog may be descended from Tibetan Sheepdogs that arrived during the massive invasions from the East. Related to the Hungarian Kuvasz, this dog guards the flocks in the high valleys of the Tatra range (the highest peaks of the Carpathians), protecting them from bears and wolves. Almost wiped out during WWII, this breed was recognized by the FCI in 1967. A very popular breed in its country of origin.

Strong, compact build. Rectangular body ouline.

1

SHEEPDOGS

COUNTRY OF ORIGIN
Poland

ORIGINAL NAME
Owerzarek Podkalanski

OTHER NAMES
Tatra Mountain Sheepdog
Owczarek Tatrzanski

Large Breeds
between
25 and 45 kg
(55-100 lb)

HEAD
Clean and broad. Marked stop. Large muzzle. Broad forehead.

EYES
Medium size, set slightly oblique. Dark brown color. Dark rims.

EARS
Medium size, drop, set on high. Triangular, fairly thick.

BODY
Long, sturdy and muscular. No dewlap. Deep chest. Broad, well-knit loin. Ribs sloping and rather flat. Belly moderately tucked up. Sloping croup. Straight, broad back.

LIMBS
Strong-boned legs. Oval, strong feet. Strong, hard pads.

TAIL
Set on low. Carried below the topline, curving slightly at the tip. Covered with thick hair forming a flag.

COAT
Short and thick on the head and front of the forelegs. Long, thick and straight on the neck and body. Thick mane. Heavy undercoat.

COLOR
Uniform white. Cream markings are not desirable.

SIZE
Dog: 65 to 70 cm (25.6-27.5 in).
Bitch: 60 to 65 cm (23.6-25.6 in).

WEIGHT
30 to 45 kg (66-99 lb).

· Guard dog.
· Pet.

Character, special skills and training
This hardy breed is courageous, lively and alert. He is an agile, swift runner. He is naturally gentle and calm and must never be treated harshly. Loyal to his owner and affectionate with children, he watches over his territory and family.

Care and functions
This dog must not live in an apartment. He needs considerable space and exercise. Weekly brushing is sufficient. During seasonal shedding, stripping the coat is recommended.
· Sheepdog.

Saarloos Wolfhond

Around 1930 in Rotterdam, L. Saarloos crossed a German Shepherd with a Russian wolf in an attempt to increase the German Shepherd's endurance and hardiness. In 1975, the Saarloos Wolfhond was recognized in the Netherlands. In 1981, the FCI officially recognized the breed. The Saarloos Wolfhond is rare outside its country of origin.

Lupoid. Balanced construction. Gait resembles that of the wolf.

1

SHEEPDOGS

COUNTRY OF ORIGIN
Netherlands

ORIGINAL NAME
Saarloos Wolfhound

Large Breeds between 25 and 45 kg (55-100 lb)

1

HEAD
Wolflike, well-balanced in relation to the rest of the body. Wide, flat skull. Slight stop. Broad muzzle. Black or liver nose, depending on the color of the coat. Tight-lipped jaws.

EYES
Medium size, almond. Preferably yellow color.

EARS
Medium size. Thick, pointed, held erect.

BODY
Powerful. Slightly longer than tall. Smooth, muscular neck. Ribs well sprung. Powerful, muscular rump. Slightly sloped croup. Straight, massive back.

LIMBS
Oval, very compact feet Long, strong-boned legs.

TAIL
At rest, carried in the shape of a saber.

COAT
Harsh and straight (in the shape of a baton). Thick, wooly undercoat.

COLOR
Light to dark black (wolf gray), light to dark brown, cream to white. Any other color is a disqualification.

SIZE
Dog: 65 to 75 cm (25.6-29.5 in). Bitch: 60 to 70 cm (23.6-27.5 in).

WEIGHT
30 to 35 kg (66-77 lb).

Character, special skills and training
This attentive, affectionate dog is reserved toward strangers. When with other dogs, his pack instinct is still strong. Independent and stubborn, this dog needs a handler capable of dominating him mentally without resorting to physical blows. It is vital to socialize this dog well during the first two years of his life.

Care and functions
The saarloos wolfhond is not suited for urban life. Even in the country, he needs regular walks. The coat does not require any special care.
· Guide dog.
. Rescue dog.
· Pet.

Czechoslovakian Wolfdog

In 1955, german shepherds and carpathian wolves were crossed in Czechoslovakia. In 1965, a project to selectively breed this animal was undertaken in the hope of combining the best of the wolf and the dog. In 1982, the Cesky Vlcak was recognized as a national breed by the Czechoslovakian committee of breeder associations. In 1994, the FCI recognized the breed.

1

SHEEPDOGS

COUNTRY OF ORIGIN
Czech Republic

ORIGINAL NAME
Cesky Vlcak

Wolflike (gait, coat, mask). Robust constitution. Gait: smooth, relaxed, trot with good reach.

Large Breeds between 25 and 45 kg (55-100 lb)

HEAD
Obtuse cone-shape. Slightly domed forehead. Stop moderately pronounced. Rectangular nose bridge. Oval nose.

EYES
Narrow, set obliquely in the skull. Amber color.

EARS
Held erect. Narrow, short, triangular.

BODY
Robust. Rectangular body outline. Smooth, muscular neck. Full chest. Short, muscular loin. Short, slightly sloped croup. Rectangular back.

LIMBS
Powerful hind legs. Solid forelegs with dry joints. Large front feet turned slightly out.

TAIL
Set on high, hanging straight down at rest. Sickle tail when in action.

COAT
Straight, close-lying. Undercoat is abundant in winter.

COLOR
Wolf coloring or silvery gray with characteristic light mask. Light hairs at the base of the neck and on the chest. Dark gray mask is tolerated.

SIZE
Dog: at least 65 cm (25.5 in).
Bitch: at least 60 cm (23.5 in).

WEIGHT
Dog: at least 26 kg (57.5 lb).
Bitch: at least 20 kg (44 lb).

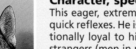

Character, special skills and training
This eager, extremely active dog has great endurance and quick reflexes. He is bold and courageous. While he is exceptionally loyal to his owner, he is distant and wary around strangers (men in particular). His sense of smell is considerably more developed than that of most dogs. With his powers of dissuasion, perhaps this breed should be trained as a guard and defense dog.

Care and functions
The cesky vlcak should be owned only by individuals who have an excellent understanding of animal behavior.
· Guard and defense dog.

Collie

The Collie is descended from Scottish herding dogs. When the Romans invaded, their dogs were crossed with native Scottish dogs. Early shepherds began crossing the short-tailed and long-tailed shepherd dogs, and the result was the superb animal with an aristocratic bearing that we know today. The origin of this breed's name is disputed. Some believe the name comes from the word "colley", an early variety of Scottish sheep with a black mask and tail. Others believe the breed is named for its beautiful collar. The smooth Collie is much less common than the Rough Collie.

Extremely beautiful. Dignified carriage.

1

SHEEPDOGS

COUNTRY OF ORIGIN
Great Britain

ORIGINAL NAMES
Two varieties:
Smooth Collie
Rough Collie

OTHER NAME
Scotch Collie

Between 10 and 45 kg (20-100 lb)

1

HEAD
Long, clean, wedge-shaped. Size in proportion to body. Flat skull. Slight stop.

EYES
Medium size, almond, set obliquely in the skull. Dark brown color, except blue merles that often have blue or blue flecked eyes.

EARS
Medium size, fairly wide set. Carried forward and semi-erect.

BODY
Medium size, longer than tall. Powerful neck. Deep chest. Ribs well sprung. Straight back with a slightly arched loin.

LIMBS
Oval feet. Compact, arched toes. Muscular legs with a fair amount of bone.

TAIL
Long, reaching the hocks. Generally carried low. Profuse covering of hair.

COAT
Rough Collie: straight, harsh, long and dense; soft, dense undercoat; abundant on the mane and frill; feathering on the legs. Smooth collie: flat and harsh; dense undercoat.

COLOR
Three colors are recognized: sable – from light gold to dark mahogany. Tricolor – predominantly black with tan shadings on the head and legs and white markings. Blue merle (marbled) – blue-gray marbled or mottled with black.

SIZE
Dog: 56 to 61 cm (22-24 in).
Bitch: 51 to 56 cm (20-22 in).

WEIGHT
Dog: 20 to 29 kg (44-64 lb).
Bitch: 18 to 25 kg (39.5-55 lb).

Character, special skills and training
This active, lively dog is typically well-balanced, but can be anxious and timid. This gentle, sensitive lassie dog is a faithful companion. The Collie is reserved toward strangers, but not aggressive. He should receive firm, but gentle training.

Care and functions
The Collie can live in the city but he will be happier with a yard and space to run. Regular exercise is required. Brushing two times per week is adequate.
· Sheepdog.
· Police dog, guide dog.
· Pet.

Bearded Collie

Some writers believe the Bearded Collie's oldest ancestor is the Magyar Komondor of central Europe. Others contest that this breed is the result of a cross between a Scottish sheepdog and the Polski Owczarek Nizinny, a Polish sheepdog, and was developed in the Highlands of Scotland. This breed almost disappeared in the 20th century, replaced by the Old English Sheepdog. But thanks to the efforts of a Scottish breeder, the breed began a comeback in 1950 and continues to flourish today.

Solid construction. Free, supple gait.

1

SHEEPDOGS

COUNTRY OF ORIGIN
Great Britain

OTHER NAMES
Highland Collie
Beardie

Between
10 and 45 kg
(20-100 lb)

HEAD
Wide and flat. Strong muzzle. Moderate stop. Large, squarish nose.

EYES
Large and wide-set. Color varies according to coat color. Eyebrows arched to the sides, framing the head.

EARS
Medium size, hanging close to the head.

BODY
Long. Deep chest. Ribs well sprung. Strong loin Straight back Underline fairly high off the ground.

LIMBS
Oval feet. Compact, arched toes. Thick pads. Legs with substantial bone.

TAIL
Set low and covered with abundant hair. Not kinked or twisted. Carried low and curving up slightly at the tip.

COAT
Long, flat, harsh, strong and shaggy. Sometimes wavy. Coat increases in length at the cheeks and chin, forming the characteristic beard.

COLOR
Slate, dark fawn, black, blue, any shade of gray, with or without white markings. Coat does not take on its definitive color until the age of three, lightening and darkening several times over the first three years.

SIZE
Dog: 53 to 56 cm (21-22 in).
Bitch: 51 to 53 cm (20-21 in).

WEIGHT
20 to 30 kg (44-66 lb).

Character, special skills and training
This well-balanced, lively dog is neither shy nor aggressive. He is self-confident, affectionate, and always ready to play. The bearded Collie, which becomes very attached to his owner and adores children, does not like to be left alone. Though he barks a lot, he does not make a very good guard dog. His good sense of smell is put to use searching for truffles. Early, firm (though not harsh) training is required.

Care and functions
The bearded Collie can adapt to being a house dog if he has many opportunities to go out and is not left alone. Regular brushing, at least twice per week, is required to keep his coat tangle-free. Otherwise, it will be impossible to brush out all of the knots.
· Pet.

Kelpie

This breed is probably the result of a cross between the Dingo (an Australia wild dog) and the short-haired Scottish Collie brought to Australia in the late 1860s. The breed's name is said to have been taken from a novel by R.L. Stevenson in which a devil river called Kelpie is mentioned. Thought not very well-known in Europe, the Kelpie is the primary working dog used on Australia and New Zealand ranches.

Hardy. Solid. Flexible

HEAD
LOng, narrow, fox-like. Slightly domed skull. Pronounced stop. Tight, clean lips.

EYES
Almond-shaped. Brown, in harmony with coat color.

EARS
Carried erect, coming to a fine point at the tip. Thin ear leather. Interior of the earflap is well-clad with hairs.

BODY
Moderately long neck without dewlap. Full collarette. Topline is strong and horizontal. Chest well let down, deeper than broad. Ribs well sprung. Strong, muscular loin. Rather long, sloped croup.

LIMBS
Muscular legs strong of bone. Round, strong feet. Thick pads. Compact, arched toes. Short, strong nails.

TAIL
Hangs down in a slight curve reaching the hocks. Well-clad, brush.

COAT
Thick, straight, hard, close-lying, short (2-3 cm) (0.8-1.2 in). Longer on the underbody and back of the legs. Collarette at the neck. Short, dense undercoat.

COLOR
Black, black and tan, red, red and tan, chocolate (brown), and smoky blue.

SIZE
Dog: 46 to 51 cm (18-20 in).
Bitch: 43 to 48 cm (17-19 in).

Medium Breeds between 10 and 25 kg (20-55 lb)

1

SHEEPDOGS

COUNTRY OF ORIGIN
Australia

ORIGINAL NAME
Australian Kelpie

OTHER NAME
Bard

WEIGHT
11 to 20 kg (24-44 lb).

1

Character, special skills and training
This tireless working dog is extremely active and full of life. The Kelpie is naturally gentle and calm and is a very loyal, devoted dog. The breed has a natural instinct for working sheep, whether in open fields or in the farmyard.

Care and functions
The Kelpie needs exercise and room to run. Weekly brushing is sufficient.
· Herder.

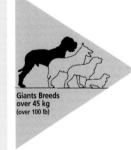

Komondor

This breed is a native sheepdog brought to hungary around 1,000 years ago by the nomadic magyars. The komondor is descended from various asian sheepdogs, including the tibetan Mastiff. This dog has long been used to protect the flocks from wolves and bears and to chase away other pests.

Imposing stature. Noble, dignified gait. Highly pigmented skin. Relaxed gait: walk and stretched out trot.

1

SHEEPDOGS

COUNTRY OF ORIGIN
Hungary

ORIGINAL NAMES
Komondor
kiraly

Giants Breeds
over 45 kg
(over 100 lb)

HEAD
Broad. Size in proportion to the rest of the body. Covered with abundant hair. Domed skull. Pronounced stop. Bridge of nose is straight. Very broad muzzle.

EYES
Oval. Dark color.

EARS
Long and hanging, u-shaped.

BODY
Slightly longer than tall. No dewlap. Broad breast. Deep, barrel chest. Broad loin. Slightly sloping croup. Short back.

LIMBS
Large, round feet. Thick pads. Strong, slate-colored

nails. Front legs look like vertical pillars, with massive bone.

TAIL
Carried hanging down at rest and at the level of the back when in action.

COAT
Long - 20 to 27 cm (8-10.5 in) on the rump; 15 to 22 cm (6-8.7 in) on the back, chest and shoulders; 10 to 18 cm (3.9-7 in) on the head, neck and legs. Hair is harsh, corded and bushy, with a fine, wooly undercoat. At birth, a puppy's coat is made up of soft, fine, curly or wavy white hairs.

COLOR
White.

SIZE
Dog: approx. 80 cm (32 in).
Bitch: approx. 70 cm (28 in).

WEIGHT
Dog: 50 to 60 kg (110-132 lb).
Bitch: 40 to 50 kg (88-110 lb).

Character, special skills and training
This dog is not very affectionate, but is loyal and devoted to his owner and gentle with children. The komondor is a rustic breed that needs vigorous exercise. He is a superb guard dog, protecting the flock and the home with unfailing courage and daring. This dog will fight to the death to protect his owner. When he attacks, it is in determined silence. Particularly firm training is required for this breed.

Care and functions
This dog is not suitable as a house dog; he needs space and a lot of exercise. Komondors are never brushed. Instead, begin separating the cords with your fingers once the dog reaches the age of eight months. The komondor should be bathed only once or twice per year.
· Sheepdog.
· Guard dog.
· Pet.

Kuvasz

Some writers believe the Kuvasz was imported by primitive Hungarians, while others contest that it was brought to the Carpathians by the Kumans, nomadic shepherds of Turkish origin that came to Hungary in the thirteenth century as they tried to escape the invading Mongols. What is certain is that this breed is descended from Asian sheepdogs. In the fifteenth century, King Mathias I used Kuvasz for hunting big game, though this breed is more skilled at guarding flocks than hunting wild boar. Until the nineteenth century, the Kuvasz was used as a flock guard. Later, he was used almost exclusively to guard large estates. This breed is not common outside of its native Hungary, though it is bred in the United States.

Noble and powerful. Almost square body outline. Muscular without bulkiness. Strong-boned. Slow, heavy walk. Swaying trot.

SHEEPDOGS

COUNTRY OF ORIGIN
Hungary

Giants Breeds
over 45 kg
(over 100 lb)

HEAD
Nobel and strong. Long (but not pointed) skull. The longitudinal midline of the forehead is pronounced. Moderate stop. Nose bridge is broad and long. Straight muzzle. Lips closely cover the teeth.

EYES
Set obliquely in the skull, almond shape. Dark brown color.

EARS
relatively small, set on high. Drop, v-shaped. Held slightly away from the head.

BODY
Solidly built and muscular. Powerful neck. Deep chest. Shoulders broad and sloping. Croup slightly sloped. Short loin Straight back. Deep brisket. Highly pigmented skin (slate gray).

LIMBS
Round, compact feet. Strong, slate-colored nails.

TAIL
Bushy, set fairly low. Reaches the hocks, curving up slightly at the tip.

COAT
Strong, wavy and long on the body. Mane on the neck and feathering on the back of the legs. Short, straight hair on the head and front of the legs. Wooly undercoat.

COLOR
White. Ivory is tolerated.

SIZE
Dog: 71 to 75 cm (28-30 in).
Bitch: 66 to 70 cm 26-28 in).

WEIGHT
Dog: 40 to 52 kg (88-115 lb).
Bitch: 30 to 42 kg (66-93 lb).

Character, special skills and training
This loyal dog meets any challenge head on. He is hardy and serious and not overly demonstrative. The kuvasz has a keen sense of smell, which he used in the past to hunt wolf and wild boar.

Care and functions
This dog is not a city-dweller. He needs space and exercise. Daily brushing is required to keep the coat from knotting.
· Sheepdog.
· Guard dog, police dog.
· Pet.

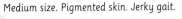

Mudi

This breed is thought to have been developed in the late nineteenth and early twentieth centuries. Some believe it is the result of a cross between a Puli and a Spitz-type breed. The Mudi has always been used to guard and herd sheep and cattle, as well as to hunt wild boar.

Medium size. Pigmented skin. Jerky gait.

1

SHEEPDOGS

COUNTRY OF ORIGIN
Hungary

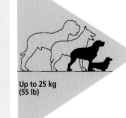

Up to 25 kg
(55 lb)

HEAD
Long and snippy. Slightly domed skull. Straight muzzle. Pointed nose.

EYES
Oval, set slightly oblique. Dark brown color.

EARS
Held erect, pointed, in the shape of an upside-down "v".

BODY
Oblong. Short straight back. Short, sloping croup. Topline sloping from rump to withers. Long, deep chest.

LIMBS
Round, compact feet. Strong, slate nails. Dewclaws not desirable.
Legs plants slightly back.

TAIL
Short or docked at the length of two or three fingers.

COAT
Straight, short and smooth on the head and front of the legs. Longer (5 to 7 cm) (2-3 in), thick, wavy and glossy on the rest of the body.

COLOR
Black, white, or black and white pied, with spots of medium size over all the body. Color of the feet is always that of the dominant coat color.

SIZE
35 to 47 cm (14-18.5 in).

WEIGHT
8 to 13 kg (18-29 lb).

Character, special skills and training
This rustic, hardy, lively, vigorous dog is always on the alert, rather vocal and has a seemingly unlimited supply of energy. Docile and affectionate, the mudi bonds to only one person and must receive firm training. He needs someone in control who can give him a mission or a job to do. Having a tendency to bite, this dog is respected for its ability to guard the herd and the home. His keen sense of smell makes him a good dog for hunting boar.

Care and functions
This dog is not made for living indoors. He needs space and exercise. Daily brushing is required.
· Herder (cattle).
· Hunting dog (large game).
· Guard dog.
· Pet.

Puli

The Puli is very much like the Tibetan Terrier. He is thought to be descended from the Persian sheepdog or ancient Asian sheepdogs. The Puli arrived on the Hungarian Plains when the nomadic Magyars invaded in the eleventh century. The Puli has always been used as a herder. As the breed became rarer, its role began to change to that of guard dog, protecting the farm. The puli has even been used for police work. In 1930, the puli was introduced in the United States, then recognized by the American Kennel Club six years later. The standard for the Puli was established in 1955.

Square body outline. Cobby. Skin is of slate color. Quick-stepping, light-footed.

SHEEPDOGS

COUNTRY OF ORIGIN
Hungary

OTHER NAME
Hungarian sheepdog

Medium Breeds between 10 and 25 kg (20-55 lb)

1

1

HEAD
Small and fine. Round skull. Pronounced stop. Short muzzle. Large nose. Pronounced superciliary arches.

EYES
Round. Dark brown color. Partially obscured by long fall. Black rims.

EARS
Hanging, v-shaped, broad and rounded.

BODY
Square. Powerful neck. Deep brisket. Short loin. Croup slightly sloping. Medium length back

LIMBS
Hind legs have well-bent stiples, dry hocks. Strong, straight front legs. Front feet short, round and compact. Slate nails.

TAIL
Medium length, carried curved over the rump, blending into the backline because its long hairs intermingle with those of the croup.

COAT
Bushy, wavy, with a tendency to become feltlike. Wooly undercoat. The corded coat is made up of long hairs that clump together. Longest hair (8 to 18 cm) (3-7 in) is on the croup, loin and thighs. Shortest hair is on the head and feet.

COLOR
Solid color, rusty black. Shades of gray and white are common.

SIZE
Dog: 40 to 44 cm (16-17 in). Bitch: 37 to 41 cm (14.5-16 in).

WEIGHT
Dog: 13 to 15 kg (29-33 lb). Bitch: 10 to 13 kg (22-29 lb).

Character, special skills and training
This rustic, lively breed is very agile and a good jumper. The puli is a happy, affectionate, loyal dog. Both independent and possessive, he needs his family to be near. The puli is excellent with children. Suspicious of strangers, the puli is always on the alert and ready to raise the alarm with his throaty bark. Training should begin early and be done gently.

Care and functions
This dog can adapt to living indoors, but he needs exercise. His corded coat should not be brushed or combed. Once his coat starts to grow around the age of eight to twelve months, groom the coat regularly by running your fingers through the cords from the skin the tips of the cords. This dog should be bathed when he is dirty. Extra attention is required for the cords on the flews and around the anus to keep the hair from clumping.
· Excellent herder (sheep, cattle, goats).
· Hunting dog (retriever) (ducks).
· Guard dog.
· Pet.

Pumi

The Pumi, developed in the seventeenth and eighteenth centuries, was bred from prick-ear sheepdogs imported from France and Germany and crossed with the Puli. For many years, the Pumi and the Puli were not considered separate breeds. It was not until around 1920 that the Pumi was officially recognized as a breed separate from the Puli and the standard was written for the breed.

Square body outline. Smooth gait. Light-footed gallop. Topline sloping toward the croup.

1

SHEEPDOGS

COUNTRY OF ORIGIN
Hungary

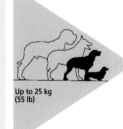

Up to 25 kg
(55 lb)

HEAD
Long with a long bridge. Domed forehead. Indistinct stop. Straight muzzle. Long, pointed nose.

EYES
Set slightly oblique. Dark brown color.

EARS
Set on high. V-shaped. Held erect with tips breaking forward slightly. Medium size, well-proportioned.

BODY
Medium size. Sturdy. Pronounced withers. Short back. Ribs relatively flat. Deep, broad, long chest. Short, slightly sloping crop.

LIMBS
Round, compact feet. Dewclaws not desirable. Hard, slate nails.

TAIL
Set high, carried horizontally or slightly above the level of the back. One-third of the tail is removed.

COAT
Medium length with undercoat. Curly, forming ringlets, but not cords. Never feltlike. Short hair on the legs.

COLOR
Solid colors preferred. Any shade of gray (slate, silvery gray). Black, reddish brown, white. Brindle not permitted.

SIZE
35 to 44 cm (14-17 in).

WEIGHT
8 to 13 kg (18-29 lb).

Character, special skills and training
This high-spirited, energetic dog is remarkably daring. Suspicious of strangers, he barks at even the most innocent sound. He is affectionate with his owner and has a keen sense of smell.

Care and functions
Regular brushing is required. The pumi needs exercise and room to run.
· Herder.
· Hunting dog, hunter of vermin.
· Guard dog.
· Pet.

Schapendoes

At the turn of the century, the Schapendoes was well-known in the Netherlands, particularly in the northern province of Drenthe where he worked large sheep flocks. The Schapendoes is related to the Bearded Collie, the Puli, the Polski Owczarek Nizinny, the Old English Sheepdog, the Briard, the Bergamasco and others. The dog fancier P.M.C. Toepoel was responsible for preserving this breed. After the ravages of World War II, he used the few remaining Schapendoes to resurrect the breed. The Schapendoes club was created in 1947 and a standard was written in 1954, though it was not officially approved until 1971. The FCI recognized the breed in 1989.

Light structure. Light, elastic gait. Remarkable jumper.

1

SHEEPDOGS

COUNTRY OF ORIGIN
Netherlands

ORIGINAL NAME
Nederlandse Schapendoes

OTHER NAME
Dutch Sheepdog

Medium Breeds
between
10 and 25 kg
(20-55 lb)

1

HEAD
Covered by abundant hair making it look larger than it is. Nearly flat skull. Marked stop. Moderately short muzzle. Full mustache and beard.

EYES
Round, moderately large. Brown color.

EARS
Set on relatively high. Medium size. Drop.

BODY
Slightly longer than tall. Belly slightly tucked up. Chest well let down. Ribs well sprung. Powerful neck.

LIMBS
Wide, oval feet. Compact toes. Dewclaws on hind legs permitted. Legs lightly boned.

TAIL
Long, hanging down at rest. Carried at the level of the back when at a gallop. Elevated at attention. Feathering.

COAT
Long, fine, dry, slightly wavy, tending to have a tufted, tousled look, particularly on the hindquarters. Must not be curly. Abundant undercoat.

COLOR
All colors acceptable. Blue gray to black preferred.

SIZE
Dog: 43 to 50 cm (17-20 in). Bitch: 40 to 47 cm (16-18.5 in).

WEIGHT
10 to 18 kg (22-40 lb).

Character, special skills and training
This rustic, lively, tireless dog is courageous. He is never nervous or aggressive. He is affectionate, cheerful, playful and loyal, but rather independent and stubborn. The owner that does not assert his authority over this dog will quickly find himself with an out-of-control dog.

Care and functions
This dog can live in the city if he can get out to expend his energy every day. A good brushing once or twice per week is sufficient.
· Herder.
· Pet.

Schipperke

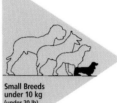

The smallest sheepdog. Bouncy step.

The Schipperke, which looks rather like spitz dogs and Belgian sheepdogs, is thought by some to be descended from the Leauvenaar, a small sheepdog from Louvain in the Flemish provinces of Belgium. Others think that he is descended from northern spitz dogs. This tailless dog, the most popular guard dog in Belgium, guarded the canals. He was also a much loved companion. Shown for the first time in 1880, the breed was officially recognized by the Royal Schipperkes Club of Brussels in 1888. An official standard was written in 1904. Today, the Schipperke is a popular breed in England and South Africa.

1

SHEEPDOGS

COUNTRY OF ORIGIN
Belgium

OTHER NAME
Schip

Small Breeds
under 10 kg
(under 20 lb)

HEAD
Resembles that of a fox. Moderately broad forehead, slightly rounded skull. Distinct, but not pronounced stop. Tapered muzzle. Small nose.

EYES
Ideally oval. Dark brown color.

EARS
Placed high on the head. Small, triangular. Held erect, very mobile.

BODY
Short and thickset. Deep, broad chest. Belly moderately tucked up. Broad loin. Straight, horizontal back.

LIMBS
Fine-boned legs.

Small, round, compact feet. Strong, straight, short nails.

TAIL
Tailless or docked.

COAT
Abundant and dense. Short on the head, body and front of legs. Longer on the neck (ruff), shoulders, chest (apron) and back of legs (breeching).

COLOR
Solid black.

SIZE
32 to 36 cm (12.5-14 in).

WEIGHT
3 to 8 kg (6.5-18 lb), depending on size.

Character, special skills and training
This perky, cheerful, seemingly tireless dog is constantly alert, always in motion. He raises the alarm with hispiercing bark at the slightest provocation. Loyal and gentle with his owners and children, he is reserved with strangers. He is highly trainable.

Care and functions
This is an ideal house dog, though he does require regular exercise. He should be brushed and combed two or three times per week.
· ratter and vermin hunter.
· guard dog.
· pet.

Slovak Cuvac

*Originating in the Carpathian mountains,
this large sheepdog looks much like the Hungarian Kuvasz.
Characteristics for this breed were fixed in the 1960s
based on native Sheepdogs.*

SHEEPDOGS

COUNTRY OF ORIGIN
Slovakia

OTHER NAME
Slovensky Tchouvatch

Large Breeds
between
25 and 45 kg
(55-100 lb)

HEAD
Broad skull. Nose bridge is straight. Fairly broad muzzle.

EYES
Oval. Dark color.

EARS
Set on high. Drop, with rounded lower border reaching the level of the mouth. Covered in fine hair.

BODY
Broad forechest. Solid, relatively broad, muscular rump.

TAIL
Set low. Richly clad. Hangs down when at rest; carried in an arch at the level of the croup when in action.

COAT
5 to 10 cm (2-4 in) long. Thicker and harsher on the neck. Slightly wavy on the back and hindquarters. Short on the head and ears. Mane at the neck.

COLOR
White. A small amount of yellow on the ears and

neck is permissible.

SIZE
Dog: 60 to 70 cm (23.5-27.5 in).
Bitch: 55 to 65 cm (21.5-25.5 in).

WEIGHT
Dog: 35 to 45 kg (77-99 lb).
Bitch: 30 to 40 kg (66-88 lb).

Character, special skills and training
This impressive dog is courageous, vigorous and always alert. He is an obedient, gentle, affectionate and loyal companion. With his solid constitution, the slovak cuvac effectively defends his flock against wolves and bears.

Care and functions
The slovak cuvac needs space and exercise. Weekly brushing is required.
· Sheepdog.
· Guard dog.
· Pet.

69

Welsh Corgi

The two Welsh Corgi varieties have similar origins. However, some writers hold that their history differs. The Cardigan is thought to have been introduced in Wales by the Celts, then crossed with Nordic breeds and British sheepdogs. The Pembroke, on the other hand, is said to have been introduced by Flemish weavers during the Middle Ages and may be related to some Nordic breeds. The two varieties were crossed in the 19th century, making them more similar in appearance. Since 1934, each variety has had its own standard. The pembroke, the most common variety, owes his royal connections to King George VI who introduced the breed to the court when he gave a Pembroke to his daughter, Queen Elizabeth II.

Sturdily built and strong. Relaxed gait.

1

SHEEPDOGS

COUNTRY OF ORIGIN
Great Britain

ORIGINAL NAMES
Two varieties:
Cardigan Welsh Corgi
Pembroke Welsh Corgi

Medium Breeds between 10 and 25 kg (20-55 lb)

HEAD
Foxy in shape and appearance. Broad, flat skull. Stop not pronounced. Tapered muzzle.

EYES
Medium size, round. Variations of brown in harmony with the coat color.

EARS
Held erect. Moderately long, rounded at the tips.

BODY
The cardigan is larger than the pembroke, but his chest is not as broad. Belly slightly tucked up. Straight back.

LIMBS
Large, round, compact feet. Forelegs turned slightly outward.

TAIL
Cardigan: relatively long, richly clad, carried low at rest. Pembroke: naturally short or docked at birth.

COAT
Cardigan: short or medium length, harsh and straight; short, thick undercoat. Pembroke: medium length, straight, thick, neither harsh nor soft; dense undercoat.

COLOR
Cardigan: all colors acceptable, with or without white markings, but white must not be dominant color. Pembroke: self colors—red, sable, fawn, tan—with or without white markings on the legs, forechest, neck and head.

SIZE
Cardigan: approx. 30 cm (12 in).
Pembroke: 25 to 30 cm (10-12 in).

WEIGHT
Cardigan: 12 to 15 kg (26.5-33 lb).

Pembroke:
Dog: 12 to 15 kg (26.5-33 lb).
Bitch 10 to 11 kg (22-24 lb).

Character, special skills and training
This robust, lively, tireless dog is very active, always alert and a hard worker. He is loyal, very gentle with children and not shy or aggressive. This breed requires firm but gentle training.

Care and functions
This dog adapts readily to living indoors provided he receives regular exercise and room to run. The cardigan requires daily brushing; the pembroke requires weekly brushing.
· Herder.
· Utility dog: assistant, drug search, rescue.
· Guard dog.
· Pet.

Australian Cattle Dog

This breed is thought to be the result of crossbreeding of the now extinct Smithfield (closely related to the Old English Sheepdog), the Dingo, the Collie and the Bull terrier. Around 1840, Dalmatian and Kelpie blood may have been introduced. The Australian Cattle Dog is also called the heeler for his ability to nip at the heels of cattle without being injured. The breed was recognized around 1890, but it was not introduced in the United States and Europe until the 1970s.

Conveys the impession of great agility, strength and endurance. True, free, supple action.

2

1

CATTLE DOGS

COUNTRY OF ORIGIN
Australia

OTHER NAMES
Blue Heeler
Australian Queensland Heeler

Medium Breeds
between
10 and 25 kg
(20-55 lb)

HEAD
Strong. Broad, slightly convex skull. Slight stop. Muscular cheeks. Powerful, medium-length nose bridge. Tight, clean lips.

EYES
Oval, medium size. Dark brown color.

EARS
Moderately small, pointed, broad at the base, muscular. Held erect.

BODY
Longer than tall. Compact, balanced construction. Exceptionally strong neck without dewlap. Strong back. Chest well let down and muscular. Ribs well sprung. Shoulders strong, sloping and muscular. Deep

flanks. Horizontal topline. Broad, strong, muscular loin.

LIMBS
Round feet. Short, strong, arched, compact toes. Strong legs.

TAIL
Hangs down forming a slight curve at rest. Richly clad (brush).

COAT
Weather-resistant. Short (2,5 to 4 cm) (1 to 1,5 in), straight, smooth, close-lying, dense, harsh. Double coat. Longer on the back of the legs and on the underbody. Short, dense undercoat.

COLOR
Blue: blue, blue-mottled or speckled, with or without

black, blue or tan markings on the head. Red speckle: small, even red speckle all over the body.

SIZE
Dog: 46 to 51 cm (18-20 in).
Bitch: 43 to 48 cm
(17 to 19 in).

WEIGHT
15 to 20 kg (33-44 lb).

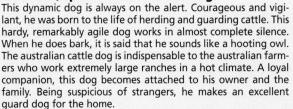

Character, special skills and training
This dynamic dog is always on the alert. Courageous and vigilant, he was born to the life of herding and guarding cattle. This hardy, remarkably agile dog works in almost complete silence. When he does bark, it is said that he sounds like a hooting owl. The australian cattle dog is indispensable to the australian farmers who work extremely large ranches in a hot climate. A loyal companion, this dog becomes attached to his owner and the family. Being suspicious of strangers, he makes an excellent guard dog for the home.

Care and functions
This dog is not a city dweller. If forced to live indoors, he will get into mischief for lack of space or adequate activity. The australian cattle dog needs considerable exercise every day. Regular brushing is sufficient.
· Herder, herd guard, cattle dog.
· Guard dog.

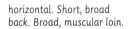

Molossian type. Cobby. Square body outline.
Normal gaits: walk and trot.

2
CATTLE DOGS

1

COUNTRY OF ORIGIN
Belgium

ORIGINAL NAME
Vlaamse Koehond

Large Breeds
between
25 and 45 kg
(55-100 lb)

Belgian Cattle Dog

Originating in Flanders, the Belgian Cattle Dog was produced by crossing several breeds in order to produce an ideal working dog for the farm. Some believe this breed was brought to Flanders by Spanish invaders. Others think large barbets, Mastiffs and Picardy Shepherds were crossed to produce the breed, or perhaps that he is descended from the Beauceron and the Griffon. During World War I, the Belgian Cattle Dog was almost eliminated. Flemish breeders rebuilt the breed from the few survivors. Its standard was established by the FCI in 1965.

HEAD
Massive, chiseled, size in proportion to the body. Stop not pronounced. Broad, powerful, well filled out muzzle, tapering toward the nose. Flat, clean cheeks. Pronounced superciliary arches.

EYES
Medium size, slightly oval in shape. Dark color.

EARS
Held erect, set on high. Triangular if cropped. Naturally drop.

BODY
Short and thickset. Strong, muscular neck. Broad, deep forechest. Deep brisket. Short flanks. Croup almost horizontal. Short, broad back. Broad, muscular loin.

LIMBS
Strong, muscular legs. Short, round, solid feet. Compact toes. Strong, black nails.

TAIL
Docked, leaving two or three vertebrae (approx. 4 in). Carried gaily in action. Some dogs born tailless.

COAT
Medium length (2 in). Harsh, dry, dull and tousled. Shorter on the head. Full mustache and beard. Fine, dense undercoat.

COLOR
Black to fawn, often brindle or pepper and salt passing through gray. White star on the chest is allowed. Light, washed out coats not desirable.

SIZE
Dog: 62 to 68 cm
(24.5-27 in).
Bitch: 59 to 65 cm
(23-25.5 in).

WEIGHT
Dog: 35 to 40 kg (77-88 lb).
Bitch: 27 to 35 kg (60-77 lb).

Character, special skills and training
This rustic, energetic, bold breed is dominant and bonds to only one person. He is calm, wise and steady. He is alert, well behaved and docile, though can be a bit surly. This active dog has energy to spare. He must receive firm, consistent training. Strangers will find his forbidding countenance very dissuasive. This dog has always worked on the farm, guarding and herding the cattle as sled dog and even turning a wheel in the butter-churning process. His superb sense of smell makes him useful for police work.

Care and functions
This breed must be brushed once or twice per week and taken to a professional groomer three or four time per year for stripping. This is not a house dog. He requires considerable space and exercise.
· Herder.
· Police dog (tracking, messenger).
· Guard dog.
· Pet.

Group 2

SECTION 1

AFFENPINSCHER
DOBERMANN PINSCHER
PINSCHER
AUSTRIAN SHORTHAIRED PINSCHER
SCHNAUZER
DUTCH SMOUSHOND
BLACK RUSSIAN TERRIER

SECTION 2

AIDI
BOXER
DANISH BROHOLMER
BULLDOG
BULLMASTIFF
CANE CORSO
ANATOLIAN SHEPHERD DOG
CENTRAL ASIAN SHEEPDOG
CAUCASIAN SHEEPDOG
KARST SHEEPDOG
CAO DE CASTRO LABOREIRO
GREAT PYRENEES
ESTRELA MOUNTAIN DOG
GREAT DANE
ARGENTINEAN MASTIFF

FRENCH MASTIFF
MALLORQUIN BULLDOG
TIBETAN MASTIFF
FILA BRASILEIRO
HOVAWART
LANDSER
LEONBERG
MASTIFF
SPANISH MASTIFF
NEAPOLITAN MASTIFF
PYRENEAN MASTIFF
RAFEIRO DO ALENTEJO
ROTTWEILER
ST. BERNARD
SARPLANINAC
SHAR-PEI
NEWFOUNDLAND
TOSA

SECTION 3

APPENZELLER
BERNES MOUNTAIN DOG
ENTELBUCHER
GREATER SWISS MOUNTAIN DOG

Tibetan Mastiff

75

Affenpinscher

Affenpinscher, meaning "Monkey-like terrier" in german, received its name because of its small head with a monkey-like expression. It is thought that this breed is descended from the brussels griffon, or perhaps the other way around. The Affenpinscher has been around a long time; paintings prior to the seventeenth century depict similar looking dogs. Beginning in the late 1930s, the popularity of this little dog took off when he began to make a name for himself at dog shows.

Small and compact.

1A

PINSCHERS

2

COUNTRY OF ORIGIN
Germany

OTHER NAME
Diabletin moustachu
(mustached little devil)

Small Breeds
under 10 kg
(under 20 lb)

Character, special skills and training
This dog exhibits a mixture of exuberance and serenity. He is lively, alert, loyal, affectionate, bold, and rather obstinate. The affenpinscher is a hunter of vermin and an excellent guard dog that will bark a warning to alert his owner.

Care and functions
This breed can make a good house dog. Daily brushing and combing is required.
· Guard dog.
· Hunter of vermin.
· Pet.

HEAD
Round. Monkey-like expression. Short muzzle. Slightly undershot bite. Black lips.

EYES
Round. Dark color.

EARS
Small, set on high. If cropped, held erect and forward. If natural, v-shaped, drop or held erect.

BODY
Square body outline. Short neck. Ribs slightly sprung. Well developed breast. Underline slightly tucked up at the loin. Straight short back sloping slightly from withers to croup.

LIMBS
Small, round feet. Compact, arched toes. Hard pads.

TAIL
Docked to approximately three vertebrae. Set high and carried erect.

COAT
Harsh and dense on the body. Less harsh on the head, standing off and framing the face. Bushy eyebrows, full beard.

COLOR
Preferably black. Brown or gray markings or nuances permissible.

SIZE
25 to 30 cm (10-12 in).

WEIGHT
4 kg (9 lb) or less.

Doberman Pinscher

This breed's history begins in Apolda, a small German village in the province of Thueringen. F. L. Doberman developed this fearless guard dog to protect him as he made his rounds collecting taxes. Around 1870, he crossed a number of aggressive breeds (many ancestors of the Rottweiler), including local black and tan Sheepdogs, the German Pinscher, the German Shepherd, the Beauceron, and the Rottweiller. The result was a vigilant working dog, farm dog, guard dog and police dog. For hunting, the Doberman was used to fight off predators. Later, new blood was added, notably the Black and Tan Terrier and probably the greyhound. In 1910, the standard for the doberman was established.

Mesomorph. Elegant, pure lines. Solidly built and muscular without bulkiness. Highly pigmented skin. Elastic, supple, relaxed gait.

1A

PINSCHERS

COUNTRY OF ORIGIN
Germany

Large Breeds between 25 and 45 kg (55-100 lb)

2

During World War I, the Doberman served as a patrol, as a sentry at military bases and as a guide dog for soldiers blinded during the fighting.

HEAD
Long and dry. Strong, blunt wedge-shape. Stop not pronounced. Muzzle line almost at level with topline of skull. Powerful, broad jaws. Lips smooth, lying close to the jaws.

EYES
Medium size. Oval. Dark color.

EARS
Set on high. Cropped, erect, length in proportion to length of the head. If not cropped, semi-drop with the front edge lying alongside the cheek.

BODY
Square body outline. Dry, well muscled neck. Powerful forechest. Clearly defined

hocks. Well developed chest with slightly sprung ribs. Belly well tucked up. Rounded croup. Solid, short back

LIMBS
Solid legs. Short feet with compact, arched toes. Black nails.

TAIL
Set high, short, docked after the second caudal vertebra.

COAT
Short, hard, thick, smooth and close-lying. No undercoat.

COLOR
Black or brown with clearly defined tan markings on the muzzle, cheeks, throat, forechest, legs and feet.

SIZE
Dog: 68 to 72 cm (27-28 in).
Bitch: 63 to 68 kg (25-27 in).

WEIGHT
Dog: 40 to 45 kg (88-99 lb).
Bitch: 32 to 35 kg (70-77 lb).

Character, special skills and training
Lively, courageous, vigilant and energetic, the doberman has a slightly disquieting, resolute expression. This proud, determined, impulsive breed must be stable, composed and sociable. This is not a dog for everyone. He requires an authoritative owner who is fair, calm and will assert himself with patience and gentleness. The doberman is blindly loyal and devoted to his owner and can be trusted with children. He is a born guardian and is extremely wary of strangers. Fundamentally peace-loving, the doberman is an emotionally sensitive dog and does not like conflict.

Care and functions
This dog needs space and exercise to burn off energy. He will not tolerate being tied up. Regular brushing is required.
· Working dog: police dog, army dog.
· Guard and defense dog.
· Pet.

Pinscher

The origin of the Pinscher is not clear. Some writers believe it is descended from a very old german breed related to the schnauzers, which is descended from the black and tan terrier. The blood of the standard pinscher contributed to the development of the Doberman Pinscher. The breed was recognized in 1879 and the Pinscher Club was created in 1895. The standard Pinscher is less common than the miniature Pinscher.

Well-balanced construction.
Square body outline.

1A

PINSCHERS

2

COUNTRY OF ORIGIN
Germany

OTHER NAMES
Standard (German) Pinscher
Miniature Pinscher
(Zwergpinscher)

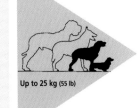

Up to 25 kg (55 lb)

HEAD
Robust, long. Slight stop. Rectangular nose bridge. Blunt, wedge-shaped muzzle. Lips smooth, lying close to jaws.

EYES
Medium size. Oval. Dark color.

EARS
If cropped, prick. If natural, drop, v-shaped.

BODY
Compact. Dry neck. Moderately broad chest. Ribs slightly sprung. Well developed forechest. Belly moderately tucked up. Short back. Heavily muscled legs.

LIMBS
Short, round feet. Compact, arched toes.

TAIL
Docked to approximately three vertebrae. Set high, carried erect.

COAT
Short, thick, smooth and close-lying.

COLOR
Solid color: fawn or shades of brown to stag red. Bi-color: black with tan, red, or lighter markings above the eyes, on the neck, forechest, lower legs, feet, inside of hind legs and around the anus. Markings also on the cheeks, flews and lower jaw in the miniature pinscher.

SIZE
43 to 58 cm (17-23 in).
Miniature Pinscher:
25 to 30 cm (10-12 in).

WEIGHT
12 to 16 kg (26.5-35 lb).
Miniature Pinscher:
2 to 4 kg (4.5 to 9 lb).

Character, special skills and training
This spirited, courageous, playful dog is vigilant, well-balanced and good-tempered. Very fond of family, the pinscher is a good playmate for children provided the dog is not man handled. The miniature pinscher is more high-strung and has a stronger personality than the standard pinscher. They need firm, consistent training.

Care and functions
This is a very clean breed. The pinscher can live in the city if he receives a fair amount of exercise. Regular brushing is required.
· Guard dog (standard pinscher); excellent ratter.
· Pet.

Austrian Shorthaired Pinscher

The origins of this breed are not known. It is closely related to the standard Pinscher, but the Austrian Shorthaired Pinscher was raised to be a good farm dog rather than a pet. This breed is rare outside of its native Austria.

Austrian shorthaired Pinscher. Cobby. Elegant.

1A

PINSCHERS

COUNTRY OF ORIGIN
Austria

ORIGINAL NAMES
Osterreichischer Kurzhaariger Pinscher

Medium Breeds between 10 and 25 kg (20-55 lb)

2

HEAD
Pear-shaped. Broad skull. Pronounced stop. Strong, short muzzle. Large nose. Lips smooth, lying close to jaws.

EYES
Large. Dark color.

EARS
Rose or v-shaped. Held erect or semi-erect.

BODY
Thickset. Powerful neck. Long, deep, barrel chest.

Long, broad loin. Short, broad back and loin. Broad chest.

LIMBS
Compact feet with well arched toes.

TAIL
Set high. Typically carried curved over the back. May be docked.

COAT
Short, flat, straight, with undercoat.

COLOR
Most common are yellow, golden brown, fawn, reddish-brown, black, black and tan, brindle, almost always with large white markings on the throat, forechest, legs and head (flare).

SIZE
35 to 50 cm (14-20 in).

WEIGHT
12 to 18 kg (26.5-40 lb).

Character, special skills and training
This spirited, hardy, active animal makes a remarkable guard dog. He is cheerful, kind and very open to training. His terrier instinct drives him to chase rabbits and foxes.

Care and functions
This breed needs space and plenty of exercise. Weekly brushing is sufficient.
· Guard dog.
· Pet.

Schnauzer

Square body outline. Robust, yet elegant. Sound gait.

1B

SCHNAUZERS

2

COUNTRY OF ORIGIN
Germany

OTHER OAMES
Giant Schnauzer
Standard Schnauzer
Miniature Schnauzer

Up to 45 kg
(100 lb)

GIANT SCHNAUZER

HEAD
Strong, elongated. Pronounced stop. Rectangular nose bridge. Shaggy muzzle ending in a blunt wedge. Black lips.

EYES
Oval. Dark color.

EARS
If cropped, carried erect. If natural, v-shaped, breaking at skull level or small and held erect.

BODY
Square outline. Arched neck. Medium width chest with

moderately sprung ribs. Belly moderately tucked up. Short back sloping gently toward the croup

LIMBS
Short, round feet. Compact, arched toes. Dark nails. Muscular legs.

TAIL
Set high and carried erect. Docked to three vertebrae.

COAT
Hard, wiry, thick. Dense undercoat. Wiry beard on the muzzle; eyes slightly hidden by bushy eyebrows.

"Schnauze" means "muzzle" in German, so this breed was named for its characteristic shaggy muzzle. Up to the nineteenth century, Schnauzers were considered rough-haired Pinschers. There are three schnauzer varieties. The Standard Schnauzer's ancestry is unknown since it has been around for a very long time. Perhaps its roots can be traced to the Biberhund and a rough-haired ratter, or shepherd breeds. The Standard Schnauzer was primarily used to clear vermin. The Giant Schnauzer is thought to be the result of crossbreeding of the Standard Schnauzer, the Great Dane and the Belgian Cattle Dog. Of course, the Giant Schnauzer may simply be an enlarged model of the Standard Schnauzer. Depicted in one of artist Albrecht Dürer's works, the Giant Schnauzer was probably developed in the Wurtemberg region. These dogs guarded farm carts and kept stables free of vermin.

The Miniature Schnauzer was developed around 1880 by selectively breeding small Standard Schnauzers. In Europe, the Giant Schnauzer is the most popular variety, but in English-speaking countries, the Miniature Schnauzer is more common.

MINIATURE SCHNAUZER

STANDARD SCHNAUZER

COLOR
Solid black or pepper and salt. Dark mask. White markings are not desirable.

SIZE
Giant Schnauzer:
60 to 70 cm (23.5-27.5 in).
Standard Schnauzer:
45 to 50 cm (18 to 20 in).
Miniature Schnauzer:
30 to 35 cm (12-14 in).

WEIGHT
Giant Schnauzer:
30 to 40 kg (66-88 lb).
Standard Schnauzer:
approx. 15 kg (33 lb).
Miniature Schnauzer:
4 to 7 kg (9-15.5 lb).

Character, special skills and training
The schnauzer is high-spirited, energetic, impetuous (though stable), hardy, proud and dominant. The Giant Schnauzer is calmer than the spunky miniature. This devoted, affectionate dog loves children and makes an excellent pet. Constantly alert, wary of strangers and very reliable, the Standard and Giant Schnauzers are excellent guard dogs. This breed requires firm authority and a lot of attention.

Care and functions
Schnauzers should not be confined indoors. They are active dogs and need space and considerable exercise to stay fit and maintain their mental health. Daily brushing and professional grooming once every three months is required.
· Guard dog, defense dog, military dog.
· Pet.

Dutch Smoushond

The Smoushondje, which means dog of the jews in Dutch, were very common in the Netherlands in the past. The Dutch Smoushond was considered a stable dog. He kept the stable clear of rats and accompanied horses and drivers.

Square body outline

1C

SMOUSHOND

COUNTRY OF ORIGIN
Denmark

ORIGINAL NAMES
Hollandse Smoushound
Hollandse Smoushondje

2

Small Breeds
under 10 kg
(under 20 lb)

Character, special skills and training
This affectionate, cheerful, well-balanced dog makes an excellent family pet.

Care and functions
Weekly brushing is required.
· Pet.

HEAD
Short and broad. Domed skull. Distinct stop. Moderately short jaws. Fine lips.

EYES
Large, round. Dark color. Dark rims.

EARS
Small, fine, set on high, falling forward along the cheeks.

BODY
Sturdy. Short neck. Broad chest. Well sprung ribs. Muscular croup. Belly very slightly drawn up. Straight, broad back.

LIMBS
Round feet. Black nails. Legs with strong bone.

TAIL
Natural or cropped to one third its length. If natural, relatively short length, carried gaily.

COAT
Body: 4 to 7 cm (1.5 to 3 in) long; harsh, straight, slightly shaggy, not wavy or curly; adequate undercoat. Legs: medium length. Tail: bushy, without feathering. Head: short on the skull and long on the cheeks; mustaches, beard and long eyebrows.

COLOR
Any shade of solid yellow. Preferably dark straw color. Ears, mustaches, beard and eyebrows are darker than the rest of the coat.

SIZE
Dog: 37 to 42 cm (14.5-16.5 in).
Bitch: 35 to 40.5 cm (14-16 in).

WEIGHT
9 to 10 kg (20-22 lb).

Black Russian Terrier

The Black Russian Terrier was created in Russia in the early twentieth century by crossing the Airedale Terrier with the Giant Schnauzer and the Rottweiler. The breed was used to guard military installations. The largest of all terriers, the Black Russian Terrier is rare outside of Russia. The breed was recognized by the FCI in 1984.

Massive skeleton and musculature. Relaxed, graceful gait.

Large Breeds between 25 and 45 kg (55-100 lb)

1

2

COUNTRY OF ORIGIN
Russia

OTHER NAME
Chiornyi

HEAD
Long. Flat skull. Pronounced stop. Massive muzzle. Thick, fleshy lips.

EYES
Small, oval, set obliquely in the skull. Dark color. Coarse, bushy eyebrows.

EARS
Set on high, small, triangular, drop.

BODY
Massive. Long, dry neck. Broad, deep chest. Short, broad, muscular loin. Belly is tucked up. Broad, muscular

croup sloping slightly to the tail. Broad, straight, muscular back.

LIMBS
Muscular legs. Large, round feet.

TAIL
Thick, set high. Docked short, leaving three or four vertebrae.

COAT
Harsh, hard, 2 to 4 in long, with mustaches, beard and mane. Thick, well developed undercoat.

COLOR
Black or pepper and salt.

SIZE
Dog: 66 to 72 cm (26-28 in).
Bitch: 64 to 70 cm
(25- 27.5 in).

WEIGHT
Approx. 40 kg (88 lb).

Character, special skills and training
This sturdy, rustic, hardy dog has a strong, steady personality. The Russian Black Terrier is very devoted to his owner. An excellent guard dog, the breed is suspicious of strangers, has an active defense reaction and will bite. Firm training is a necessity.

Care and functions
This breed can adapt to life in the city if born to it. Long daily walks are required. Regular brushing and professional grooming are needed.
· Guard dog.

Aidi

No sheepdog breed exists in the Atlas mountains. This Moroccan dog, probably originating in the Sahara, lives in the mountains and defends his owner and property from wildcats, but he has never worked as a flock guard. This explains why his 1963 standard, which was published under the name Atlas Sheepdog, was nullified in 1969.

2B

MOUNTAIN TYPE MOLOSSIANS

2

COUNTRY OF ORIGIN
Morocco

ORIGINAL NAMES
Kabyle Dog
Chien de l'Atlas

Strong construction. Muscular.

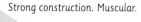

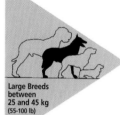

Large Breeds between 25 and 45 kg (55-100 lb)

Character, special skills, and training
This very rustic breed has remarkable power and agility. He is always on the alert and ready for action. He will protect his owner and loved ones from predators and strangers with great courage. This breed can even sniff out snakes. The sensitive, lively Aidi must receive firm, but kindly, training.

Care and functions
The Aidi can live indoors provided he gets exercise every day. Weekly brushing is required.
· Guard dog.
· Pet.

HEAD
Like that of a bear. Dry. Size in proportion to the body. Flat, broad skull. Stop not pronounced. Tapered muzzle. Black or brown nose, matching coat color. Strong jaws. Black or brown tight lips.

EYES
Medium size. Dark color. Dark, slightly oblique rims.

EARS
Medium size with rounded tips, semi-drop.

BODY
Powerful. Muscular neck without dewlap. Broad, very deep chest. Ribs slightly sprung. Powerful, arched loin. Belly tucked up.

LIMBS
Slightly rounded feet with strong nails (color of coat). Broad, muscular back. Solid, fairly muscular legs.

TAIL
Long, carried down, reaching the hock joint, in the form of a scimitar at rest. Very thick fur (plume).

COAT
Very thick, slightly long (6 cm) (2,5 in) except on the head and ears where it is very short and not as thick.

Mane at the neck (particularly impressive in dogs).

COLOR
Wide range of colors: white, tawny, fawn, red, black and white, fawn and white, shades of gray, tri-color, etc.

SIZE
52 to 62 cm (20.5 to 24.5 in).

WEIGHT
Approx. 30 kg (66 lb).

Boxer

Like all Mastiffs, the Boxer's ancestors included eastern Molossians, breeds used for fighting and defending their charges against wild animals. The German Bullenbeisser (now extinct) was crossed with the English Bulldog to create the modern Boxer in 1890. The Boxer was first shown in 1896 in Munich and a standard was established some ten years later. This breed was used by the German army during World War I. The Boxer is very popular as a pet and guard dog.

Sturdy appearance. Well developed muscles. Tight-fitting coat without wrinkles. Lively, noble, powerful gait.

2A

MASTIFF TYPE MOLOSSIAN

COUNTRY OF ORIGIN
Germany

2

Large Breeds between 25 and 45 kg (55-100 lb)

HEAD
Harmonious proportions. Clean and square. Domed skull. Distinct stop. Muzzle as broad and powerful as possible. Lower jaw protrudes beyond the upper jaw and curves slightly upward (prognathism).

EYES
Not too small, not protruding. Dark brown color. Dark rims.

EARS
Set on high. Not too broad. Cropped to a point, held erect.

BODY
Square. Round, powerful neck. Broad, deep forechest. Deep brisket. Well sprung ribs. Short, muscular loin. Straight, muscular back.

LIMBS
Straight, sturdy legs with plentiful bone. Small, round feet.

TAIL
Set high. Docked and carried erect.

COAT
Short and lying close to the body, hard, thick and shiny.

COLOR
Fawn or brindle. Shades of fawn from light tan to mahogany, preferably golden-red. Black mask. Brindle coat has dark or black streaking on a fawn background. White markings are permissible.

SIZE
Dog: 57 to 64 cm (22.5-25 in).
Bitch: 53 to 60 cm (21-23.5 in).

WEIGHT
25 to 30 kg (55-66 lb)

Character, special skills and training
This is an energetic, impetuous, dominant, self-assured breed. The boxer must be calm, well-balanced and sociable. He forms a strong bond with his family and remains loyal at all cost. Alert and wary toward strangers, he demonstrates fearless courage in his role as protector and guard. Training should start at a very young age.

Care and functions
The boxer can make a good house dog, but he must be given a considerable amount of exercise. His short coat requires little care.
· Guard and defense dog.
· Utility dog: police dog, guide dog.
· Pet.

Danish Broholmer

This Molossian-looking shepherd dog belongs to an old Danish breed, which was the result of crossings between Mastiffs and German dogs of undetermined breeds. The breed appeared in Denmark in the 19th century, although it really spread out during the two World Wars. It is almost unknown in France.

Large. Very powerful.
Mastiff-type square body.

2A

MASTIFF TYPE MOLOSSIANS

2

COUNTRY OF ORIGIN
Denmark

Giants Breeds
over 45 kg
(over 100 lb)

Character, special skills and training
This is a steadfast, peace-loving, well-balanced, good-natured breed. The broholmer is well known for his even temper and courage. Firm training is required to temper any aggressive tendencies he may have toward strangers.

Care and functions
This dog needs space and a lot of exercise. Weekly brushing is sufficient.
· Herder.
· Guard dog.
· Pet.

HEAD
Strong and broad. Carried slightly down. Relatively short muzzle. Pendulous lips.

EYES
Round. Black or dark amber color.

EARS
Small. Set on moderately high.

BODY
Square body outline. Thick neck. Broad forechest. Long back. Croup slightly sloping.

LIMBS
Strong, thick, solid feet. Powerful legs.

TAIL
Medium length, thick. Carried low at rest, saber when in action.

COAT
Short, thick, weather-resistant.

COLOR
Fawn (light yellow, golden) with black mask; black. White markings on the forechest, feet and tip of the tail are permissible.

SIZE
Dog: at least 75 cm (30 in).
Bitch: at least 70 cm (28 in).

WEIGHT
50 to 60 kg
(110-132 lb).

Bulldog

The Bulldog is thought to be descended from ancient Mastiffs of asiatic blood, combat dogs that were introduced in Great Britain by early phoenician navigators. Its name reflects its original purpose; the Bulldog was used for bull-baiting. Organized dog fights were also the rule of the day. In 1835, the cruel practice of bull-baiting was outlawed in England. In 1875, the first Bulldog standard was published. Selective breeding since that time has turned the Bulldog into a loving family pet.

Thickset. Low-swung. Broad, powerful and compact. Heavy gait.

2A

MASTIFF TYPE MOLOSSIANS

COUNTRY OF ORIGIN
Great britain

OTHER NAME
English Bulldog

Medium Breeds between 10 and 25 kg (20-55 lb)

2

HEAD
Kassive. Short face. Broad skull. Loose, wrinkled skin. Deep stop. Well developed cheeks. Short, broad, upturned muzzle. Broad nostrils. Thick, pendulous flews. Broad, square jaws. Lower jaw protrudes beyond the upper jaw and curves slightly upward.

EYES
Very wide set. Medium size, round. Very dark color.

EARS
Ket on high and placed wide apart. Small and thin. Rose ear, in which the ear folds in such a way as to show the inside of the burr.

BODY
Short, well-knit. Very thick neck with dewlap. Shoulders broad and slanting outward. Capacious, round brisket. Ribs well sprung. Elevated, strong hindquarters. Belly tucked up. Short, strong back. Arched loin.

LIMBS
Round, compact feet. Slightly out-turned. Forelegs set wide apart. Strong, muscular legs.

TAIL
Set low, round, moderate length. Carried low, hanging straight, not curving up.

COAT
Fine, short, smooth and thick.

COLOR
Uniform color with black mask or muzzle. Uniform colors: red, fawn. Brindle, white, or piebald (white with the above colors). Liver, black and tan are undesirable.

SIZE
30 to 40 cm (12-16 in).

WEIGHT
Dog: 24 to 25 kg (53-55 lb). Bitch: 22 to 23 kg (48-51 lb).

Character, special skills and training
The Bulldog is vigorous, courageous, hardy, uniform and dignified. Despite his frightening appearance, he is an affectionate, calm, quiet dog of excellent character. He makes a marvelous playmate for children and develops a strong bond with his owner. Firm training is required.

Care and functions
The Bulldog can adapt to city living provided he exercises regularly. He does not tolerate heat well. Daily brushing is required. Special attention must be given to the folds on his to ward off possible skin irritation.
· Guard dog.
· Police dog, army dog.
· Pet.

Bullmastiff

Created by crossing the Bulldog and a Mastiff, the Bullmastiff is fast and active like the Bulldog, large and heavy like a Mastiff. This breed was developed in the nineteenth century to guard large estates. The breed was recognized in 1924.

Powerful. Harmonious build. Powerfully built without bulkiness.

2A

MASTIFF TYPE MOLOSSIANS

2

COUNTRY OF ORIGIN
Great britain

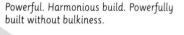

Giants Breeds
over 45 kg
(over 100 lb)

Character, special skills and training
Active, agile, showing great endurance and of solid build, the Bullmastiff has a symmetrical appearance. He is earnest, courageous and alert, making him an excellent guard dog. He is also loyal and gentle, an excellent playmate for children. The Bullmastiff has a very keen sense of smell and a dominant personality. Early, firm (though gentle) training is required.

Care and functions
The Bullmastiff is not a good house dog. He needs a lot of space and exercise. Regular brushing of the coat and cleaning of his folds are required.
· Guard and defense dog
· Police and army dog
· Pet.

HEAD
Broad. Strong, square skull. Skin on face is wrinkled when dog is alert. Distinct stop. Well developed cheeks. Short, broad muzzle. Flews must not be pendulous.

EYES
Medium size. Dark or hazel color.

EARS
Small, v-shaped, set on high and placed wide apart. Darker color than the rest of the coat.

BODY
Powerful. Very muscular neck. Broad chest. Muscular shoulders. Broad loin. Short, straight back.

LIMBS
Strong, muscular legs with plenty of bone. Small, round cat feet with rounded, well-arched toes. Dark nails.

TAIL
Set high, strong at the base and tapering to the tip. Carried straight or curved and reaching the hocks.

COAT
short, hard, close-lying.

COLOR
Any shade of brindle, red or fawn. White spot on the chest is acceptable. Black mask on the muzzle. Dark markings around the eyes.

SIZE
Dog: 63 to 68 cm (25 to 27 in).
Bitch: 61 to 66 cm (24-26 in).

WEIGHT
Dog: 50 to 59 kg (110 to 130 lb).
Bitch: 41 to 50 kg (90.5 to 110.5 lb).

Cane Corso

The Corso is the direct descendant of the ancient Roman molosser dogs. In the past, the breed was common throughout Italy, but it is now found only in the southern Italian province of Puglia and neighboring regions. The name is derived from the Latin word Cohors (farmyard or enclosure) meaning protector, guarder of farms, courtyards, and enclosed property. The breed first appeared in the sixteenth century and was used for hunting and guard duties.

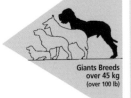

Solid. Powerfully muscled. Elegant. Agile. Rather thick skin. Preferred gait: Trot.

2B

MOUNTAIN TYPE MOLOSSIANS

Giants Breeds over 45 kg (over 100 lb)

COUNTRY OF ORIGIN
Italy

ORIGINAL NAME
Cane Corso Italiano

2

HEAD
Broad, like that of molossians. Pronounced stop. Strong, square muzzle is shorter than the skull. Straight nose bridge. Very broad, thick jaws.

EYES
Medium size. Almost oval shape. Darkest colors preferred; in harmony with coat color.

EARS
Triangular, broad at the base, hanging. Often cropped to an equilateral triangle.

BODY
Slightly longer than tall.

Sturdy neck. Withers higher than croup. Straight, very muscular back. Prominent chest. Solid, short loin. Long, broad, slightly sloped loin.

LIMBS
Powerful legs. Hind feet are round and more compact than forefeet.

TAIL
Set on high. Very thick at the root. Docked at the fourth vertebra.

COAT
Short, very thick. Thin undercoat.

COLOR
Black, lead gray, slate gray, light gray, light fawn, fawn

red, dark fawn, brindle (streaks on fawn or gray background of various nuances). Fawn and brindle subjects have a black or gray mask. Small white spot on the chest, on the tip of the feet, and on the nose bridge is permissible.

SIZE
Dog: 64 to 68 cm (25-27 in).
Bitch: 60 to 64 cm (23.5-25 in).

WEIGHT
Dog: 45 to 50 kg (99-110 lb).
Bitch: 40 to 45 kg (88-99 lb).

Character, special skills and training
This rustic, hardy dog is full of energy and is extremely courageous. The Corso is proud and well-balanced, gentle and affectionate with his owner. This breed tolerates children well and is playful with them. The Corso is wary of strangers. This breed is easy to train.

Care and fonctions
The Corso needs exercise and room to run. Weekly brushing is sufficient.
· Guard and defense dog.
· Herder.
· Hunting dog.
· Pet.

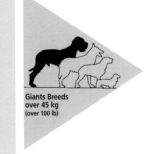

Anatolian Shepherd Dog

Descended from molossus of Asian origin, the Anatolian Shepherd Dog's roots can be traced to the high plateaus and mountains of Turkey. This breed was used to guard sheep and protect them from predators, such as wolves. The Anatolian Shepherd Dog is also used as a hunting dog and army dog.

Powerful. Tall. Relatively streamlined. Supple, stretched out gait, like that of a cat.

2B

MOUNTAIN TYPE MOLOSSIANS

2

COUNTRY OF ORIGIN
Turkey

ORIGINAL NAME
Goban Kopegi

OTHER NAME
Anatolian Karabash Dog

Giants Breeds
over 45 kg
(over 100 lb)

Character, special skills and training
His habit of living and working outdoors in all weather conditions and his rugged past make this a sturdy, hardy breed. The Anatolian Shepherd Dog has a strong personality and is often stubborn and requires an owner with an alpha personality. While he is loyal and gentle with his owner and children, this dog is very distrustful of strangers, making him a superb guard dog.

Care and functions
The Anatolian Shepherd Dog should live in the country where he can get the vigorous daily exercise that he requires. Regular brushing is sufficient.
· Flock guard.
· Guard dog.
· Pet.

HEAD
Strong and broad. Slightly domed skull. Slight stop. Muzzle is slightly shorter than the skull. Black lips.

EYES
Small. Golden to brown color depending on coat color.

EARS
Medium size, drop, triangular with rounded tips.

BODY
Powerful. Thick, muscular neck. Deep chest. Belly well tucked up. Chest well let down. Ribs well sprung.

LIMBS
Solid, muscular legs. Solid, oval feet with arched toes.

TAIL
Long, carried low and slightly curled.

COAT
Thick, short or moderately long. Thick undercoat. Longer on the neck, shoulders and thighs.

COLOR
All colors permissible. Preferred colors are tawny and fawn with black mask and ears.

SIZE
Dog: 74 to 81 cm (29-32 in).
Bitch: 71 to 79 cm (28-31 in).

WEIGHT
Dog: 50 to 65 kg (110-143 lb).
Bitch: 40 to 55 kg (88-121 lb).

Central Asian Sheepdog

This breed is most likely descended from the Asian molussus. The Central Asian Sheepdog is found in all Central Asian republics and in some neighboring regions. The dog is used to defend herds from wolves and thieves.

HEAD
Massive, broad. Flat forehead. Very slight stop. Large black or brown nose.

EYES
Wide set, round. Dark color.

EARS
Set on low, small, triangular, drop. Often cropped.

BODY
Powerful. Short neck. Deep, broad brisket. Rounded ribs. Short, broad, slightly arched loin. Belly moderately tucked up. Broad, muscular, almost horizontal croup. Strong, straight, broad back.

LIMBS
Strong, oval, compact feet.

TAIL
Docked. Set high, carried down in the shape of a saber.

COAT
Harsh, straight and coarse. Long-haired variety: 7 to 8 cm (2.5-3 in) in length; Short-haired variety: 3 to 5 cm (1-2 in) in length, smooth. Thick undercoat.

COLOR
White, gray, black, straw, reddish-brown, tiger, pied or mottled.

SIZE
Dog: at least 65 cm (26 in). Bitch: at least 60 cm (24 in).

WEIGHT
40 to 50 kg (88-110 lb).

Rugged construction. Massive bone structure. Powerfully muscled. Thick skin. Gait: slow, collected trot and gallop are most common.

2B

MOUNTAIN TYPE MOLOSSIANS

Large Breeds between 25 and 45 kg (55-100 lb)

COUNTRY OF ORIGIN
Asia
Russia

ORIGINAL NAME
Sredneasiatskaya Ovtcharka

2

Character, special skills and training
This rustic breed requires little care and adapts easily to all climates. The Central Asian Sheepdog is well-balanced and peaceable. Nevertheless, he is bold and suspicious of strangers and will react instantaneously to defend his charges with valor. Firm training is required.

Care and functions
The Central Asian Sheepdog is not a house dog. He needs exercise and room to run. Weekly brushing is sufficient.
· Flock guard
· Guard dog

Caucasian Sheepdog

Originating in the Caucasus, this large sheepdog is most likely one of the most direct descendants of the Tibetan Mastiff, which was introduced in Russia during the Asian invasions. This dog can be found throughout most of the former Soviet Union. The Caucasian Sheepdog of the steppes is taller and rangier than the Caucasian Sheepdog found in mountainous regions.

Large. Robust. Rugged construction. Massive bone structure. Heavily muscled. Gait: Lumbering gallop and clipped trot.

2B

MOUNTAIN TYPE MOLOSSIANS

2

COUNTRY OF ORIGIN
Russia

ORIGINAL NAME
Kavkazskaya Ovtcharka

OTHER NAME
Caucasian Owtcharka

Giants Breeds
over 45 kg
(over 100 lb)

Character, special skills and training
This very rustic breed requires little care and adapts easily to all climates. The Caucasian Sheepdog is well-balanced, active and even-tempered. However, he is suspicious of strangers and may bite. Firm training is required.

Care and functions
The Caucasian Sheepdog requires space and exercise. Weekly brushing is sufficient.
· Flock guard
· Guard and defense dog.
· Pet.

HEAD
Massive and broad. Distinct stop. Relatively short muzzle with large black or brown nose. Thick, though tight, lips.

EYES
Small, oval. Dark color.

EARS
Set on high, drop, cropped short.

BODY
Slightly longer than tall. Powerful, short neck. Deep, broad, slightly rounded chest. Short loin. Belly moderately tucked up. Broad, muscular back. Broad, muscular, almost horizontal croup.

LIMBS
Large, oval, compact feet. Solid legs.

TAIL
Set high, hanging down in the shape of a sickle, hook or ring. Docked tails are permitted.

COAT
Straight and coarse. Shorter on the head and front of the legs. Extremely thick undercoat of lighter color.
Three types:
- Long hair with mane, feathering, breeching and plume.
- Short hair without mane, feathering, etc.
- Medium length hair, long, but without mane, feathering, breeching or plume.

COLOR
Gray in patches with a variety of nuances, normally light and tending toward red, white, reddish-brown, brindle and piebald and speckled.

SIZE
Dog: at least 65 cm (26 in).
Bitch: at least 62 cm (24 in).

WEIGHT
45 to 65 kg (99-143 lb).

Karst Sheepdog

This sheepdog lives in the mountainous region of Karst (or Kras). He is a tireless defender of the herd. This breed was mentioned for the first time in 1689 and was officially recognized in 1939 under the name of Illyrian Sheepdog, which also included the future Sarplaninac. The Karst Sheepdog and the Sarplaninac were separated in 1968.

Medium size. Robust. Dark-colored skin. Preferred gait: trot.

Large Breeds between 25 and 45 kg (55-100 lb)

2B

MOUNTAIN TYPE MOLOSSIANS

COUNTRY OF ORIGIN
Slovenia

ORIGINAL NAME
Kraski ovcar

2

HEAD
Broad and noble. Slightly convex skull. Stop not accentuated. Straight, broad forehead.

EYES
Almond-shaped eyes set slightly oblique. Chestnut or dark brown color.

EARS
Lie flat against the head in a V.

BODY
Strong, slightly rectangular, and well-muscled. Broad, muscular neck. The deep chest long is well let down. Sloped croup.

LIMBS
Forelegs oval, compact feet. Hind legs round, compact feet. Arched toes.

TAIL
Set on high, of medium length. Saber tail. Richly clad with long hair.

COAT
Short on the head and front of legs. Long and abundant over the rest of the body. Lies flat. Mane at neck; flag tail. Feathering on the hind legs.

COLOR
Iron gray, dark nuances desirable, particularly on the withers, the abdomen, and the feet. Dark mask on the head.

SIZE
Dog: 57 to 63 cm (22.5-25 in).
Bitch: 54 to 60 cm (21-23.5 in).

WEIGHT
Dog: 30 to 42 kg (66-93 lb).
Bitch: 25 to 37 kg (55-82 lb).

Character, special skills, and training
This dog is brave and courageous, but not fearless. He is of excellent character and easy-going. Devoted to his owner, he makes an excellent pet. Wary of strangers and not easily won over, he is a good guard dog and will protect his owner. Firm, but not harsh training is appropriate for this breed.

Care and functions
This breed needs space and exercise. Regular brushing is required.
· Sheepdog.
· Guard dog.
· Pet.

Cao de Castro Laboreiro

*The Cao de Castro Laboreiro is one of the oldest breeds on the Iberian peninsula.
Springing from the village Castro Laboreiro, this typical Portuguese breed is widespread in the region
bordered by the Minho and Limia rivers between the Peneda and Suajo mountain
chains in northern Portugal. The Cao de Castro Laboreiro, a mastiff, protects herds from wolves.
He is also used as a guard dog and police dog.*

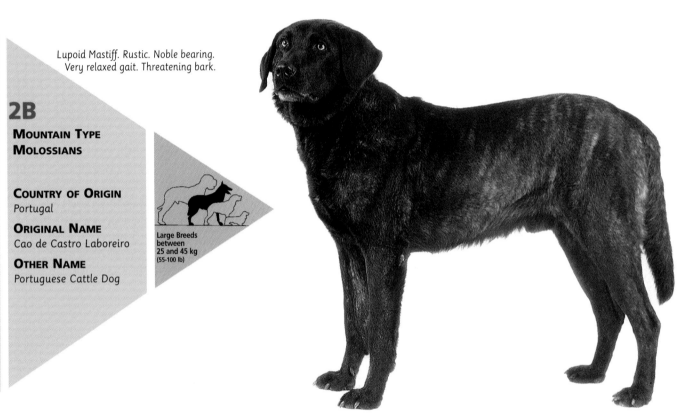

Lupoid Mastiff. Rustic. Noble bearing.
Very relaxed gait. Threatening bark.

2B

**MOUNTAIN TYPE
MOLOSSIANS**

2

COUNTRY OF ORIGIN
Portugal

ORIGINAL NAME
Cao de Castro Laboreiro

OTHER NAME
Portuguese Cattle Dog

Large Breeds
between
25 and 45 kg
(55-100 lb)

Character, special skills and training
This robust, loyal, docile breed is affectionate, calm
and even-tempered. Constantly on the alert, this dog's
great courage and wariness of strangers make him a
superb guard dog. Firm training is required.

Care and functions
The Cao de Castro Laboreiro needs exercise and room
to run. Regular brushing is required.
· Flock guard.
· Guard dog. Police dog.
· Pet.

HEAD
Medium size, dry, no wrinkles. Stop not pronounced.
Long, strong, straight nose
bridge. Powerful jaws.

EYES
Set obliquely in the skull.
Medium size. Light brown
color in light-coated varieties
and dark brown in dark-
coated varieties.

EARS
Medium size, slightly thick,
almost triangular with
rounded tips, drop.

BODY
Rectangular. Short neck
without dewlap. Broad, deep
chest. Narrow through the

belly. Broad, short, strong,
muscular loin. Croup slightly
sloped.

LIMBS
Muscular legs with substantial bone. Almost round feet
with thick toes and black or
dark gray nails.

TAIL
Thick and bushy, carried in
the shape of a saber, reaching the hock joint.

COAT
Thick, coarse, short
(5 cm) (2 in), harsh, close-
lying and smooth.

COLOR
Wolf gray most common.

Any shade of gray, with or
without a black mask;
brindle.

SIZE
Dog: 55 to 60 cm
(21,5-23,5 in).
Bitch: 52 to 57 cm
(20.5 to 22.5 in).

WEIGHT
Dog: 30 to 40 kg
(66 to 88 lb).
Bitch: 20 to 30 kg
(44-66 lb).

Great Pyrenees

Like many Molossians, the Great Pyrenees'distant ancestor may be Tibetan Mastiff, which was introduced in Europe during Asian invasions. Identified as early as the 12th century, the Great Pyrenees protected the shepherd and his flock from wolves and bears, guarded homes and castles, and even sat in the royal court of Louis XIV. The Argeles and Cauterets clubs, founded in 1907, established the first standard for this breed. This standard was officially accepted in the 1960s. The Great Pyrenees is one of the few French breeds that is common outside of France. The breed is particularly popular in the United States and Japan.

Majestic. Powerfully built. Elegant.

2B

MOUNTAIN TYPE MOLOSSIANS

Giants Breeds over 45 kg (over 100 lb)

COUNTRY OF ORIGIN
France

ORIGINAL NAME
Montagne des Pyrénées

OTHER NAME
Pyrenean Mountain Dog

2

SIZE
Dog: 70 to 80 cm (27.5-31,5 in).
Bitch: 65 to 72 cm (25.5-28 in).

WEIGHT
Dog: approx. 60 kg
(132 lb).
Bitch: approx. 45 kg (99 lb).

HEAD
Size in proportion to body. Slightly domed skull. Stop not pronounced. Broad muzzle tapering toward the nose. Black, very slightly drooping lips.

EYES
Fairly small. Dark amber color. Black rims.

EARS
Small and triangular with rounded tips, hanging flat against the head.

BODY
Powerful. Strong, moderately short neck. Deep, broad brisket. Ribs slightly sprung. Belly slightly tucked up. Croup slightly sloped. Broad, straight, level back. Slightly elongated, compact feet with arched toes.

LIMBS
Solid legs with feathering. Double dewclaw on hind legs.

TAIL
Fairly long and bushy (plume). Carried low at rest and carried over the back making a wheel when alert.

COAT
Long, flat, resistant and thick. Longer on the tail, thighs and neck, where it may be slightly wavy. Thick, wooly undercoat.

COLOR
White with or without gray spots (badger coat) or pale yellow or orange on the head, ears and root of the tail. Badger coat is preferred. A few body spots are permissible.

Character, special skills and training
The Great Pyrenees has a rather independent nature and is proud, dominant and fairly strong-willed. Firm training from a very young age is required to bring this dog under control. This dog is tolerant, affectionate, gentle with children and very protective, making him an excellent pet. Reserved around strangers, this dog is a born protector. His size and demeanor can make him appear fearsome indeed.

Care and functions
This dog is not suited to city living. He needs exercise and room to run, or he will develop behavioral problems. He does not like to be shut in. Brushing three times per week and bathing several times per year are required.
· Flock guard.
· Guard dog.
· Pet.

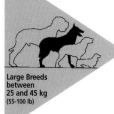

Estrela Mountain Dog

The origins of the Estrela Mountain Dog, which is fairly popular in Portugal, are not known, but it is thought to be the oldest breed on the Iberian peninsula. Descended from the Asian Molussus and related to the Spanish Mastiff, this breed was developed on Serra da Estrela mountain. Traditionally used as a sheepdog to protect the flock from wolves, the Estrela Mountain Dog is also used as a draft dog. This breed's standard was established in 1934. The Estrela Mountain Dog is still quite uncommon outside of Portugal.

Molossian. Mastiff type. Well balanced body proportions. Rustic.

2B

MOUNTAIN TYPE MOLOSSIANS

2

COUNTRY OF ORIGIN
Portugal

ORIGINAL NAME
Cao da Serra da Estrela

OTHER NAME
Portuguese Sheepdog

Large Breeds between 25 and 45 kg (55-100 lb)

HEAD
Strong and capacious. Convex profile to the skull. Stop not pronounced. Powerful jaws. Elongated nose bridge.

EYES
Medium size, oval. Dark amber color preferred. Black rims.

EARS
Small, narrow, triangular with rounded tips, drop. Cropped ears are permissible.

BODY
Compact. Short, thick neck. Deep, broad, rounded brisket. Short, broad loin. Short back. Croup slightly sloped.

LIMBS
Muscular legs with substantial bone and dry joints. Feet neither too long nor too round. Thick, compact toes. Dark or black nails.

TAIL
Long, carried down reaching the tip of the hock joint. Richly clad (feathering in long-haired variety).

COAT
Thick, slightly coarse, rather goatlike, smooth or slightly wavy. Two varieties exist; the long-haired variety is the most common, while the short-haired variety has almost disappeared.

COLOR
Only shades of fawn, wolf gray and yellow, solid color or parti-color.

SIZE
Dog: 65 to 72 cm (25.5 to 28 in).
Bitch: 62 to 68 (24.5 to 27 in).

WEIGHT
Dog: 40 to 50 kg (88-110,4 lb).
Bitch: 30 to 40 kg (66 to 88 lb).

Character, special skills and training
This impassive dog has quick reflexes. He is extremely hardy, energetic and courageous. The Estrela Mountain Dog is devoted to protecting the flock and works hard as a defense dog and draft dog. His exceptional sense of smell makes him a good hunter. Distrustful of strangers and even aggressive, he is known as an excellent guard dog. Docile and calm with his owners, he makes an excellent family pet. Firm, but gentle, training must be started at a very early age.

Care and functions
This dog is not suited to city living. He needs exercise and room to run to expend his energy. Regular brushing is required for the long-haired variety.
· Flock guard.
· Guard dog, police dog, army dog.
· Pet.

Great Dane

This large Mastiff is thought to be descended from the tibetan Mastiff introduced in europe by the phoenicians, then by the nomadic persian alans. In the middle ages, there were two varieties of this Mastiff: a smaller alaunt, powerful, agile, streamlined dogs that hunted in packs for boar, wolf and bear and a heavier, more compact alaunt used for guard duties. The immediat ancestors are the Bullenbeisser (now extinct) crossed with large hunting dogs descended from the more streamlined alaunt.

Large. Powerful. Harmonious build. Robust, strong, elegant, regal. The Apollo of dogs. Proud. Pigmented skin. Harmonious, supple gait.

Later, names such as Ulm Dog, Great Dane, and Siberian Dog were used to indicate the different types of this breed. In 1878, all varieties were placed under the one name, Great Dane. The standard was written around 1890 in Germany.

2A

MASTIFF TYPE MOLOSSIANS

Giants Breeds over 45 kg (over 100 lb)

COUNTRY OF ORIGIN
Germany

ORIGINAL NAME
Deutsche Dogge

OTHER NAME
German Mastiff

2

HEAD
Finely chiseled. Elongated, narrow. Very expressive. Always carried high. Strongly pronounced stop. Well developed superciliary arches. Broad nose bridge. Deep, rectangular muzzle. Black nose (lighter in the harlequin).

EYES
Medium size. Round. As dark as possible. Lighter eyes permissible in blue danes. Lighter eyes or eyes of different color permissible in harlequin danes.

EARS
Set on high, naturally drop. Cropped to a point, carried rigid and erect.

BODY
Square outline. Long, dry, muscular, well arched neck. Prominent forechest. Ribs well sprung. Wide croup sloping slightly. Belly well tucked up. Short, almost rectangular back. Broad, slightly arched loin

LIMBS
Strong, muscular legs Round cat feet. Very compact, arched toes.

TAIL
Medium length reaching the hocks. Set high, broad at the root tapering to a narrow tip. Curved slightly in the form of a saber when in action.

COAT
Very short, thick, smooth, shiny, lying close to the skin.

COLOR
Brindle: background color is light to dark yellow gold always with strong, black cross stripes; a black mask is preferred.
Fawn: light to dark yellow gold; a black mask is preferred.
Black: glossy black; white

markings are permissible. Blue: pure steel blue; white markings on the chest and feet are permissible. Harlequin: pure white background with glossy black torn patches of differing sizes well distributed over the entire body.

SIZE
Dog: at least 80 cm (31,5 in). Bitch: at least 72 cm (28 in).

WEIGHT
50 to 70 kg (110.5-154.5 lb).

Character, special skills and training
The great dane may be the most peace-loving of all the Mastiffs. He is a gentle, tender, kind, sensitive and affectionate dog, particularly with children. This stable, calm dog rarely barks and is never aggressive unless the situation warrants. He is alert, protective of his territory and his owner's property, wary around strangers and not easily swayed. His formidable size is enough to dissuade almost anyone. Training must start early. It should be firm, but undertaken with patience.

Care and functions
The great dane can be content living in an apartment, but he must get out daily to stretch his long legs. This athletic dog needs space and exercise. However, he should not exercise too vigorously until he has stopped growing, or he may damage his joints and ligaments. This dog has a short life expectancy of only eight years.
· Guard dog.
· Pet.

Argentinean Mastiff

This breed was created in Argentina by the Martinez brothers in the early twentieth century. The root stock was the Fighting Dog of Cordoba, a ferocious Mastiff. As the breed was developed it was crossed with the Spanish Mastiff, the Great Pyrenees, the Great Dane, the Boxer, Mastiffs, the Bulldog, Pointers, and the Irish Wolfhound. The result was a versatile breed that could be used for hunting, fighting, guard duties and more. The first standard was written in 1928 and approved by the Argentina Kennel Club in 1965. In 1973, the FCI established a standard for the breed and, in 1975, officially recognized the first and only breed ever developed in argentina.

Molossian type. Imposing, solid, elegant.

2A

MASTIFF TYPE MOLOSSIANS

2

COUNTRY OF ORIGIN
Argentina

ORIGINAL NAME
Dogo argentino

OTHER NAME
Dogo

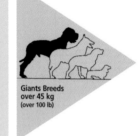
Giants Breeds
over 45 kg
(over 100 lb)

Character, special skills and training
This is a very robust, active, energetic, agile, courageous breed. The dogo argentino is calm, peaceful, affectionate and docile. He is very sociable and needs to stay close to his owner. He rarely barks. This breed is aggressive and dominant with other dogs and is fearsome indeed when defending his owner's property. Firm training is required, but be gentle with this sensitive dog.

Care and functions
The argentinean Mastiff can adjust to life in an apartment if he can get out two or three times each day and get plenty of exercise. He should be outdoors as much as possible. Brushing once or twice per week and bathing two or three times per year is recommended. It is necessary to clean his eyes regularly to avoid streaks.
· Hunting dog (large game – boar, puma, etc.)
· Utility dog: police dog, army dog, customs, search and rescue, guide dog.
· Guard dog.
· Pet.

HEAD
Molossian appearance. Strong, well chiseled. Capacious, convex skull. Deep wrinkles on forehead. Slightly hollow muzzle. Powerful jaws.

EYES
Dark or hazel color.

EARS
Set on high. Held erect or semi-erect, v-shaped. Generally cropped.

BODY
Powerful without bulkiness. Arched, strong neck. Deep, full chest. Solid back.

LIMBS
Very muscular hind legs. Long, straight forelegs. Moderately oval feet with arched toes.

TAIL
Long and thick, naturally hanging down.

COAT
Short, thick, lying close to the skin.

COLOR
White. Any color marking is a disqualification.

SIZE
Dog: 62 to 65 cm (24.5-26.5 in). Bitch: 57 to 60 cm (22.5-23.5 in).

WEIGHT
40 to 50 kg (88-110.5 lb).

French Mastiff

The Dogue de Bordeaux, one of the oldest breeds in France, is the only Mastiff of French origin. This dog may be descended from the Roman Molossus, the Spanish Mastiff and others. During the middle ages, the breed was used for hunting and dog fighting. In the eighteenth century, Buffon described it as the Dogue d'Aquitaine. This breed was long known as the "Butcher dog" because butchers often selected this breed to protect their homes. He has also been known as the "Turk dog" in reference to his asian ancestors. An official standard was recognized in 1926 after the breed had been crossed several times with Mastiffs.

Brachycephalic molossian type. Very muscular. Built fairly low to the ground. Compact, athletic build. Imposing and proud.

2A

MASTIFF TYPE MOLOSSIANS

Giants Breeds over 45 kg (over 100 lb)

COUNTRY OF ORIGIN
France

ORIGINAL NAME
Dogue de Bordeaux

OTHER NAME
Dogue d'Aquitaine

2

HEAD
Extremely capacious, angular, broad, relatively short. Viewed from the side, it has the shape of a trapezoid. The skull (perimeter equaling dog's height) is slightly convex. Strong stop. Forehead, which is wider than high, dominates the face. Deep, symmetrical wrinkles. Powerful, thick, moderately short, slightly hollow muzzle. Broad nose. Extremely powerful jaws. Undershot jaw (lower jaw protruding 0.2 to 1 in). Thick flews.

EYES
Oval, moderately wide set. Hazel to dark brown color in dogs with a black mask, lighter color permissible in dogs with a red mask.

EARS
Small, slightly darker than the rest of the coat. Drop close to head along the cheeks.

BODY
Powerful. Very strong, almost cylindrical neck with dewlap. Powerful, deep, broad chest. Ribs well sprung. Broad, muscular back. Belly tucked up. Powerful chest. Slightly sloping croup.

LIMBS
Round, strong feet with compact toes. Dark nails. Muscular legs with a lot of bone.

TAIL
Very thick, carried low with the tip reaching no further than the hocks.

COAT
Fine, short, smooth and soft.

COLOR
Fawn or dark auburn with a red or black mask. Good pigmentation preferred. Small white markings on the forechest and feet are permissible.

SIZE
Dog: 60 to 68 cm (23,5-27 in).
Bitch: 58 to 66 cm (23-26 in).

WEIGHT
Dog: at least 50 kg (110 lb).
Bitch: at least 45 kg (99 lb).

Character, special skills and training
This former fighting dog is an excellent guard dog that vigilantly protects the home with courage, though not aggression. The french Mastiff does not like to socialize with other dogs. This gentle, calm, sensitive dog forms a strong bond with his owner and is very affectionate with children. He rarely barks. This breed detests solitude and lack of activity. This dog must be exceptionally well-trained in order to keep him under control.

Care and functions
The french Mastiff is not suitable as a house dog. He needs space and exercise. No special care of the coat is required.
· Guard and defense dog.
· Pet.

Mallorquin Bulldog

*Originating on the island of Majorca, the mallorquin Bulldog was developed
for bull-baiting and dog-fighting, like the english Bulldog.
When this practice came to an end, the very existence of the Mallorquin Bulldog came
into question. The breed was saved by spanish breeders, but is still very rare.*

Mastiff. Medium size. Powerful, muscular build.

2A

MASTIFF TYPE MOLOSSIANS

2

COUNTRY OF ORIGIN
Balearic Island of Majorca, Spain

ORIGINAL NAME
Perro de Presa Mallorquin

OTHER NAME
Ca de Bou

Large Breeds between 25 and 45 kg (55-100 lb)

Character, special skills and training
This extremely courageous, independent dog has a combative personality. This breed must receive strict training.

Care and functions
This breed needs space and a lot of exercise. Regular brushing is required.
· Guard and defense dog.
· Pet.

HEAD
Massive. Broad, square skull. Broad, flat forehead. Deep stop. Broad muzzle. Very strong, bulging jaw muscles.

EYES
Large, bulging slightly and slightly out of round. Very dark color.

EARS
Short and thin. Set on high. Rose ears folded back exposing the burr.

BODY
Massive. Long, very powerful neck. Deep, cylindrical chest.

Short loin and flanks. Belly drawn up. Croup slightly higher than the withers.

LIMBS
Round, medium size, compact feet. Forelegs shorter than hind legs. Dewclaws on hind legs.

TAIL
Strong at the base and tapering to a point reaching the hocks.

COAT
Short, harsh, smooth, lying close to the skin.

COLOR
Fawn, brindle, dark striped with white markings.

SIZE
56 to 58 cm (22-23 in).

WEIGHT
Approx. 40 kg (88 lb).

Tibetan Mastiff

This Mastiff is the direct descendent of the ancient Greater Tibetan Mastiff. Originating in the high plateaus of central Asia, the breed migrated into the rest of central Asia, into Asia Minor, eastern Europe and finally central Europe. Many modern-day mastiffs are descended from this breed, which can be found on the steppes and in the foothills of the Himalayas guarding flocks and villages alike with great ferocity. This breed was much larger in the past than today's version. In fact, the Tibetan Mastiff used to be so big that Marco Polo claimed the dog was "as big as a donkey"! Almost extinct by the nineteenth century, the Tibetan Mastiff was saved by British fanciers.

Formidable. Powerful. Massive. Well constructed. Beautiful expression. Gait: Light, elastic movement. Slow, measured walk.

2B

MOUNTAIN TYPE MOLOSSIANS

Giants Breeds over 45 kg (over 100 lb)

COUNTRY OF ORIGIN
Tibet
Sponsored by Great Britain

2

ORIGINAL NAME
Do-Kyi (meaning "dog that can be tied up")

HEAD
Thick and strong. Massive skull. Pronounced stop. Square muzzle. Strong jaws. Broad nose. Thick lips.

EYES
Medium size, oval, set slightly oblique and well apart. Any shade of brown.

EARS
Medium size, drop, triangular.

BODY
Strong, with length being slightly greater than height. Strong, arched neck without dewlap and with a thick mane. Deep forechest. Moderately deep and broad brisket. Straight back. Croup almost imperceptible.

LIMBS
Strong, round, compact feet. Heavy-boned legs.

TAIL
Medium to long length, not reaching beyond the hock joint. Richly clad and curling over the back.

COAT
Fairly long, thick, straight and harsh. Never silky, curly or wavy. Dense, thick, rather wooly undercoat.

COLOR
Jet black, black and tan, brown, shades of gold or gray, gray with gold markings. Tan and gold markings above the eyes, on the lower legs and the tip of the tail. White spot on the chest is permissible. Small white markings on the feet are tolerated, though not preferred.

SIZE
Dog: approx. 66 cm (26 in).
Bitch: approx. 61 cm (24 in).

WEIGHT
55 to 80 kg
(121.5-176.5 lb).

Character, special skills and training
This rustic, hardy, even-tempered dog is affectionate, but not demonstrative and can have a stubborn streak. He is very distant with strangers and can even become aggressive. A guard dog to the core, he is particularly vigilant at night. His loud bark can strike fear in the heart of even the hardiest soul. Firm, patient training must start very early. The Tibetan Mastiff does not reach full maturity until the age of three or four and the bitch cycles only once per year.

Care and functions
This breed should not be kept as a house dog. The Tibetan Mastiff needs exercise and room to run. Weekly brushing is required.
· Flock guard.
· Guard dog. · Pet.

Fila Brasileiro

Spanish and Portuguese conquistadors brought Mastiffs, Scenthounds and Bloodhounds to Brazil in the seventeenth century. These breeds were crossed with Brazilian dogs to create the Fila Brasileiro. The Fila was originally used to track escaped slaves. Later, the breed was used as a guard and to drive cattle. The Fila Brasileiro was recognized in 1950.

Molossian type. Rectangular, compact build.
Harmonious proportions. Great agility.
Relaxed trot. Powerful gallop.
Camel pace.

2A

MASTIFF TYPE MOLOSSIANS

2

COUNTRY OF ORIGIN
Brazil

OTHER NAMES
Brazilian Mastiff,
Brazilian molosser

Giants Breeds
over 45 kg
(over 100 lb)

Character, special skills and training
This valiant, courageous, fiery, resolute breed can be calm, self-assured, obedient and tolerant of children. However, firm training is required to achieve these traits. The fila brasileiro is distrustful of strangers.

Care and functions
This breed does not adapt well to urban living. He needs wide open spaces and plenty of exercise.
· Cattle driver.
· Guard dog, hunting dog (large game).
· Pet.

HEAD
Large, square, capacious. Broad skull. Stop not pronounced. Strong, broad, deep muzzle. Broad nose.

EYES
Medium size, almond. Deep chestnut to yellow color. Lids are often drooping.

EARS
Large, thick, v-shaped, drop.

BODY
Strong, longer than tall. Very strong neck with dewlap. Chest broad and well let down. Thick, loose skin. Broad, long, sloping croup. Withers slightly lower than croup.

LIMBS
Legs with plenty of bone. Strong feet with arched toes. Black nails.

TAIL
Thick at the base and tapering to a point reaching the hock joint.

COAT
Short, thick, soft, lying close to the skin.

COLOR
Any solid color (except white, mouse-gray, black and tan, or blue), brindle with moderately dark streaking. With or without a black mask. White markings on the feet, chest and tip of the tail are permissible provided they cover no more than a quarter of the body.

SIZE
Dog: 65 to 75 cm (25.5 to 29.5 in).
Bitch: 60 to 70 cm (23.5 to 27.5 in).

WEIGHT
Dog: at least 50 kg (110 lb).
Bitch: at least 40 kg (88 lb).

Hovawart

This old breed's name comes from the German word *Hofewart*, meaning estate dog, revealing his traditional role as guard dog for German farms in the thirteenth century. His distant ancestors were probably Asian Mastiffs. Over the centuries, the breed was gradually abandoned. It wasn't until the 1920s that the breed was resurrected by crossing German Shepherds, Leonbergers, Newfoundlands and others. The breed was recognized in 1936 and established as a utility dog by the FCI in 1964. Today, the Hovawart is quite popular in Germany and Scandinavian countries.

Medium size without bulkiness. Longer than tall.

2B

MOUNTAIN TYPE MOLOSSIANS

COUNTRY OF ORIGIN
Germany

Between 10 and 45 kg (20-100 lb)

2

HEAD
Robust. Broad, arched forehead. Pronounced stop. Long muzzle. Black lips.

EYES
Dark color.

EARS
Triangular, pendulous, hanging flat against the head.

BODY
Muscular and streamlined. Powerful neck without dewlap. Broad, deep brisket. Croup slightly sloped. Straight, solid back.

LIMBS
Robust, very muscular legs. Solid, oval feet.

TAIL
Long, richly clad, reaching just below the hocks. Carried low at rest.

COAT
Long with slightly wooly undercoat. Coarse with slight wave. Short on the head and front of the legs. No streaking or curl.

COLOR
Fawn (blond) becoming lighter on the legs and abdomen. Black. Black and tan (most common) with fawn markings (above the eyes, on the chest, legs and under the root of the tail). Each of the three varieties allows one small white spot on the forechest and mixture of a few lighter colored hairs, particularly on the tip of the tail.

SIZE
Dog: 63 to 70 cm (25 to 27.5 in). Bitch: 58 to 65 cm (23 to 25.5 in).

WEIGHT
25 to 40 kg (55 to 88 lb).

Character, special skills and training
This weatherproof, hardy, energetic dog loves to swim and is an excellent runner and jumper. He also has a keen sense of smell. The Hovawart is always on the alert, but is never aggressive without cause. This breed can fill several roles. The Hovawart is calm, even-tempered, affectionate with his owners and gentle with children. He is highly trainable, but training must be firm and undertaken with patience. He rarely barks, but when he does, his bark is loud, deep and resonant. This breed reaches full maturity around two years of age.

Care and functions
While this dog can adapt to city living, he needs exercise and room to run. Weekly brushing is sufficient to maintain the coat.
· Flock guard.
· Utility dog: rescue (avalanches), tracker (drugs), guide dog.
· Guard dog.
· Pet.

Landseer

Bred from the Newfoundland, the Landseer was named after the artist Sir Edwin Landseer who depicted the breed in paintings around 1837. He has been wrongly considered a black and white version of the Newfoundland, a variety British and Americans called the Landseer Newfoundland. The breed almost disappeared in the early twentieth century, but was saved by German breeders who introduced mountain dog blood, including that of the Great Pyrenees. In 1960, the FCI recognized the Landseer as a separate breed, distinct from the Newfoundland.

Large. Robust. Harmonious proportions. Longer legs and more powerfully built than the Newfoundland.

2B

MOUNTAIN TYPE MOLOSSIANS

2

COUNTRY OF ORIGIN
Germany

Giants Breeds
over 45 kg
(over 100 lb)

Character, special skills and training
This alert, courageous dog loves the water. He is affectionate and gentle.

Care and functions
This breed does not like to be closed in. He needs exercise and room to run. Daily brushing is required.

· Hunting dog.
· Rescue dog.
· Guard dog.
· Pet.

HEAD
Broad and massive. Skin on the head is not wrinkled. Covered with short, fine hairs. Distinct stop, but less pronounced than that of the St. Bernard. Firm flews.

EYES
Medium size. Brown to dark brown color.

EARS
Medium size, triangular, set on close to the eyes and hanging close against the head. Covered with short, fine hairs.

BODY
Powerful. Muscular neck. Deep, broad brisket. Ribs well sprung. Straight, broad, robust back. Broad, rounded croup.

LIMBS
Round feet. Muscular legs with substantial bone.

TAIL
Strong, bushy, carried down and reaching the hocks.

COAT
Long, smooth, fine to the touch, the thicker the better. Undercoat is not as thick as that of the Newfoundland.

COLOR
Clear white with distinct black spots on the body and croup. The neck, forechest, underbelly, legs and tail must be white. The head is black with a white muzzle.

SIZE
Dog: 72 to 80 cm (28-31.5 in). Bitch: 67 to 72 cm (26.5-28 in).

WEIGHT
50 to 70 kg (110-154 lb).

Leonberger

This breed is named after a town in Wurtemberg, Germany where it is thought to have existed for many years, or perhaps after the town of Löwenberg in Switzerland. Some experts believe it is descended from the Tibetan Mastiff, while others believe that H. Essig, from the town of Leonberg, crossed Newfoundlands, St. Bernards and Great Pyrenees in 1846. However, it is more likely that this breed is the last descendant of the Greater Swiss Mountain Dog, a breed distinct from the St. Bernard. The first standard was established in 1895 and the FCI established a standard in 1973.

Well proportioned. Powerfully built. Elegant. Light-footed.

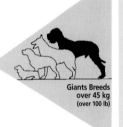

2B

MOUNTAIN TYPE MOLOSSIANS

Giants Breeds over 45 kg (over 100 lb)

COUNTRY OF ORIGIN
Germany

ORIGINAL NAME
Leonberger

2

HEAD
Fairly narrow, longer than wide. Moderately domed skull. Moderate stop. Slightly aquiline nose bridge (like that of a ram). The muzzle is never pointed. Black, tight lips.

EYES
Medium size. Light to dark brown color.

EARS
Set on high, drop, falling flat against the head.

BODY
Slightly longer than tall. Powerful neck. Deep chest. Robust loin. Strong back.

LIMBS
Strong, muscular legs with plenty of bone. Rounded feet with compact toes and black pads.

TAIL
Very richly clad (brush). Carried half down, never too high or curled over the back.

COAT
Medium fine to coarse, thick, long, smooth, lying close to the skin. Presence of undercoat. Beautiful mane on the neck and forechest.

COLOR
Lion-colored: fawn, gold yellow or reddish-brown with black mask. A small white spot on the forechest is permissible. Sable with a black overlay is also permissible. The collarettes, trousers (feathering on the back of the legs), culottes and feathering on the tail may be lighter in color than the rest of the coat.

SIZE
Dog: 72 to 80 cm (28-31.5 in). Bitch: 65 to 75 cm (26-30 in).

WEIGHT
60 to 80 kg (132-176 lb).

Character, special skills and training
The "weatherproof" Leonberger an excellent swimmer. He is lively, calm and self-assured. He will only bark to warn of danger. This breed is loyal, docile, very loving with his owner and extremely gentle with children. Though he can appear formidable indeed to strangers, he generally will not bite. Due to his size, early training is required to teach this dog to be gentle. The Leonberger reaches full maturity at the age of three.

Care and functions
The Leonberger needs exercise and room to run. He does not like to be tied up or left alone. Weekly brushing is sufficient, except during the twice-yearly seasonal shedding, when more frequent brushing is required.
· Flock guard.
· Rescue dog (mountain rescues and drowning accidents).
· Pet.

Mastiff

The Mastiff, which is of British origin, is descended from Assyrian Mastiffs (descended from the Tibetan Mastiff imported to Europe by the Phoenicians), through the Roman Molossus. Originally bred as a fighting dog, the Mastiff later was used as a guard dog for English Seigneurs'herds and estates and as a hunting dog for large game. This breed was given the name Mastiff toward the end of the fourteenth century. The first Old English Mastiff standard was published in 1883. During World War II, this mighty breed almost disappeared, but was saved and restored from a few remaining Mastiffs that were imported into the United States.

Massive. Powerful. Well-balanced proportions. Well constructed. A combination of grandeur and courage.

2A

MASTIFF TYPE MOLOSSIANS

2

COUNTRY OF ORIGIN
Great Britain

OTHER NAME
Old English Mastiff

Giants Breeds
over 45 kg
(over 100 lb)

Character, special skills and training
This peaceable, gentle dog is affectionate with his owner and children. Courageous and not easily swayed, he is a guard dog through and through. This breed requires rigorous training because he can present a danger to strangers.

Care and functions
The Mastiff needs a lot of space and exercise. Regular brushing is required.
· · Guard dog.
· Pet.

HEAD
Square. Broad skull. Flat forehead with distinct wrinkles when at attention. Pronounced stop. Short, blunt muzzle (squarish). Slightly pendulous flews.

EYES
Small, set wide apart. Hazel color (the darker the better).

EARS
Small, thin, wide set and set on high. Hang flat against the cheeks.

BODY
Massive, broad and tall. Slightly arched, very muscular neck. Ribs well sprung.

Broad, muscular back and loin. Deep flanks. Broad, well let down chest.

LIMBS
Large, round feet with arched toes and black nails. Heavy boned legs set wide apart.

TAIL
Set high. Broad at the root and tapering toward the tip. Carried straight down at rest and hanging to the hock joint.

COAT
Short, lying very close to the body. Not too fine on the shoulders, neck and back.

COLOR
Fawn, apricot, silvery fawn or fawn-brindle. All have black mask, ears and nose. Eyes surrounded by black.

SIZE
Dog: 75 to 82 cm (29.5-32 in).
Bitch: at least 66 cm (26 in).

WEIGHT
70 to 90 kg
(154-198 lb).

Spanish Mastiff

Developed in Extremadura in southwestern Spain, the Spanish Mastiff is possibly descended from the Mastiff and Roman Molossus. In the past, this breed was used for dog fighting, in war and for hunting boar and other large game.

Tall. Very large. Balanced proportions. Solid construction. Very powerful and muscular. Compact bone structure. Thick, pink skin with darkly pigmented areas.
Preferred gait: Trot.

2B

MOUNTAIN TYPE MOLOSSIANS

Giants Breeds over 45 kg (over 100 lb)

COUNTRY OF ORIGIN
Spain

ORIGINAL NAME
Mastín Español

OTHER NAMES
Mastín de Extremadura
Mastín de Leon
Mastín de la Mancha

2

HEAD
Solid, massive, size in proportion to the body. Moderately domed skull. Stop not pronounced. Rectangular muzzle. Large nose.

EYES
Small, almond. Dark color preferred (hazel). Black rims.

EARS
Medium size, triangular, drop, hanging against the cheeks.

BODY
Massive, elongated (longer than tall). Solid, tapered neck. Thick, double dewlap.

Withers slightly pronounced. Deep, broad brisket. Ribs well sprung. Long, broad loin. Broad, sloped croup. Powerful, muscular back.

LIMBS
Powerful, muscular legs. Dewclaws sometimes present on hind legs. Round cat feet with compact toes.

TAIL
Thick at the root and tapering to the tip. Hair on the tail is longer than on the rest of the body. Carried low at rest, reaching the hocks.

COAT
Heavy, thick, moderately

long, smooth. Shorter on the legs.

COLOR
Any color. Solid colors are preferred: yellow, fawn, red, black, wolf gray and piebald.

SIZE
Dog: at least 77 cm (30 in).
Bitch: at least 72 cm (28 in).

WEIGHT
50 to 65 kg (110-143.5 lb).

Character, special skills and training
This rustic, lively, self-confident breed has a noble bearing. He is calm, affectionate, gentle with children and forms a close bond with his owner. The Spanish Mastiff holds his ground with predators and strangers. His bark is deep, resonant, husky and powerful.

Care and functions
The Spanish Mastiff needs a lot of exercise and room to run. Regular brushing is required.
· Flock guard.
· Hunting dog (boar).
· Guard and defense dog.
· Pet.

Neapolitan Mastiff

The Neapolitan Mastiff is descended from the Tibetan Mastiff through the large Roman Molossus described by agronomist Columella in the first century. This breed fought with the Roman legions and was spread throughout Europe during the Roman invasions. The Neapolitan Mastiff has also been used as a circus dog. This breed was the progenitor of many mastiff breeds in other European countries. The breed survived for many centuries. Spanish Mastiff blood was later introduced. The breed has been selectively bred since 1947.

Heavy. Massive. Noble. Majestic.
Thick, abundant, loose skin.
Gait: walk is slow and bearlike. Rarely gallops.

2A

MASTIFF TYPE MOLOSSIANS

2

COUNTRY OF ORIGIN
Italy

ORIGINAL NAME
Mastino Napoletano

Giants Breeds
over 45 kg
(over 100 lb)

Character, special skills and training
This calm, loyal, devoted dog is very affectionate with his owners and gentle with children. Dominant with other dogs, he is courageous and suspicious of strangers. This breed is not aggressive and will not bite without cause. Formidable in appearance, he is even more fearsome if provoked. Early, firm training is vital. The Neapolitan Mastiff should not be trained to attack, because he could become overly aggressive and dangerous.

Care and functions
This breed needs wide open spaces and a lot of exercise. The Neapolitan Mastiff should not be allowed to sleep on hard surfaces or unsightly calluses may form on his elbows and knees. Regular brushing is required. Special attention should be given to the folds in the skin and drooping eyelids.
· Guard dog.
· Police dog.
· Pet.

HEAD
Short, massive, imposing. Broad, flat skull. Loose skin with wrinkles and folds. Pronounced stop. Broad, deep muzzle. Powerful jaws. Large nose. Thick, fleshy, pendulous lips.

EYES
Wide set, round, of a darker color than that of the coat.

EARS
Small, triangular, flat, lying against the cheeks. If cropped, they are the shape of an equilateral triangle.

BODY
Massive, longer than tall. Tapered neck with double dewlap. Broad withers (not pronounced). Large brisket. Ribs well sprung. Broad back. Broad, powerful, sloping croup.

LIMBS
Heavy boned legs. Round, large feet with arched, compact toes.

TAIL
Broad and thick at the root, tapering slightly toward the tip. If left natural, tail hangs down reaching the hock joint. Typically, one-third of the tail is removed.

COAT
Short, harsh, hard, thick and smooth (maximum length (1.5 cm) (0.6 in).

COLOR
Preferred colors: gray, lead gray and black, brown, fawn, stag-red, sometimes with small white spots on the chest and feet. All colors may be brindle.

SIZE
Dog: 65 to 75 cm (25.5-29.5 in).
Bitch: 60 to 68 cm (23.5-27 in).

WEIGHT
Dog: 50 to 70 kg (110 to 154 lb).
Bitch: 50 to 60 kg (110 to 132 lb).

Pyrenean Mastiff

The Pyrenean Mastiff was developed on the southern slopes of the Pyrenees Mountains in Spain. It is not to be confused with a closely related French breed, the Great Pyrenees. Some experts believe the Pyrenean Mastiff is the product of a cross between the Great Pyrenees and the Spanish Mastiff. Over the centuries, they guarded flocks during the Transhumante, the formal mass migration of the flocks up and down the mountainside with the change of the seasons. The breed was recognized in the late nineteenth century.

Tall. Massive proportions. Balanced construction. Balanced proportions. Very powerful and muscular. Compact skeleton. Thick, pink skin with spots of darker pigmentation.

2B

MOUNTAIN TYPE MOLOSSIANS

Giants Breeds over 45 kg (over 100 lb)

2

COUNTRY OF ORIGIN
Spain

ORIGINAL NAME
Perro Mastin de los Pirineos

OTHER NAMES
Mastin d'Aragon
Mastin de Navarre

WEIGHT
55 to 70 kg
(121-154 lb).

HEAD
Large and solid. Broad, slightly rounded skull. Stop not pronounced. Rectangular muzzle tapering toward the large nose.

EYES
Small, almond. Hazel, preferably dark, color. Black rims. Mild droop of lower lid slightly revealing the conjunctiva.

EARS
Medium size, triangular, dropping flat against the cheeks.

BODY
Slightly longer than tall. Very strong and robust. Tapering neck with double dewlap. Withers slightly pronounced. Broad, deep brisket. Ribs well sprung. Belly moderately tucked up.

Powerful, muscular back. Broad, solid, sloped croup.

LIMBS
Round, compact cat feet with arched toes. Muscular legs.

TAIL
Thick at the root, supple, richly clad with fur (plume). Carried low at rest reaching the hocks, with the last third always curving up.

COAT
Stiff, thick, dense. Moderate length (6 to 9 cm) (2,4-3,5 in). Longer on the shoulders, neck, underbelly and back of the legs.

COLOR
White with a well-defined mask. Sometimes the body has distinct markings of the same color as the mask. Ears are always dark. Tri-colors and solid white coats not preferred. Tip of the tail and feet must be white. Mask clearly visible, with a light-colored background. Preferred colors are white (solid white or snow white with medium gray or bright golden yellow markings), brown, black, silvery gray, light beige, yellowish sable, mottled.

SIZE
Dog: at least 77 cm (30 in).
Bitch: at least 72 cm (28 in).

Character, special skills and training
This breed is affectionate and calm and has a noble bearing. But he is also courageous and can be formidable with strangers, never backing down if property, owner, or animals under his charge are threatened. The Great Pyrenean has a deep, loud bark. His temperament is benign with other dogs. Firm training should start early.

Care and functions
This dog is not made for city living. He does not like to be closed in. Brushing once or twice per week is required.
· Flock guard.
· Guard and defense dog.
· Pet.

Rafeiro do Alentejo

The Rafeiro do Alentejo was developed from local breeds
in the Alentejo region, an area in southern Portugal with a continental climate.
A good herder, this breed is now used as a flock guard.
The Rafeiro do Alentejo is the largest dog of its type in Portugal.

Large. Strong. Long back. Massive head.

2B

**MOUNTAIN TYPE
MOLOSSIANS**

2

COUNTRY OF ORIGIN
Portugal

ORIGINAL NAME
Rafeiro do Alentejo

Large Breeds
between
25 and 45 kg
(55-100 lb)

Character, special skills and training
This rustic, powerful, hard-working dog is courageous and dedicated. He is loyal and affectionate
with his owner. The Rafeiro do Alentejo is aggressive
toward strangers, as with predators. Firm training is
required.

Care and functions
This dog is not suited to city living. He needs exercise
and room to run. Weekly brushing is sufficient.
· Flock guard.
· Guard and defense dog.
· Pet.

HEAD
Bearlike. Broad, domed
skull. Slight stop. Domed
nose bridge. Strong jaws.
Oval nose. Thin lips.

EYES
Small, oval. Dark color.
Dark rims.

EARS
Small, folded, triangular,
drop.

BODY
Strong and long. Strong,
short neck. Deep, broad
chest. Broad loin. Straight

back. Broad, slightly sloped
croup.

LIMBS
Strong, compact feet with
long toes

TAIL
Long, thick, carried down
and curving slightly.

COAT
Short or medium length
(preferred), smooth, coarse
and thick.

COLOR
Black, wolf gray, fawn or
yellow, with or without

white; or white with spots,
stripes or brindle.

SIZE
Dog: 66 to 74 cm (26-29 in).
Bitch: 64 to 70 cm (25 to
27.5 in).

WEIGHT
Dog: 40 to 50 kg
(88 to 110,5 lb).
Bitch: 35 to 45 kg
(77-99 lb).

Rottweiler

Some writers believe this very German dog is descended from the Bavarois Bouvier. Others contest that it is descended from Roman Molosser dogs brought to Germany during the Roman invasions. By the Middle Ages, this powerful, courageous dog was already guarding the herd and defending cattle merchants against bandits in the village of Rottweil in Wurtemberg, Germany. Butchers commonly kept this dog and as a result, the breed became known as the "butcher dog". The first Rottweiler club was formed in 1907. During World War I, the Rottweiler served in the German army. The breed was officially recognized in 1966 and it became well-known worldwide around 1970.

Compact. Powerful. Harmonious proportions. Power and agility. Gait: Trot.

2A

MASTIFF TYPE MOLOSSIANS

COUNTRY OF ORIGIN
Germany

ORIGINAL NAME
Rottweiler

OTHER NAMES
Rottweiler Metzgerhund (Butcher dog)
Rottie

2

Giants Breeds
over 45 kg
(over 100 lb)

HEAD
Strong. Broad, moderately convex skull. Pronounced stop. Rectangular nose bridge. Large nose. Powerful jaws. Black, tight lips.

EYES
Medium size, almond. Dark brown color.

EARS
Set on high, medium size, triangular, very wide set. Drop, hanging forward tightly against the head.

BODY
Compact. Powerful neck

without loose skin (no dewlap). Well pronounced forechest. Roomy chest. Ribs well sprung. Short loin. Straight, powerful back. Broad, slightly rounded croup.

LIMBS
Round feet with arched, compact toes and black nails. Muscular legs.

TAIL
Docked (to one or two vertebrae) or natural.

COAT
Medium length, coarse to the

touch, dense and lying flat. Presence of undercoat.

COLOR
Black with distinct tan markings on the cheeks, above the eyes, on the muzzle, on the underside of the neck, on the forechest, legs and under the root of the tail.

SIZE
Dog: 61 to 68 cm (24 to 27 in).
Bitch: 56 to 63 cm (22 to 25 in).

WEIGHT
Dog: approx. 50 kg (110 lb).
Bitch: approx. 42 kg (93 lb).

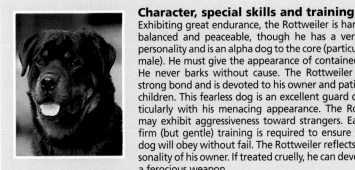

Character, special skills and training
Exhibiting great endurance, the Rottweiler is hardy, well-balanced and peaceable, though he has a very strong personality and is an alpha dog to the core (particularly the male). He must give the appearance of contained power. He never barks without cause. The Rottweiler forms a strong bond and is devoted to his owner and patient with children. This fearless dog is an excellent guard dog, particularly with his menacing appearance. The Rottweiler may exhibit aggressiveness toward strangers. Early, very firm (but gentle) training is required to ensure that this dog will obey without fail. The Rottweiler reflects the personality of his owner. If treated cruelly, he can develop into a ferocious weapon.

Care and functions
The Rottweiler requires considerable space and exercise. He does not like to be closed in or tied up. This breed does not tolerate heat well. Daily brushing is required.
· Guard dog.
· Police and army dog.

St. Bernard

The St. Bernard is thought to be descended from ancient Molosser dogs that crossed the Alps with the Roman legions. This breed's roots can be traced to Switzerland where monks at the Grand Saint Bernard Hospice (founded in the Middle Ages) developed the breed around the twelfth century. The St. Bernard quickly developed a reputation as a mountain rescue dog. The most famous St. Bernard in history, Barry, born in 1800, saved forty people over a period of ten years. Prior to 1830, St. Bernards had short coats. They were later crossed with the Newfoundland and the long-haired variety was created. It is the long-haired variety that is now most common. Called at different times in history the Mountain Dog, the Alpine Mastiff and the Barry Dog, this breed was officially recognized as the St. Bernard in 1880. The Swiss St. Bernard club was formed in Basel in 1884, and the St. Bernard's standard was fixed in Bern as of 1887.

Heavy. Powerful. Harmonious proportions.

2B

MOUNTAIN TYPE MOLOSSIANS

2

COUNTRY OF ORIGIN
Switzerland

ORIGINAL NAME
Bernhardiner

Giants Breeds
over 45 kg
(over 100 lb)

Character, special skills and training
This tranquil, calm, gentle, friendly dog is very sociable, devoted to his owners and adores children. Wary around strangers, the St. Bernard can be aggressive if the situation warrants. Firm training is required.

Care and functions
This breed requires considerable space and long walks every day. Energetic daily brushing is required. The St. Bernard does not tolerate heat well.
· Guard dog.
· Mountain rescue dog.
· Pet.

HEAD
Powerful and imposing. Broad, slightly domed skull. Straight nose bridge. Short muzzle. Large nose.

EYES
Fairly large. Dark brown color. Dark rims.

EARS
Medium size, set on high, triangular, drop.

BODY
Imposing. Powerful neck. Withers strongly pronounced. Ribs well sprung. Broad back.

LIMBS
Well-developed hindquarters with powerful, muscu-larthigs. Large, straight, compact, solid feet with high knuckles. Dewclaws are permissible on the back legs.

TAIL
Long, heavy, hanging down and reaching the hocks.

COAT
Two varieties:
- Short-haired: Dense, tough, lying smooth; abundant undercoat.
- Long-haired: Straight. Breeching, feathering, bushy tail. Short on the face and ears. Abundant undercoat.

COLOR
White with moderately large reddish-brown markings.

Reddish-brown brindle is permissible. Dark shadings on the head are favored.

SIZE
Dog: at least 70 cm (27.5 in).
Bitch: at least 65 cm (25.5 in).

WEIGHT
55 to 100 kg (121.5 to 221 lb).

Sarplaninac

This breed's name is taken from the mountain in southwest yugoslavia where it originated, the Sarplanina. This breed is believed to have been bred by shepherds in the region around 2,000 years ago to protect their flocks of sheep from predators such as wolves and bears. Some writers hold that this breed was brought to europe from asia during times of migration and may be descended from the Tibetan Mastiff. Registered by the FCI in 1939, this breed has spread throughout all of Yugoslavia and is becoming more popular in other countries.

Powerfully constructed. Imposing. Well-balanced. Preferred gait: high-stepping trot.

2B

MOUNTAIN TYPE MOLOSSIANS

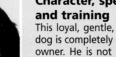

Giants Breeds over 45 kg (over 100 lb)

COUNTRY OF ORIGIN
Former Yugoslavia

ORIGINAL NAME
Illirski Ovcar

OTHER NAMES
Sar Planina
Illyrian Sheepdog

2

HEAD
Size in proportion to body. Slightly convex skull. Straight bridge. Stop not pronounced. Broad muzzle.

EYES
Almond. Dark or light chestnut color. Black rims.

EARS
Medium size. Drop, v-shaped, hanging flat against the cheeks.

BODY
Slightly longer than tall. Broad neck without dewlap. Deep chest. Ribs moderately well sprung. Belly well tucked up. Sloping croup. Topline slightly sloping from withers to croup. Broad back.

LIMBS
Solid legs. Strong, oval feet. Compact, arched toes.

TAIL
Long, narrowing at the tip, curving in the form of a saber. Thick feathering.

COAT
Long, thick, fairly coarse on the neck (collarette), body, back of legs and tail (feathering). Short on the head and the front of the legs. Short, fine, very thick undercoat.

COLOR
Solid color. Any shade ranging from white to dark brown. Iron gray and greenish gray preferred. Pied or white markings not permissi-

ble. On all pigmented dogs, the darkest hairs are on the top of the head, neck, and body.

SIZE
Dog: average 62 cm (24.5 in).
Bitch: average 58 cm (23 in).

WEIGHT
Dog: 35 to 45 kg (77 to 99 lb).
Bitch: 30 to 40 kg (66 to 88 lb).

Character, special skills and training
This loyal, gentle, calm, sensible dog is completely devoted to his owner. He is not easily swayed. Alert, with a strong defensive instinct, and distrustful, even potentially aggressive toward strangers, the sarplaninac is an exemplary guard dog. Be aware that this extraordinarily courageous dog will never retreat. He also exerts his dominance over other dogs.

Care and functions
This dog can adapt to living indoors, but he needs access to wide-open spaces and a lot of exercise. This dog despises solitude. His strong personality demands early training. Weekly brushing is required; daily brushing during seasonal shedding.
· Herder.
· Pet.

Shar-Pei

This ancient Chinese breed has endured for centuries and still lives in provinces bordering the China Sea to the south. The Shar-Pei has been used as temple guard, fighting dog, hunting dog (boar) and herd guard. In 1947, dogs were officially outlawed in China, but some Shar-Peis were exported to the United States from Hong Kong in 1970 and to Europe in 1980. One of the most unusual breeds in existence, the Shar-Pei is much sought after by fanciers who love its eclectic appearance. A miniature Pei (weighing 15 lb and measuring approximately 35 in at the withers) also exists, but is not recognized by the FCI.

Compact. Solid. Close-coupled.
Square in profile. Well proportioned.
Loose skin folds.

2A

MASTIFF TYPE MOLOSSIANS

2

COUNTRY OF ORIGIN
China

OTHER NAME
Chinese Fighting Dog

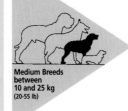

Medium Breeds
between
10 and 25 kg
(20-55 lb)

Character, special skills and training
This dominant dog is often aggressive toward other dogs, but is calm, dignified and affectionate with his owner. He loves children. His training must be firm, but gentle.

Care and functions
This breed makes a good house dog as long as daily exercise is provided. Weekly brushing is sufficient. This dog must be kept extremely clean and the folds in his loose skin require special care.
· Guard dog.
· Pet.

HEAD
Broad, flat skull. Slight stop. Profuse, fine wrinkles covering the forehead and cheeks continuing into side wrinkles and abundant dewlap. Large nose. Bluish-black tongue.

EYES
Deep set, small, almond shape. Dark color.

EARS
Small, fairly thick, triangular. Set on high, lying flat against the head.

BODY
Powerful and muscular. Strong neck with abundant dewlap. Broad, deep chest. Short back.

LIMBS
Legs with substantial bone. Compact feet.

TAIL
Medium length. Carried erect, straight, or tightly curled across the back.

COAT
Extremely short, horse coat. Extremely harsh to the touch

(Shar Pei means sand skin in Chinese).

COLOR
Only solid colors, black, tan, brown, beige and cream.

SIZE
40 to 51 cm (16 to 20 in).

WEIGHT
Approx. 20 kg (44 lb).

Newfoundland

Experts speculate that this breed may be descended from the Scandinavian "bear dogs" brought over from Norway in the sixteenth century, or perhaps from the Labrador, or Molosser dogs introduced by the Vikings, or the Leonberger, or the St. Bernard, or the Great Pyrenees introduced by Basque fisherman. In reality, it is not know how the ancestors of the Newfoundland found their way to Newfoundland in Canada. In the nineteenth century, French cod fisherman brought the Newfoundland to France. In England, the breed was lauded by Byron and immortalized in Landseer's paintings.

Noble. Majestic. Powerful. Massive bone structure. Relaxed, slightly rolling gait.

Giants Breeds over 45 kg (over 100 lb)

2B

MOUNTAIN TYPE MOLOSSIANS

COUNTRY OF ORIGIN
Canada – Newfoundland
Scandinavian Countries
Great Britain, etc.

OTHER NAME
Newfie

2

HEAD
Broad and massive. Stop not too pronounced. Short, rather squarish muzzle.

EYES
Small and wide set. Dark brown color.

EARS
Small, lying close to the head.

BODY
Massive. Strong neck. Chest well let down. Broad back. Strong, muscular loin.

LIMBS
Large, webbed feet.

TAIL
Thick at the root. Moderately long, reaching slightly past the hocks and carried down forming a slight curve.

COAT
Long, straight, coarse. Oily feel, water-resistant. Feathering on the legs. Soft, wooly undercoat.

COLOR
Acceptable colors: black (dull jet black), brown (chocolate or bronze), Landseer (British-American type, only black and white permissible).

SIZE
Dog: average of 71 cm (28 in).
Bitch: average of 66 cm (26 in).

WEIGHT
Dog: 64 to 69 kg (141 to 152 lb).
Bitch: 50 to 54.5 kg (110-120 lb).

Character, special skills and training
This gentle, friendly, extraordinarily loyal dog is even-tempered and affectionate. He loves children. While his appearance may be formidable, the Newfoundland is not a guard dog. By instinct, he is a rescue dog. Because of his willingness to dive into the water and swim for hours to save a drowning victim, he has been called the "St. Bernard of the sea." Training must be firm, but undertaken with patience because this gentle giant does not reach emotional maturity until two years of age.

Care and functions
The Newfoundland can adapt to life as a housedog provided he is not left alone too often. He needs room to romp. This breed does not tolerate heat well. Brushing twice per week is sufficient.
· Water rescue dog.
. Pet.

Tosa

This Japanese fighting dog was developed in the late nineteenth and early twentieth centuries. The breed was created by crossing the native Kochi, the Bull Terrier, the Bulldog, the Great Dane and the Saint Bernard, creating a truly imposing specimen.

Large. Robust conformation.
Imposing bearing. Energetic, powerful gait.

2A

MASTIFF TYPE MOLOSSIANS

2

COUNTRY OF ORIGIN
Japan

OTHER NAME
Tosa Inu

Giants Breeds
over 45 kg
(over 100 lb)

Character, special skills and training

This breed is remarkably patient, calm, courageous and bold. The Tosa forms a strong bond with his owners but is distrustful of strangers. He can be a formidable adversary if necessary. Firm training is required.

Care and functions

Brushing once per week is required. This breed needs space and exercise.
· Guard dog.
· Pet.

HEAD
Strong. Broad skull. Fairly abrupt stop. Straight nose bridge. Square muzzle. Solid jaws. Large nose.

EYES
Moderately small. Dark brown color.

EARS
Relatively small, thin, set on high, falling along the cheeks.

BODY
Powerful. Muscular neck with dewlap. Elevated withers. Deep, broad chest. Broad, muscular loin. Belly well tucked up. Straight back.

LIMBS
Solid legs. Slightly arched loin. Compact feet. Hard, dark nails.

TAIL
Set high. Strong at the root tapering toward the tip. Carried low reaching the hock joint.

COLOR
Solid red is preferred. All shades of fawn permissible. White and red markings are tolerated.

SIZE
Dog: at least 60.5 cm (24 in).
Bitch: at least 54.5 cm (22 in).

WEIGHT
Approx. 40 kg (88 lb).

Appenzeller

Originating in Appenzell canton in eastern Switzerland, the Appenzeller was first described in an early work as a "quite vocal, multi-colored, short-haired drover of medium size". The breed is thought to be descended from Tibetan Molosser dogs and Nordic breeds. The Appenzeller was established as a distinct breed in 1898. Max Siever, a great promoter of the Appenzeller, worked on the first standard for the breed. The Swiss Appenzeller club was created in 1906. The breed is rare outside of its native Switzerland.

Compact. Balanced proportions. Not massive. Gait: Long strides.

3

MOUNTAIN TYPE MOLOSSIANS

Medium Breeds between 10 and 25 kg (20-55 lb)

COUNTRY OF ORIGIN
Switzerland

ORIGINAL NAME
Appenzeller Sennenhund

OTHER NAME
Appenzell Mountain Dog

2

HEAD
Slightly wedge-shaped. Stop not pronounced. Rectangular nose bridge. Black or brown nose. Tight lips.

EYES
Small, almond. Dark brown to chestnut color.

EARS
Set on high, triangular, drop, lying against the head.

BODY
Robust, compact. Strong, dry neck. Broad chest is well let down. Prominent forechest. Belly slightly tucked up.

Muscular legs. Short croup.

LIMBS
Straight, solid back. Short, well-arched, compact feet.

TAIL
Set high, strong, moderately long, bushy. In action, carried curled over the croup, falling to the side or along the midline.

COAT
Short, thick, lying close to the skin. Thick undercoat.

COLOR
Black or tan background

with symmetrical tan or white markings. Tan markings above the eyes and on the cheeks, forechest and legs. White flare, white patch from chin to forechest. White markings on the feet and tip of the tail.

SIZE
Dog: 50 to 58 cm (20-23 in).
Bitch: 48 to 56 cm (19-22 in).

WEIGHT
22 to 25 kg (49-55 lb).

Caracter, special skills and training
This courageous, robust, self-confident dog is energetic and has a lively temperament. The Appenzeller fills many roles. This affectionate, gentle breed makes a good pet. Wary of strangers and possessing the defense instinct, he is also a good guard dog. The breed is also used as a draft dog and rescue dog.

Care and functions
The Appenzeller is not suited to city living. He needs a lot of exercise and room to run. Regular brushing is required.

· Herder (rounds up cattle).
· Draft dog (pulls milk carts).
· Utility dog: (rescue: avalanches, earthquakes, etc.).
· Guard dog.
· Pet.

Powerful. Supple. Balanced proportions.

3

MOUNTAIN TYPE MOLOSSIANS

2

COUNTRY OF ORIGIN
Switzerland

ORIGINAL NAME
Berner Sennenhund

Giants Breeds
over 45 kg
(over 100 lb)

Bernese Mountain Dog

This ancient breed was developed near Bern, primarily in Duerrbach and Burgdorf. The Bernese Mountain Dog is descended from the Roman molussus fighting dog brought with the Roman legions and later used to guard the flock. This breed began appearing in dog shows in 1902 and a standard was published in 1907. In 1949, Newfoundland blood was introduced. The Bernese Mountain Dog is now the most common of the Swiss mountain dogs. In 1990, the Bernese Mountain Dog was crossed with the Labrador, creating the still experimental

Character, special skills and training
This hardy, well-balanced, peaceable dog naturally has a sweet, happy temperament. He is loyal and affectionate with his owners, but is wary around strangers and will courageously defend his owners and their property if necessary, though he is not aggressive and does not bark often. This breed despises being left alone. Firm, but gentle, training must be undertaken with patience because the breed does not reach emotional maturity until eighteen months to two years of age.

Care and functions
The Bernese Mountain Dog does not like to be locked up in a house. He loves wide open spaces and exercise. Weekly brushing is sufficient.
· Herder (large animals).
· Guard dog, police dog, draft dog (light carts).
· Pet.

HEAD
Powerful. Slightly domed skull. Well-defined stop.

EYES
Almond shape. Dark brown color.

EARS
Set on high, triangular, drop when at rest.

BODY
Thickset. Broad chest is well let down. Belly not tucked up. Straight, solid back. Slightly rounded croup.

LIMBS
Short, rounded, compact feet. Strong legs with substantial bone.

TAIL
Bushy, carried low at rest.

COAT
Long, straight or slightly wavy.

COLOR
Tri-color. Black background with tan (rich rust) markings on the checks, above the eyes and on the legs and

chest. White markings on the head (flare), on the neck extending down the forechest, on the feet and tip of the tail.

SIZE
Dog: 64 to 70 cm (25-27.5 in).
Bitch: 58 to 66 cm (23-26 in).

WEIGHT
40 to 50 kg (88-110 lb).

Entelbucher

This small Swiss mountain dog is closely related to the Appenzeller. He is named after the region where he originated, Entlebuch in the canton of Lucerne. Bred to guard and drive cattle, the Entelbucher was very popular in the past. The breed almost disappeared, but then began a comeback in 1913.

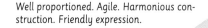

Well proportioned. Agile. Harmonious construction. Friendly expression.

3

MOUNTAIN TYPE MOLOSSIANS

COUNTRY OF ORIGIN
Switzerland

ORIGINAL NAME
Entlebucher Sennenhund

2

Medium Breeds between 10 and 25 kg (20-55 lb)

HEAD
Well proportioned. Flat forehead. Slight stop. Powerful jaws.

EYES
Fairly small. Brown color. Lively expression.

EARS
Set on high, not overly large, hanging flat against the head. Tip of ear well rounded.

BODY
Slightly longer than tall.

Short, compact neck. Broad, deep chest. Strong legs. Strong, straight back.

LIMBS
Strong, compact feet. Dewclaws not desireable.

TAIL
Docked at birth.

COAT
Short, thick, hard, shiny, lying close to the skin.

COLOR
Black with markings ranging from yellow to rust above

the eyes, on the cheeks and on all four legs. Symmetrical markings on the head (flare), neck, forechest and feet. Yellow to rust markings must always appear between the black and white.

SIZE
Dog: 40 to 50 cm (16-20 in).

WEIGHT
15 to 25 kg (33-55 lb).

Character, special skills and training
This robust, agile, stable dog is an excellent guard, both of cattle and its owner's property. The friendly Entelbucher also makes an excellent pet. The breed is used to transport milk and cheese. Naturally good tempered, the Entelbucher is easy to train.

Care and functions
This breed needs exercise and room to run. Regular brushing is required.
· Cattle drover.
· Guard dog.
· Pet.

Greater Swiss Mountain Dog

Robust. Sturdy skeletal structure. Extremely muscular. Agile. Long stride.

3

MOUNTAIN MOLOSSIANS

2

COUNTRY OF ORIGIN
Switzerland

ORIGINAL NAME
Grosser Schweizersennenhund

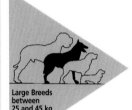

Large Breeds between 25 and 45 kg (55-100 lb)

The ancestors of the Greater Swiss Mountain Dog are the powerful tri-color dogs referred to as "butcher mastiffs." In the latter Middle Ages, this breed went to battle with Swiss soldiers. In 1908, two "Short-haired Bernese Mountain Dogs" were exhibited at a show. Dr. Albert Heim was present at the show and recognized them as survivors of the large butcher mastiffs that were on the verge of extinction. In 1909, the Swiss registry recognized the variety as a distinct breed. The Swiss Greater Swiss Mountain Dog club, created in 1912, implemented a breeding program to restore the breed. The standard for the Greater Swiss Mountain Dog was published for the first time by the FCI in 1939.

Character, special skills and training
This attentive, alert dog has remarkable endurance. He is easy to train and serves many purposes, such as guard dog protecting cattle, farms and homes, draft dog and rescue dog searching out victims buried in avalanches. As a pet, he is loyal and gentle and very fond of children.

Care and functions
The Greater Swiss Mountain Dog is not suitable as a house dog. He needs a lot of exercise and room to run. Regular brushing is required.
· Cattle drover.
· Draft dog.
· Guard dog.
· Rescue dog.
· Pet.

HEAD
Powerful without bulkiness. Broad, flat skull. Stop not pronounced. Powerful muzzle. Black lips.

EYES
Medium size, almond shape. Hazelnut or chestnut color.

EARS
Medium size, set on moderately high, triangular, hanging flat against the cheeks.

BODY
Powerful but not massive. Powerful, thick neck without dewlap. Broad, well let down chest. Broad forechest. Belly and flanks slightly tucked up. Long, broad croup. Straight, solid back.

LIMBS
Solid legs. Solid, compact feet with arched toes.

TAIL
Thick, hanging down and reaching the hocks at rest.

COAT
Medium length, dense. Thick undercoat.

COLOR
Black background with symmetrical rich rust and white markings. Rust markings between the black and white markings on the cheeks, above the eyes, inside the ears, on each side of the chest, on all four legs and under the tail. White blaze and muzzle; white markings on forechest, feet and tip of the tail.

SIZE
Dog: 65 to 72 cm (25.5-28 in).
Bitch: 60 to 68 cm (23.5-27 in).

WEIGHT
Dog: approx. 40 kg (88 lb).
Bitch: approx. 35 kg (77 lb).

Part 2

Dogs in Art

Fresco by Andrea Mantegna (1431-1506), Italy.
The couple's bedroom. Leaving for hunting.
Detail: Lower segment (after restoration).
Gal. E. Museo Di Palazzo Ducale, Mantoue.
Alinari-Giraudon Collection, Paris.

Dogs in Art and History

*Thèbes: Bibân el Molouk.
Vases, furniture, and various subjects painted
in the tombs of kings, Anubis, god of the dead,
bending over the mummy of the Pharaoh.
Selva Collection, Paris.*

Since the beginning of history, humans have created images of the animals around them. Cave art, archeology, sculpture and paintings illustrate the important role dogs have played in both daily life and imagination. Watchdog, hunting dog or companion, guardian of the dead or protector of the gates of hell, symbol of vigilance, loyalty and obedience, the dog was also cursed and associated with death and evil. He is often featured on coats of arms, coins and, more recently, postage stamps.

Dogs in Archeology

Dogs account for a large number of the animal representations that have been discovered by archeologists. These representations give evidence of the dog's status in society—from slave to god, depending on place and time. The oldest is a cave painting in Spain's Cueva Vieja from about 10,000 B.C. In it, a dog is apparently blocking a deer's path to safety—the hunt is on!

Deified Dogs

The best known example of the deified dog in Egypt is Anubis, the half-dog, half-jackal god found beginning in the 19th Dynasty (around 1200 B.C.). Because dogs were often seen lurking around cemeteries at night, Anubis was the god of the dead. He presided over funerals and burial rites, particularly embalming.

In Greek mythology, the dog was a creature forged by Hephaestus, the god of fire and blacksmith to the other gods. The dog's divine origin earned him a place of privilege among the animals.

Working Dogs and Warrior Dogs

Since the beginning of time, humans have relied on dogs as helpmates. Used as slaves in Asia Minor (the ideogram for "dog" is the same as that for "slave" in cuneiform writing from around 2000 B.C.!), dogs gradually gained a respected role in human work.

Nearly all early hunting scenes show dogs alongside humans. For example, paintings on the walls surrounding Çatal Hüyük, a Neolithic settlement in Asia Minor, depict humans using hounds to hunt big cats. Prior to the 18th Dynasty in Egypt, dogs helped humans hunt antelope and gazelle. By about 1500 B.C., dog breeding and breed specialization had produced greyhounds, which were faster than earlier dogs. In ancient Greece and Rome, just as in Egypt, dogs helped in the hunt and were often represented in art.

They also began serving as watchdogs, like Cerberus, known in Greek mythology for guarding the entrance to the underworld or Hades. In the Far East, toy dogs were the guardians of eunuchs (3470 B.C.). In ancient Rome (first century A.D.), dogs on leashes guarded homes (thus the inscription *cave canem*—beware of dog—on a mosaic from Pompei).

Dogs also aided soldiers at war. In the Far East around 1000 B.C., Mesopotamian dogs, especially hounds, were highly sought after for tracking down humans, such as escaped slaves. Sculptures of the mastiffs used in wars decorate a door of a Buddhist temple in Sanshi-Tope, India. Warrior dogs in ancient Rome had various specialties. Defense dogs protected the back lines, attack dogs were sent to the front lines and liaison dogs ensured communication between army posts. Liaison dogs were perhaps the worst off: They were forced to swallow messages and sacrificed upon arrival.

Mosaic, Tunisian Dog, 3rd century.
Cogis, Paris

Dogs in the Home

Although dogs seem to have held a less-than-desirable position in ancient times, evidence shows that they were sometimes treated with kindness and respect. In the New Dynasty in Egypt, dogs were so highly regarded that to mistreat or kill one was punishable by law. Ancient Greek artists depicted dogs as animals who had earned the privilege of human company. The sculptors of Assourbanipal in Mesopotamia evoke this privilege in Jeune satyre au repos [Young Satyr at Rest], a piece held by the Louvre Museum in Paris. But the first sign that dogs were truly a part of family life is an earthenware piece from Gaul depicting a couple embracing in a bed with a dog sleeping soundly at their feet. Surprisingly, this sculpture portraying an entirely modern notion of "love" for dogs dates to around 50 A.D.

Dogs in Paintings

Since the dawn of civilization, paintings of dogs have hinted that the dog is "man's best friend". The first cave paintings of dogs date as far back as prehistoric times, around 4500 B.C. Although dogs appear less frequently in cave paintings than game animals—the main inspiration for this art—they are nevertheless present as hunting dogs unlike any currently known breed. More recent paintings from ancient Egypt show breeds similar to those of today.

Roman Empire: Watchdogs

In the Roman Empire, the status of dogs in society was changing. In fact, dogs were fully accepted as domestic animals who also protected the home and were a precious resource for hunting. They were constant companions, loyal and completely devoted to their owners. The dogs of the Roman Empire were essentially regal yet ferocious mastiffs who defended their home from strangers.

Jean le Bon surrounded by the nobles.
Selva Collection, Paris.

Middle Ages: Primarily Hunting Dogs

From the fall of the Roman Empire to the Middle Ages, dogs are nearly absent in art, perhaps because painters of the time feared stray dogs as aggressive, dangerous beasts who hungrily devoured carcasses. In Islam, dogs were seen as cursed symbols of death and the force of evil.

The use of dogs in hunting helped change public opinion. Still, in the early Middle Ages, dogs were valued only for their aggressiveness. Dogs reappear in paintings of this time usually in packs, rather than alone. Some paintings show kings hunting with their dogs, sometimes in packs of a thousand.

Over time, the portrayal of dogs in art became closer and closer to reality. Still, it is not always easy to determine exactly which breed is depicted in a piece, since subjects may be the result of cross-breeding. Nevertheless, each type of dog had his own specialty. Scenthounds are shown hunting only mammalian game, tracking it by its scent. These breeds with a similar appearance but different coat colors include the French Chien de Saint-Hubert, Chien Blanc du Roy, Fauve de Bretagne and Gris de Saint-Louis. Their names show quite clearly to whom they belonged or where they came from. Pointers are shown with falcons, hunting large game. These dogs were used to kill prey before the invention of rifles.

Renaissance: Dogs Are Domesticated

Companion dogs begin to appear in paintings in the late Middle Ages. Renaissance ladies are shown with small dogs on their lap or at their feet. These greyhounds and other small breeds seem to enchant their mistresses, who show them a great deal of affection. Renaissance artists used dogs as subjects much more frequently than their predecessors. All sorts of breeds appear in sixteenth-century paintings, from the small companion dogs of ladies and damsels to dignified greyhounds to the larger dogs who accompanied lords.

In Renaissance times, dogs became closer to humans. Dogs are shown lying under the table at banquets, savoring the tidbits tossed by guests. They finally became full-fledged companion animals. Artists from many different countries used dogs as subjects: In Venice, for example, artists painted toy dogs reclining on cushions, being doted on by their mistresses during a gondola ride. Yet dogs were still indispensable hunting companions. Painters began to make a clearer distinction between the different kinds of hunting dogs (scenthounds, pointers, etc.).

Seventeenth Century to Today: Breeds Diversify

Starting in the seventeenth century, the number of breeds began to grow, once again because of hunting, at least at first. As hunting techniques and game diversified, so did hunting dog breeds.

Pol Limobourg
(15th century).
"Très riches heures
du Duc de Berry".
Calendar, January:
The Duke of Berry dining
(with zodiac).
Chantilly, Musée Condé,
France.
Giraudon Collection,
Paris.

Detail: Two dwarf dogs
on the table.

Nevertheless, by the late seventeenth century, the focus had switched to smaller dogs like the King Charles, a favorite of royalty.

Little by little, dogs began to appear in paintings alone or at least as the focal point. Some artists began to specialize in animal subjects, including François Desportes (1661-1743, the official painter of King Louis XIV), Paul de Vos (1596-1678), and Jean-Baptiste Oudry (1686-1755).

Dogs were depicted with striking realism, both in terms of anatomy and expression. The postures and expressions characteristic to each breed were copied directly from reality. In some pieces, it seems as though the artist included a dog only to immortalize him!

More recently, in the nineteenth and twentieth centuries, artists—and contemporary society as a whole—began to show a growing interest in dogs. In paintings, the packs of large hunting dogs that once served royalty are replaced almost entirely by domestic breeds and, in some cases, by sheepdogs and watchdogs. The painters of this period give an almost sentimental image of these dogs.

Soon the style became abstract. Dogs began to be portrayed as symbols, making it impossible to determine which breed had inspired a particular piece. Still today, dogs continue to be a source of endless admiration and inspiration, appreciated by all.

Saint-Hubert.
Miniature by Jean Bourdichon, copy of
"Heures d'Anne de Bretagne", 15th century.
Selva Collection, Paris.

Dogs in Sculpture

As humans evolved, they invented art to express their feelings about the world around them. They began by drawing what they saw on cave walls, using pigments on engravings in stone. Later, they discovered pottery and sculpture. Animals naturally became artistic subjects. They also became religious symbols, either feared or respected.

Prehistoric Times: Figurative Art

The first sculptures of dogs are earthenware objects in a very simple style. This purely figurative art is based primarily on the form of the animal seen as a companion in hunting, herding, and everyday life. Some pieces show evidence of claw and tooth marks. These early sculptures depict animals with oversized bellies and short legs.

Precolumbian art is also very simple. Dogs are depicted not realistically, but with the qualities of the god with whom they were associated. Precolumbian sculpture became an expression of the spiritual and mystical world, a trend that reached its peak in ancient times.

Egypt: Dogs as Stylized Symbols

Ancient Egyptians worshiped all sorts of animals, including the dog, considered the earthly incarnation of the god Anubis and sometimes Thot. In their very elaborate and stylized sculptures, Egyptian artists sought to evoke one of the dog's characteristics while retaining the animal's form, generally based on that of the desert greyhound. The limestone dog at the Louvre Museum in Paris—depicting a sheepdog wearing a collar—is a perfect example of this. Egyptian bas-reliefs often show dog racing or hunting scenes including dogs.

Ancient Egyptians also used dogs to decorate tombs and cemeteries. The sarcophagus of Madja from the 18th Dynasty clearly shows a dog with a fox's tail in a reclining position. Two statues of dogs stand guard at the entrance to all Egyptian temples as a symbol of the sovereign's watchfulness over his people.

Asia: Lion-Dogs

The dog occupies a very unique position in Asia, where he has been considered either a god or a delicacy, earning either respect or scorn. At the entrance to most Chinese temples and palaces stand two "lion-dogs" with clear similarities to the mastiff breeds native to the region. Even in everyday sculpted objects, dogs are depicted with exaggerated features and embellished with ornaments of various sizes.

Assyria: Fine Animal Sculpture

The animal art of Assyria is abundant and of very high quality. In this civilization, art was inspired by religion and the worship of royalty. Dogs are generally depicted alone in incredible detail, in hunting scenes, or alongside their master.

Ancient Greece and Rome: Geometric Style

Closer to modern times, the art of ancient Greece and Rome is primarily geometric in style, with clean lines. Like human sculpture, animal sculpture became more refined, to the point of near perfect realism. Very few statues of dogs have been found from this period. This is not surprising, since in these cultures dogs were no longer seen as gods.

Middle Ages: Imaginative Representations

In the Middle Ages, art became focused on the imagination and on symbolic representation. Next to religion, good and evil were the main sources of inspiration. Dogs played a limited, mainly decorative, role in art.

In Renaissance times, artists focused on anatomical and morphological studies in an effort to find the ideal proportions. Horses were the main subjects; dogs apparently had limited appeal.

Seventeenth Century to Today: Popular Subjects

Following the Renaissance, the dog was a subject more for experimental sculpture than for true art. But beginning in the nineteenth century, true animal artists started to use dogs as primary subjects. For example, Antoine Louis Barye (1796-1875) created anatomically accurate bronze sculptures based on dissections. Hunting breeds were his favorite.

Diana the Huntress. Ceramic dish. "L'œuvre de Bernard Palissy" by C. Delange and C. Borneman, Paris, 1869.

129

The Dog: Myths and Symbols

Humans have always used objects and creatures from daily life to represent the invisible and the mystical. For nearly fifteen thousand years, dogs have lived alongside humans. Therefore, it is only natural that dogs are an important element in mythical and symbolic art. The dog's appearance and especially his behavior have been used to symbolize situations, special powers, and even divinities.

Guardian of the Gates of Hell

Dogs watch over the home, howl at the moon, and often hunt at night. For these reasons, many cultures have associated dogs with death. Both Cerberus, the three-headed black dog of Greek mythology, and Garm, the guardian of Niefheim in Germanic civilization, protected the gates of hell, maintaining the separation between the living and the dead.

Guide to the Spirits of the Dead

Dogs were seen as everyday companions in life as in death. They symbolized the force that guided spirits in their journey to the kingdom of the dead. The best known dog-guide is Anubis, an ancient Egyptian god with the head of a jackal. His role was to oversee the embalming of the dead before leading them to the place where spirits were judged. At the judgment, Anubis weighed the heart of the dead against the feather of truth.

Anubis' counterpart in ancient Mexican civilization is the god Xolotl, a lion-colored dog who accompanied the sun god in his journey to the underworld. Traditionally, a dog of the Xoloitzcuintli breed, with a yellow coat like the sun, was sacrificed at funerals. The dog of the deceased person might also be sacrificed, to ensure that his owner would be protected until arriving at the gates of death. In Guatemala, dog figurines were traditionally placed at the four corners of the tomb, a practice still observed today.

In Eastern cultures, the dead and dying were entrusted to dogs who might guide them to heaven, the seat of the divine.

Messenger between the Living and the Afterworld

Dogs have also been seen as a link between the world of the living and the afterworld. Two variations on this theme can be found: Some Sudanese cultures and the Bantus of the former Zaire believed that dogs delivered messages to a sorcerer in a trance. Other Sudanese tribes and the Iroquois of North America believed that dogs themselves carried messages to the dead after being sacrificed.

From these examples, it is easy to understand how the dog's association with death, combined with his nocturnal hunting habits, might have fueled rumors of sorcery and evil spells with regard to dogs.

Dual Symbol

Islam adopted this negative view of dogs, considering them impure creatures, like pigs. Dogs were seen as carcass eaters who frightened the angels and heralded death with their barking. People were to avoid dogs, and anyone who killed one became as impure as the dog himself. However, Muslims believed they could protect themselves from evil spells by eating the flesh of a puppy, and they appreciated a dog's loyalty to his owner. Paradoxically, Muslims revered the greyhound as a noble animal and a symbol of goodness and luck.

Dogs can also be found as dual symbols in the cultures of the Far East. In China, the dog was seen either as the destroyer—the huge, hairy beast T'ien K'uan—or the loyal companion who escorted immortals to heaven. The philosopher Lao Tzu portrays the dog as an ephemeral creature, describing the ancient Chinese custom of burning straw effigies of dogs to ward off evil spells. On the contrary, in Japanese culture the dog was a good animal who protected children and mothers. In Tibet, dogs were symbols of sexuality and fertility, providing the spark of life. This leads to another aspect in the symbolism of dogs, that of fire.

Dogs on Fire

Strangely, in most cases the dog did not symbolize fire itself but instead was seen as the creature who transmitted fire to humans. The dog was therefore is the equivalent of Prometheus in certain African and Native American tribes. On the South Sea Islands, the dog was the master of fire, growling and sleeping beside the flames. For the Aztecs he was fire itself, while for the Mayas he was simply the guardian of the sun at night.

Alternately, dogs could symbolize war and victory, as for the Celts. In Celtic culture, the dog was praised, and being compared to a dog was an honor.

Ambiguous Symbol

Over time, the dog became an important symbol. Yet the symbolism of dogs throughout history shows the apparent ambiguity with which different cultures regarded them. Protector and watchdog for some, evildoer and demon for others, the symbolism of dogs changed constantly before being completely forgotten by modern civilization.

Dogs do still appear in current expressions but, paradoxically, nearly always with negative connotations. Used as an attribute, "dog" yields "to have a dog's life", "to be dog-tired", and "to have a dog's chance". Used in the comparative sense, "dog" expresses scorn, degradation, and dissention, as in the phrases "to treat someone like a dog", "to work like a dog", "to be as ugly as a dog", "to be as sick as a dog", and "to fight like cats and dogs". Other negative expressions include "going to the dogs" and "it's a dog-eat-dog world". Expressions in which "dog" is used in a positive sense are rare: "Dog is man's best friend".

Who knows? Given the growing importance of dogs in our lives, perhaps future generations will create a more respectable cultural image of our four-legged friend.

Other Representations of Dogs in Art

Images of dogs have been used for various purposes on coats of arms, coins, and, more recently, postage stamps.

Dogs in Heraldry

Coats of arms were used beginning in the eleventh century, during the Crusades. Because lords had trouble recognizing one another in their heavy armor, they decided to wear a personalized sign that all could identify. The coat of arms was born. Nobility in France and abroad, especially in England, used highly imaginative designs to express the qualities they wished to represent. At first, imaginary animals were used most often. Gradually, they were replaced by real animals.

THE FRENCH GENDARMERIE'S COAT OF ARMS

Each different section of the French Army has a coat of arms. The School of Non-commissioned Officers of the Gendarmerie (Police Force) Training Center for Dog Handlers in Gramat is no exception. Its insignia was created by heraldry expert Robert Louis in 1948 and approved December 10, 1948.

The coat of arms is combined with the gendarmerie's characteristic insignia: a fifteenth-century plumed helmet in a three-quarters view atop a shield with a sword and a civic crown. On the shield below the helmet's throat-piece is the gendarmerie's grenade ornament. The plumed helmet is specific to this army corps. It evokes the origins of the gendarmerie, established in the fifteenth century by the High Provost Marshal as the Compagnie de la Connétablie et de la Maréchalerie [Company of the Constabulary and of the Field Marshal]. The shield features an unsheathed sword pointing straight upward as a symbol of justice over force. The circular civic crown of oak branches was bestowed upon soldiers in Rome who had risked their life to save others. The silver field is specific to specialized training centers. The entire grouping represents the mission of protecting citizens and helping those in danger. It also represents the gendarmerie's military origins and its military and civilian activities. The coat of arms itself is specific to the training center in Gramat. In the language of heraldry, the field consists of azure and sable sections with an argent grenade ornament charger. Blue and black are the gendarmerie's traditional colors, and the grenade ornament is its traditional badge. In the center of the grenade ornament is a dog standing in front of red flames, signifying that dogs fear nothing, even fire.

Coats of Arms - Charrière, "Armorial Général de l'Empire français" by H. Simon, 1812. Selva Collection, Paris.

Images of dogs were used from the very beginning. They symbolized hunting, an exclusive privilege of the nobility. Beginning in the ninth century, specific breeds of hunting and fighting dogs appeared. By the twelfth century, hounds and mastiffs adorned the coats of arms of English, Scottish, and Irish lords. Since that time, coats of arms have also been adopted as emblems of large institutions, such as the French Army.

On coats of arms, dogs symbolize the protective instinct, as well as vigilance, loyalty, obedience, and gratitude. Dogs are depicted in various postures: on the hind legs (with the back facing the edge of the insignia), in profile, passant (in heraldry, facing and walking toward the viewer's right with one foreleg raised), running, sitting, couchant (lying down with the head raised), and rampant (rearing on the left hind leg with the forelegs elevated). The colors and metals used—black, red (gules, in heraldry), green (vert), blue (azure), gold (or), and silver (argent)—form a code: a silver dog on a black field signifies a loyal, steadfast knight; a gold dog on a red field signifies a knight willing to die for his lord; and a black dog on a gold field signifies a knight in mourning for his lord. Dogs might also be used as supporters, the figures appearing on either side of a coat of arms.

Dogs on Coins

Coins from all eras feature dogs either as the dominant subject of a side, as an element in a more complex scene, or as a purely decorative symbol. Dogs are found more frequently on ancient coins than on modern ones.

The first known coins with images of dogs are in silver or bronze. On these coins from 480-440 B.C., dogs are the symbol of Segesta. The mythical origin of this city is attributed to Acestes, son of the nymph Segesta and the river god Crimisus, who took the form of a dog at their wedding. A dog appears on the reverse side of various coins featuring Segesta's head on the obverse side. In the same period, heavy bronze coins were used in certain Italic regions. In the Latium-Campania series, a dog is shown running toward the left; in the Tuder-Umbrian series (the origin of the lira) a dog is shown lying down.

After dogs were featured on several small bronze coins of the Rome-Campania series minted around 210 B.C., they appeared on the Roman Republic's silver denarius. This coin, minted extensively in Rome for economic and commercial reasons, is one of the most important, for it uses a variety of subjects to illustrate many aspects of the social, economic, historic, and religious life of the period.

Dogs are depicted on many coins from feudal times, mainly pieces of lesser value. A dog reclining with his head to the left appears on the reverse side of some coins from Tuscany, a dog tied to a tree appears on the lira from Milan under Philippe II of Spain (1556-1598), and a dog is shown as a winged figure on some smaller coins from Verona (1375-1381). The Gonzaga family showed the greatest interest in dogs, depicting the animal crawling, lying down, and climbing. Their coins are characterized by an inscription surrounding the central dog figure and reading *"Infensus feris tantum"* ("Enemy of none but the big cats"). This inscription echoes nicely the highest praise of dogs as "man's best friend".

EXAMPLES OF ROMAN COINS:

- In 82 B.C., Magistrate Caius Manilius Limetanus evokes the touching scene in which the elderly Argos recognizes his master Ulysses.
- In 69 B.C., a dog is shown running between the legs of the deer pulling Diana's chariot.
- In 64 B.C., a sprinting greyhound covers the entire reverse side of a denarius from the period of Caius Postumus.
- In 60 B.C., a hunting scene is depicted in which a dog attacks an injured wild boar.
- In 45 B.C. on a silver sesterce, Titus Crisius shows a dog running toward the right, while on a denarius from the period of Augustus, a dog appears at the feet of the goddess Diana carrying her bow and arrows.

Dogs on Stamps

Dogs are an integral part of a country's art and daily life. It is therefore only normal to find dogs on postage stamps, to the thrill of many collectors. Whether as the main figure or as a simple detail that only an expert collector would spot, dogs are one of the most coveted themes in stamp collecting (including individual stamps, books of stamps, and postal logos and slogans). In fact, there are so many dog stamps that philatelic organizations recommend that collectors limit themselves to a subgroup (a breed or specialty) to keep things under control.

Dogs first appeared on stamps from their country of origin. In 1887, for example, the first "philatelic dog", a magnificent Newfoundland, was featured on a stamp from the island by that name. The Belgian

Noblemen strolling in "Très riches heures du duc de Berry" French stamp, 1965. Selva Collection, Paris.

Sheepdog appeared on Belgian stamps, and sled dogs were featured on stamps from Scandinavian countries. Since dogs seemed to "sell" stamps, they began to appear on stamps from many countries, regardless of the origins of a particular breed. For example, an English Springer Spaniel can be found on a Nicaraguan stamp. The postal service may also use dogs for purely promotional purposes, as in France's postal logo reading, "La voix de son maître" ("His Master's Voice") for Pathé-Marconi.

Dogs may appear on stamps with cultural subject matter, as when a painting with a dog is used on a stamp or when a dog is associated with a book or comic strip.

Dogs are also featured on stamps commemorating important events. For example, the former Soviet Union published numerous stamps with Laika, the first canine cosmonaut. Sometimes, community education is the focus, as in the Parisian postal slogan, *"Apprenez-leur le caniveau"* ("Curb your dog").

True philatelic fanatics are also interested in the history of dogs in the postal service. They know, for example, that in the 1940s mail in Alaska was carried from town to town by sled dog teams; there is a post office on the Île aux Chiens (Island of Dogs), a neighbor of Saint Pierre and Miquelon in the North Atlantic Ocean; and during World War I, military kennels in France received a special "postage paid" stamp.

Dogs in Literature and the Media

Since the beginning of civilization, dogs have lived alongside humans. It's only natural, then, that these animals appear in literature throughout the centuries. In fiction, fables and fantasy, dogs generally play the same roles they occupy in real life. More recently, dog heroes from the comics have been brought to movies and television. Dogs have also appeared in the press and in advertisements that take advantage of the dog's considerable influence on people.

White Fang; Ill. André Toutain - 1926. Jonas/Kharbine - Tapabor Collection, Paris.

Robinson Crusoe. Jonas/Kharbine. Tapabor Collection, Paris.

Dogs in Literature

The dog's main role in literature mirrors the dog's role in everyday life—that of guardian angel and loyal companion.

Friend and Guardian

In Homer's classic *Odyssey*, Ulysses' dog Argos has an important role. Argos is the only character who recognizes Ulysses after his perilous voyage. Dogs in children's literature generally act as protectors and are often the main character. This is the case in *Belle et Sébastien* (Belle and Sebastian), a story by French author Cécile Aubry about the alpine adventures of a Pyrenean Mountain Dog and his young owner. The same is true of Eric Knight's *Lassie*, the story of a faithful Collie and her young owner, Joe. Both books have the same general theme: A child in trouble is saved by a big, loyal dog. The dog breeds featured in these stories have become so popular that in France, for example, many people call Collies "Lassies".

In other books, dogs appear in supporting roles, rather than as main characters. In the writings of Jules Verne (1828-1905), including *Journey to the Center of the Earth*, *A Two Years' Vacation* and *Mysterious Island*, a little dog accompanies the characters in their travels and helps them out of difficult situations using his sense of smell.

Still other stories feature dogs in a purely symbolic or even exaggerated role, sometimes helping reveal a situation or emotion. Although these depictions of dogs are brief, they are far from insignificant. In *Of Mice and Men*, John Steinbeck illustrates human selfishness, injustice and loneliness through his description of the slow death of an old dog, the hapless companion of a poor day laborer who cannot bear the loss of his friend.

Dogs and Wolves

Wolves, wild cousins to dogs, also appear frequently in literature. While dogs represent loyalty and respectfully serve their master, wolves represent freedom, the wilderness and the refusal of all constraint, even at the risk of death. As in Jean de la Fontaine's fable *The Wolf and the Dog*, wolves would rather live free than be confined.

The opposition between dogs and wolves illustrates the innate human conflict between being a "good" slave and resisting slavery at the risk of death. This is a favorite theme of Jack London, a fervent humanist who lived during the 1891 Gold Rush in Alaska. While London defends animals against man's brutality, he does not give a definite answer to the question of which path to choose: that of White Fang, a wolf-dog who chooses to live among humans, or that of Buck in *Call of the Wild*, a pet dog who goes to live among wolves. Perhaps this means that we each are a bit dog and a bit wolf, depending on the circumstances.

Portrait of Colette and her dog Toby.
"Vu", July 3, 1929.
Selva Collection, Paris.

Wild Beast

Anubis was an Egyptian god, but Cerberus guarded the underworld in Roman mythology. This dark side of the dog has inspired many writers. Poets and novelists describe the prowling beast, a frantic, demonic creature who devours dead bodies or small children. Sir Arthur Conan Doyle even uses a dog in the title of one of Sherlock Holmes' best known adventures, *The Hound of the Baskervilles*, in which a huge dog devours the inhabitants of a dreary Scottish moor.

In the poem *"Carrion"* from the collection *Flowers of Evil*, Baudelaire also evokes the dog's dark side:

> Around the rocks a restless bitch was eyeing
> Us with a look of one forsaken,
> As if from the living skeleton she were spying
> The flesh that from it had been taken.

(Baudelaire, Prose and Poetry. Translated by Arthur Symons. Albert & Charles Boni, New York, 1926.)

Within these lines is a hidden metaphor: The "restless bitch" is actually man, the dog's thinking alter ego.

What the Future Holds?

The fate of man and dog seems forever closely linked and science fiction writers often evoke this connection. For example, in his novel Pet Cemetery, Stephen King uses the description of a dog who returns from the dead to foreshadow the fate of the dog's owner.

Science fiction author Frank Herbert devotes an entire short story to dogs. In it, an epidemic decimates the canine population, causing mass hysteria and disaster for humans and dogs. In this dark depiction of the future, man and dog share the same terrible fate.

Whether as friend or foe, our canine companion continues to appear in literature as an innocent reflection of human shame, misery and loneliness so deep that even in books we need the company of our four-legged friend.

THE DOG, THE ROOSTER AND THE FOX

A dog and a rooster who were friends were walking along together. At nightfall, the rooster climbed into a tree to sleep and the dog lay down at the base of the tree, which was hollow. At daybreak, the rooster crowed, as was his habit. Upon hearing him, a fox ran to the base of the tree and asked the rooster to climb down, so that he might kiss the animal who had such a lovely voice. The rooster told the fox to wake the gatekeeper sleeping at the base of the tree and he would climb down after the gatekeeper had answered. But when the fox went to find the gatekeeper, the dog leapt forth and tore him to shreds. The moral of the story is that when enemies attack, wise people put them off by leading them to someone stronger.

Aesop, Fables. Translated from Greek by Émile Chambry, Histoire des chiens (History of Dogs), Sortilèges, Paris.

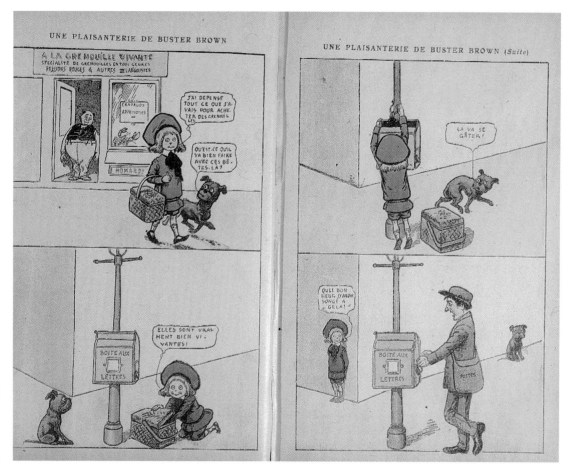

Comic strip by Richard Outcault, appeared in the New York Times in 1903 - "My Newspaper", October 26, 1907. Jonas/Kharbine - Tapabor Collection, Paris

Dogs in Comics and Cartoons

Dogs have always appeared in the favorite comic strips and cartoons of children (and adults!). The very first comic strip, published in a New York daily in the early twentieth century, takes place at a dog show. This was the beginning of fame for dogs, who later became the heroes of cartoons. Since then, they have appeared in roles of growing importance, sometimes as the main character of the story.

Everyday Hero

Some comic strip dogs remain true dogs, used essentially to help develop the main character. The first was Pluto, who later appeared in cartoons. Apart from being Mickey's companion, Pluto is the source of both disasters and happy endings. A similar character to Pluto is the Fox Terrier Milou, the faithful companion of Tintin. Milou expresses himself not through speech, but by barking at his master and through thought bubbles when he wants to communicate with the reader. He is so famous in France that his adventures have been made into cartoons and even animated films. Other dogs play a similar role in French comic strips: Rantanplan, a supporting character to cowboy Lucky Luke, is not too smart and follows his master without speaking to him. Although Rantanplan does sometimes have thoughts, the other characters are not aware of them. In this aspect, Rantanplan is similar to Jolly Jumper, the thinking horse. Another French comic strip dog, Idefix, is a tiny mutt who is inseparable from his master, the imposing Obelix. This little dog with a big heart is very loveable because he never causes trouble. The canine characters mentioned above have an important role among humans, yet retain their doglike qualities.

Almost Human

In other cases, dogs are depicted as more or less human. This is usually true when the dog is the main character of the story. Some comic strip dogs, like Charlie Brown's Snoopy, have philosophical thoughts, just like humans. But Snoopy is still a dog: He sleeps in—or on—his doghouse, eats dog food and lives like other dogs. The wise Cubitus walks on his hind legs and speaks, like the other characters in the French comic strip. He also teaches lessons. With all his good sense, Cubitus could be human, except that he looks like an Old English Sheepdog.

In the French comic *Boule et Bill* [Boule and Bill], Bill the Cocker Spaniel—probably the first purebred comic strip canine—acts like a human around other dogs but like a playful puppy at home. Still, on walks he flirts with attractive female dogs and fights off rivals, mimicking his owners and other humans.

Some comic strip dogs are hardly dogs at all. For example, the perpetually sad-faced Gai Luron, created by Gotlib, gets caught up in the events of the world around him.

Animated Films

Some comic strip dogs have become so popular that their adventures have been made into animated films. One such character is Dingo, a dog who stands on two legs like a human but has a dog's head with long, droopy ears. He has often appeared as a "spokesdog" for educational purposes, including car safety campaigns targeting young children. Sad-looking Droopy, the dog in Tex Avery's cartoons, repeatedly announces his presence with the famous line, *"You know what? I'm happy!"* He is the cartoon equivalent of Gai Luron, a French comic strip dog.

Album cover, "Pluto" by Walt Disney, Albums Roses Collection, Hachette. Selva Collection, Paris.

Other cartoon dogs live with humans, just like real pets or watchdogs. This is true of Lady and the Tramp, who live with their owners but share a romantic dinner and lead their own lives among other dogs. When Lady's owners bring home a new baby, they ignore her and humiliate her by forcing her to wear a muzzle. This serves as a brutal reminder that she is "only" a dog.

Perdita and Pongo, the leading dogs in *101 Dalmatians*, perhaps the most famous cartoon canines, are also companion animals to humans. But they become romantically involved with each other, just like their owners.

Nana the Saint Bernard protects the children in *Peter Pan* while leading a life like that of other dogs.

Sometimes, the dogs in animated features are almost caricatures in their appearance and actions. They may look generally like dogs, but one of their physical characteristics is exaggerated. Rarely the main character, they are more likely to serve as a watchdog for their owner or for another animal. Cartoons featuring a cat and mouse often include a big, burly, unfriendly dog who sits around licking his chops. In *Tom and Jerry*, for example, a bulldog defends Jerry by getting Tom into trouble. Dogs appear frequently in Disney cartoons. Disney's *Beagle Boys* are members of an international crime ring. All have the same physical features, are clumsy and not too smart and are constantly planning evil schemes to steal money.

By giving dogs many human qualities, both good and bad, the creators of comic strips and cartoons seem to use canine characters to represent our changing society.

Dogs in Movies

Dogs have appeared in movies almost since the birth of cinema. In the early twentieth century, dogs played small parts in several silent films. One of the most memorable was Charlie Chaplin's canine companion in misery in *The Kid* in 1921. Not until *Hollywood's Rin Tin Tin*, released in 1922, did a dog play the starring role in a movie.

Rin Tin Tin and Lassie

What could be more natural than acting for a dog whose past was far from the peaceful existence of a farm dog? Rin Tin Tin served as a messenger to the Germans during World War I and was found by an American aviator who brought him back to the United States after the war. When the American veteran discovered how quickly his canine companion could learn, he decided to make him a show dog. From 1922 to 1932, Rin Tin Tin appeared in twenty-two films, always in the role of an honorable and fearless hero who would do anything to defend the innocent. His popularity spread all over the world, making him a true movie star. He had his own dressing room, "signed" his own contracts and chose his own co-stars! When he died, his character was played by his pups and grandpups; his fourth-generation descendants brought Rin Tin Tin to television.

Another dog superstar was the famous Lassie. Purchased for five dollars by an animal trainer, this Collie launched her career in 1943 in *Lassie Come Home*. While Rin Tin Tin tore after the bad guys and leapt across chasms, Lassie exemplified the loyalty and unconditional love of a dog for her master, preferably a child. Like Rin Tin Tin, Lassie enjoyed worldwide popularity. Her trainer and agent demanded astronomical salaries for her—fifty thousand dollars a year and four thousand dollars per commercial appearance—as well as a dressing room, a private secretary and even paid holidays! Through the third generation, Lassie's descendants made films; then her legacy was brought to television.
The stories of Rin Tin Tin and Lassie are unique in the history of cinema. Both dogs had talented trainers who helped them gain recognition as true actors and who had the business sense to manage their career and earnings.

Friend and Guardian

Following these successes, the presence of dogs in cinema declined. Before the 1980s, a few books by Jack London were made into movies, but none featured dogs as developed characters. Instead, dogs usually served as sidekicks for their co-stars, as in *Call of the Wild* with Charlton Heston.

Not until the 1970s did Walt Disney Studios make another push for canine films. They needed to find a nice dog who was, of course, extremely loyal and had a friendly face with star quality—in short, a kid's best friend. Into the studios trotted Benji, a little Pyrenean Shepherd mix. For the first time, casting directors chose not a big, proud Sheepdog but a spunky ball of fur. Disney made five movies about Benji's wacky adventures before launching a televised series. With an annual salary of a million and a half dollars by 1974, Benji was certainly expensive to produce! Several movies pairing the police with dogs were also released but had little success. Since 1990, the new dog hero for kids is a big, fat Saint Bernard named Beethoven, whose movies have been successful worldwide. In addition, a new screen adaptation of Jack London's White Fang was produced recently by Disney.

Dogs Who Think and Talk

The current trend in movies involves dogs who think and talk, like human actors. For example, *Charly au pays des kangourous* [Charlie in the Land of the Kangaroos] follows the adventures of a Labrador puppy in Australia and Disney's *Incredible Journey* (1994) features two dogs and a cat who comb the United States in search of their young master.

Specialized Training Schools

Today's dog actors are graduates of professional training schools where they learn everything from barking on command to playing dead to whining—a true theater arts program! The result of all this effort does pay off for the trainer; only one of his students needs to be picked for him to make a fortune.

For some twenty years, film production has been monitored by animal protection organizations to ensure the well-being of canine actors.

As long as movies with dogs are successful, Hollywood will continue to make them. Of course, not all aspects of this success have been positive. Certain movies that feature a specific breed have triggered a considerable demand for the breed and the subsequent overbreeding of puppies of lower and lower quality. Hopefully, someday movies will show dogs for what they really are, not as mere caricatures of the almost human "nice doggy".

Dogs on Television

Dogs have had a television presence since the early days of this medium. First as extras and later as true characters, dogs quickly gained a permanent place on television.

In silent films, dogs often appeared as loyal, indispensable companions but also as a comic element (with Charlie Chaplin, for example). This was the beginning of dogs in acting. Dogs were featured more and more in televised series, playing roles of greater and greater significance.

Leading Dog

Soon, dogs were playing leading roles. Breeds were not chosen haphazardly. Larger breeds were favored for adventure and police shows and smaller breeds for comedies. Nevertheless, the focal point for all breeds on television has remained the dog's loyalty in his work and to his owner. There are many examples of this, from Belle, the Pyrenean Mountain Dog who protects Sebastian, to Lassie, the wandering Collie who is always ready to help those in need, to Rin Tin Tin, the German Shepherd police dog, to White Fang. Of course, one cannot forget Pollux, the most "British" of them all, who has touched the lives of so many children and adults. These examples show that the role of dogs on television (and in everyday life) is far from trivial.

Dog and Master

More and more, shows focus on the relationship between dog and master and prove the theory that dogs resemble their masters and vice versa. For example, in the French series *La loi est la loi* [The Law's the Law], the similarities between Max, a British Bulldog and the prosecutor are not mere coincidence. The same is true of Columbo's dog. More recently, dogs have appeared in numerous sitcoms. In some series, not only does a dog play a leading role, but he is also able to communicate with humans.

Dog Care Shows

More and more shows focusing on dog care have been produced. These shows discuss the dog's habits, the characteristics of each breed and the details of dog grooming, raising and training puppies and canine nutrition—all the practical tips an owner needs to live happily with his four-legged friend. Often, these shows end by showing a listing of dogs of all ages and breeds available for adoption.

Currently, the purpose of dog care shows seems to be to shed light on a particular dog or his owner by discussing the main characteristic of a breed. This appears to be successful, since trends in dog breeds closely follow television. Of course, some breeds, such as German Shepherds and Labradors, are unavoidable. More and more, these shows emphasize communication between dog and owner. Dogs try to understand their owner and communicate through specific behaviors. When we listen to a dog's habits and behaviors, we give him the ability to "talk" to us.

Dogs in Toys

Dogs are so important in our society that they have even inspired toys which provide children with a reliable friend. There are all kinds of toys involving dogs, from stuffed animals to educational materials.

Dog pull-toys for children.
Kharbine - Tapabor
Collection, Paris

Children's toys have been around much longer than movies, television and comic strips. Toys contribute to a child's emotional and creative development. The first toys based on images of dogs were made with clay, dough, or wood. At first, they were mounted on slabs of wood with wheels for children to pull. Later, they were jointed—with a mouth that opened, a tail that wagged—to make them more realistic.

Next to the bear, the dog is one of the only animals whose appeal in toys has lasted for centuries. Still today, dogs have a privileged place in children's playtime activities. Dogs are used to decorate the rooms of little and big kids, where they take the form of armchairs, clothes racks, lamps and all sorts of stuffed animals. For infants, a soft, cuddly stuffed animal friend is trustworthy, protective and, most importantly, just the right size. As in movies and television, breed is important in toys. Most often, stuffed animals are based on a character from the latest animated feature (like 101 Dalmatians), but the irresistible German Shepherd and Saint Bernard also have their place.

In the interest of early childhood education, many wood, fabric and plastic toys are created each year to enhance the development of children three months to two years old. The results include discovery mats and toys that make the noise of a dog barking. In these toys, the dog plays an instrumental role in teaching and raising the young.

Children's toys involving dogs may be so popular because real dogs require time, space and a great deal of responsibility. Wooden and stuffed dog toys give children a playmate, a friend who's just the right size and a gentle teacher who, most importantly, requires no parental attention!

Dogs in Advertising

Over some fifty years, advertising has become a vital element in our consumer society. It is no longer used simply to promote products, but also to spark trends. Advertisers began using images of dogs very early on, in an effort to please the consumer. In fact, the role of the dog in advertising has grown significantly in the past few decades. What is it about dogs that make them so popular with advertisers?

Dogs and Brand Names

Dogs were first used as selling points in the early 1900s. Perhaps one of the best known examples is Nipper, the dog shown listening intently to a Pathé-Marconi gramophone with the slogan "His Master's Voice". In this ad, Nipper thinks he hears his dead master's real voice when it is actually just a reproduction. The ad compares Nipper's loyalty to his master to the fidelity of the gramophone: If a dog is unable to tell whether the voice is real, then the gramophone's quality must be excellent! Advertisers

Development of commerce and industry: Commercial ties between Egyptians and neighboring countries.
Liebig Chromolithograph.
Selva Collection, Paris.

VÉRITABLE EXTRAIT DE VIANDE LIEBIG.

Évolution du commerce et de l'industrie.
Relations commerciales des Égyptiens avec les pays voisins.

Voir l'explication au verso.

for Black and White Whiskey chose two Scottish Terriers for the product's logo, evoking this breed's loyalty to its native land. The larger breeds favored in ads for cars evoke power and safety: A Boxer is used for Kléber tires and a mythical six-legged dog appears in the ad for Agip oil. Big dogs like the Saint Bernard give consumers a feeling of comfort and security, while mutts give ads a humorous tone.

Today, dogs are part of the family. They play with children and keep the elderly company. For these reasons, dogs commonly appear in ads portraying the typical modern family. Dogs complete the picture and create a casual atmosphere.

Unlike the private, introverted cat, the dog is an extrovert. He evokes images of freedom and the great outdoors. In ads, dogs are generally shown inside only if they've made a mess or knocked something over—the perfect situation for advertising household products. These items might include a heavy-duty floor cleaner that eliminates the traces of the puppy's "mistakes" or a new vacuum cleaner guaranteed to remove Fluffy's long hair from the carpet.

Certain breeds, including the Afghan Hound and the Dalmatian, are a symbol of elegance. These breeds appear in ads for Chanel and other cosmetics.

Marketing Tool

Whether they're shown as real dogs or given human qualities, the dogs in the preceding examples are not the advertiser's target. They are merely marketing tools often adopted at the same time by advertising agencies that may also use the same breeds. This can create harmful trends for a particular breed.

Dogs as "Consumers"

Unlike in many ads targeting humans, dogs are the focal point in ads for pet food. Dogs are the consumers of the products in these ads, at least with the help of their owner. Different brands take different approaches. France's Royal Canin portrays dogs as animals to be respected for what they are. For this reason, its ads feature puppies exploring their surroundings and a German Shepherd running across a field to his owner. This company never uses an anthropomorphic approach. Waltham's ads feature breeders discussing its product and Canigou focuses on the dog's hardiness and energy. Ads for Fido dog food show different breeds who have "tasted and approved" the product. Friskies and Frolic take a humorous approach with skits in which the actors are obviously dogs. These ads appear in all kinds of magazines and especially on television, a better medium for showing the dog in motion.

The advertising scope of veterinary medicines is much more limited. Ads for these products are generally placed only in specialized publications on animals, where they may appear side by side with ads for pet foods. Some ads for veterinary medicines strictly target medical professionals by describing a product's effectiveness and safety. Ads for veterinary medicines are quite rare compared to those for animal care products, including everything from flea powder and worm pills to grooming accessories. These ads appear more widely, sometimes as television commercials. This recent phenomenon shows the growing importance of dogs in our society. These ads commonly use humor, even mockery, to play down the "medical" aspect of the products.

In conclusion, over time dogs have become selling points either because of the qualities they represent or as potential "consumers". Dogs have been used to sell almost everything, not only products designed specifically for them. This has created the risk of media hype, which could make dogs a thing of fashion, regardless of the consequences for dogs in general.

Part 3

Dogs Helping Humans

Dogs Who Save Lives

Canine Heroes

In certain situations, a dog's loyalty to humans may cause him to go beyond his limits in order to save lives. Dogs of various breeds have thus become legends, proving through their actions just how capable they are at rescue work.

Togo and Balto: Sled Dogs

Ever since dogs were domesticated, they have been helping humans in all areas of work, from hunting to guarding to herding. Over the years, dogs have also done much more: Canine heroes have helped find missing people and save lives after avalanches, all kinds of disasters, and accidents at sea.

In February 1925 in Alaska, a diphtheria epidemic broke out and threatened to spread to Nome, a distant city on the state's west coast. At that time of year, no plane could reach Alaska from Seattle to deliver the necessary serum. Thus, the decision was made to use the train and then sled dogs for the remaining 1,000 kilometers. Leonhard Seppala, considered one of the United States' fastest sled drivers since 1920, was called in.

As the epidemic intensified, a team of mushers took turns day and night to speed the arrival of the remedy. In a raging blizzard, Seppala was forced to take incredible risks. His two lead dogs, Togo and Balto, proved their extraordinary stamina and determination, thanks to Seppala's tenacity.

Thanks to the dogs and their drivers, the serum arrived in time. It was delivered in only 127 hours and thirty minutes, with Seppala and his dogs alone covering 500 kilometers, a significant contribution to this amazing achievement!
Since then, the Iditarod—one of today's greatest northern races—is held every year to commemorate this journey.

Barry: Alpine Rescue Dog

Saint Bernards have long been used to rescue people lost in the mountains. The Cenobite monks of the Grand-Saint-Bernard Hospice in Switzerland have raised Saint Bernards since the eleventh century and, since the seventeenth century, they have trained the dogs to rescue people in the mountains.

The Saint Bernard Barry was born in the early nineteenth century. His name, meaning "bear" has traditionally been bestowed upon the finest dog in the hospice's kennel. Barry alone saved over forty people, thus becoming a legend. A statue in his honor stands in the animal cemetery in Paris. A plaque there explains that he was killed by the last person he found, who mistook him for a bear. Actually, Barry died of old age in 1814, and his body is kept at a museum in Berne. According to a popular myth, Saint Bernard rescue dogs carry a little barrel of liquor around their neck. This is as false as the story about Barry being killed by a person, since alcohol can be fatal to people suffering from hypothermia.

Rudy: Earthquake Rescue Dog

On December 11, 1988, an earthquake measuring 7.2 on the Richter scale rattled Armenia. Because of the extent of the damage—two cities were completely destroyed—international aid was requested. France took part by sending Civilian Safety Instruction and Intervention Units (UIISC) to Armenia about twenty-four hours after the disaster occurred. These units included disaster search and rescue dogs and their handlers, such as First Class Firefighter Deguerville and his dog Rudy, a four- or five-year-old Siberian Husky and German Shepherd mix. The weather was far from ideal: The temperature hovered near –3 or –4 °C during the day and dipped as low as –20°C at night. The teams of dogs and handlers worked in shifts, covering twenty-four hours a day for the first two days, then in six- to eight-hour shifts followed by a three-hour break. Inhabitants helped the search teams by showing them where victims might be caught. On the fourth day, an inhabitant led First Class Firefighter Deguerville to an elementary school, but no survivors were found there. Then he was brought to a nearby shoe factory. After several hours of searching, Rudy "marked" an area, that is, he showed his handler that he had detected a victim. When the wreckage was cleared, a woman was found alive and evacuated. She had spent several days caught beneath the wreckage with no food or water and a severely injured leg. Thanks to intensive medical care, she survived with her leg intact and recovered fully.

Rudy became a canine hero, like many other dogs who have helped save people trapped beneath the debris of earthquakes in Iran and Mexico.

Avalanche Rescue Dogs

What could be more gorgeous than the mountains in winter, when the snow sparkling in the brilliant sun attracts hordes of hikers and skiers . . . who sometimes forget that the mountains can be dangerous. Even when weather conditions seem favorable, there is always the chance of an avalanche. For this reason, ski lodges have the support of considerable safety resources, including teams of rescuers and trackers, rescue dogs and their handlers, experts who provide information and guidance to people who want to explore the mountains, and an effective weather detection system.

Search-And-Rescue Dogs

Prevention is critical, but sometimes accidents cannot be avoided. That's when the rescue teams, including search-and-rescue dogs, are called in.

Avalanche searches are a rare area of rescue work in which dogs are used immediately because of their speed, their determination, and, above all, their exceptional sense of smell. Avalanche search dogs are part of a team that also includes depth sounders and shovelers. While team members work simultaneously, the dogs are at the forefront from the start.

The dogs are important mostly because of time, an essential factor in rescuing avalanche victims, since the faster an area is explored, the more likely it is that

victims will be found alive. This is where the major advantage of using dogs becomes clear: In equal (or even more difficult) work, dogs cover terrain faster. For example, a painstaking investigation executed by twenty people requires twenty hours to complete, while a dog could complete the task in two hours and cover an area of about one hectare.

Choosing Dogs and Handlers

In France, dog rescue teams are provided by the Army, the gendarmerie, the CRS (Compagnies Républicaines de Sécurité [Republic Safety Companies] national police forces), ski lodges, and private organizations. Teams fall under two categories: Army and gendarmerie teams are trained by gendarmerie instructors, while the rest come under the domain of civilian safety. Most handlers are accustomed to the hardships of mountain life and are highly skilled skiers on all types of terrain.

The two most commonly used breeds are the Malinois Belgian Sheepdog and the German Shepherd. These breeds are popular in all types of search work, and it is easy to see why. Thanks to their large size and considerable weight, Malinois Belgian Sheepdogs and German Shepherds do not struggle through the snow, and they are tireless hard workers. Dogs are chosen based on their physical traits, personality, and overall health. Interestingly, the animals chosen adapt very quickly to their new environment. In several days, their undercoat grows thicker and retains heat better; the hair between their toes wears away less, widening the paw into a "snowshoe"; and the skin on their paw pads becomes tougher and more resistant to cold and to the salts spread on roadways to reduce slipping. Only the dogs' eyes must be protected from the sun's ultraviolet rays: During training or prolonged work outdoors, handlers administer protective eye drops.

Search Dog Teams: Training and Practice

Alpine search dogs receive several weeks of training in the mountains. This training is based on a program developed by Swiss rescue workers to teach dogs and handlers the basics.

During training, dogs gradually learn to understand what they are being asked to do, and handlers learn to "read" their dog, that is, determine the precise moment when the dog marks a location. After they complete this training, the rescue teams are ready for work.

To maintain a high level of proficiency, teams participate in regular training exercises during the winter that also give handlers the opportunity to meet and discuss their experiences.

Tracking Dogs

Tracking consists of locating people based on a number of olfactory clues (footprints, objects, possible evidence).
The goal of this work is to find one or more persons, to locate any objects or materials lost or hidden on or near the trail, or simply to indicate the direction taken.

Choosing Dogs and Handlers

In theory, all dogs have a sufficiently developed sense of smell to follow a trail left by a person. But because tracking is a complex task requiring special training to which not all dogs are receptive, animals are selected according to specific criteria.

Dogs are chosen based on the following qualities: energy, stamina, ruggedness, hardiness, a particularly well-developed sense of smell, the ability to concentrate and not become distracted by unrelated

THE TRAIL

The human body constantly emits tiny odor molecules. Tracking dogs are faced with a blend of different factors, including specific odors (of people, groups, species), chemical odors (leather, fat, clothing), broken terrain (plants that have been crushed, bacteria released through a crack in the ground, etc.), the environment (woods, prairie, fields of alfalfa or other crops, etc.), and atmospheric conditions.

Certain factors can modify a dog's sense of smell. When these factors coincide at different moments in time, tracking becomes more difficult. These factors include:

Environmental Factors

Temperature. This factor can have a favorable effect (cold weather slows the diffusion of odor molecules) or an unfavorable effect (high temperatures speed the diffusion of odors, dry mucous membranes, and decrease the resistance to fatigue).

Wind. This factor can change the direction of the trail, dry the mucous membranes, and cause considerable diffusion of odor molecules.

Precipitation. Precipitation can affect the trail favorably or unfavorably, depending on heaviness. Slight humidity, such as frost or a light snowfall, preserves the trail. Heavy precipitation "washes away" the trail and diminishes the sense of smell when water droplets or snowflakes are inhaled over the mucous membranes lining the nose. This makes tracking impossible.

Terrain. The nature of the terrain greatly affects the quality of the trail. Terrain falls under the following categories:
• Hard, dry terrain (sand, pebbles, rock, roadways, etc.), on which odors don't "stick";
• Loose and/or damp terrain (prairies, undergrowth, etc.), which retains odors for long periods (sometimes over twenty-four hours); and
• Cultivated terrain, which retains odors when the weather is cloudy or humid but loses odors quickly when the weather is dry and hot.

Electromagnetic field. Stormy weather and nearby power lines generally interfere with tracking.

Dog-Specific Factors

Breed. German Shepherds are the most commonly used breed. They are known for their exceptional sense of smell.

Gender. Dogs are greatly disturbed by the odor of another animal of their species, especially that of a bitch in heat.

Health. Dogs track well only when they are in good health.

Fatigue. Tracking takes a great deal of energy and exacts a heavy toll on the nervous system. Regular, step-by-step training delays the onset of fatigue and increases the quality of tracking.

Nutrition. Any lack in food quality or quantity affects the dog's general condition and can alter his sense of smell.

Trail-Specific Factors

Length Dogs cannot detect a body odor unless the reference (an object, such as an article of clothing) is of sufficient quality and freshness and the trail is sufficiently long before presenting difficulties. A single footprint is not enough for a dog to establish an odor; as he follows the trail, tiny amounts of body odors accumulate over time, and the dog can eventually identify the odor of the person who left the trail.

Age. Odor molecules disperse and fade into the environment. The intensity of an odor decreases gradually until it disappears completely.

Route. The route a trail follows affects tracking. Obviously, a simple, straight trail is much easier to follow than a trail with many twists and turns.

The Handler's Influence

Handlers must remain as neutral as possible, or a dog will quickly lose his effectiveness.

odors and the environment (focus and accuracy on the trail), and courage and indifference to gunfire.

Handlers must be physically fit, calm, and level-headed. In tracking, great distances must sometimes be covered at a quick and even pace. Handlers must also be observant and good at interpreting and acting on a dog's most subtle reactions.

Area-Searching Dogs

The goal of detection is to find people who are lost. This makes area seaching dogs very similar to tracking.

However, in the area search a dog is given no reference object or potential point of departure. He is let go without a harness or leash, and his job is to search for a specific odor in a defined area, as is the case in searches in disaster areas or in an avalanche.

Water Rescue Dogs

As in any area of rescue work, the dog's physical abilities and determination make him an important member of water rescue teams.

Choice of Breed : the Newfoundland

Newfoundlands possess many characteristics that make them suited for water rescue:

THE NEWFOUNDLAND'S FUNCTIONS

The Dog Alone
The Newfoundland comes to the rescue in almost any situation. He can help conscious or semi-conscious victims, tow boats or equipment, extend safety ropes in floods or other disasters, and bring boats to shallow areas or areas with exposed rocks.

The Handler And His Newfy
Newfoundlands also help human rescue workers. When a worker finds a struggling victim, he can focus on keeping the victim under control while the dog does the pulling. The dog can also pull boats away from shore or out of a dangerous area. He helps people whose boat has capsized or been damaged. In area searches, the Newfy tows the divers' Zodiac, following their trail of air bubbles.

Areas Of Activity
Newfoundlands perform water rescue work in all sorts of environments.
• **Oceans:** Responding on call or upon witnessing an accident from a rescue station; ensuring the safety of hard-to-reach areas. Restriction: assistance on beaches with large waves.
• **Rivers:** Responding on call, as a back-up to existing rescue squads; providing immediate, rapid intervention regardless of obstacles, thanks to car transport. Restriction: assistance in areas upstream from lock spillways.
• **Lakes and stretches of smooth water:** Responding on call at the request of a witness or upon witnessing an accident; helping with lifeguard duty in tourist areas. Restriction: assistance in areas upstream from dams.
• **Floods:** Responding as needed, as a back-up to transport teams; recovering equipment, carrying food or lifeboats to victims, extending support ropes.
• **Disasters:** Assisting victims, performing the same activities as in floods.
• **Nautical events:** Providing support at regattas, triathlons, and other water sports events requiring short-term surveillance; responding when an accident is sighted.

- Strength: They can tow several people or a boat weighing several tons.
- Stamina: They can swim great distances, for several hours straight.
- Resistance to the cold: This means they are ready at a moment's notice, unlike a diver, who needs about five minutes to prepare his equipment.
- Calmness: The Newfy's incredible calmness in all kinds of circumstances can be very reassuring to victims.
- Determination: Newfies never abandon their mission.
- Availability: Newfies can dive in at a moment's notice, since they need no special equipment.

Choosing a Rescue Dog

A good water rescue dog needs thorough training and must be physically and psychologically suited to the work. A lack of instinct or swimming ability are the main disqualifications. But the most problematic is hip dysplasia.

Puppies are chosen as potential water rescue dogs based on their energy, strength, and healthy bone structure. A puppy's parents are systematically x-rayed to determine his susceptibility to hip dysplasia.

Raising a Rescue Dog

Whether training a puppy or an adult dog, the key phrase is "easy does it". Adult dogs must adapt to their new job. Their muscles and joints may become overstressed if training is administered too quickly. Adult dogs must progress gradually in such activities as swimming, climbing, and running. In addition, their already developed character may have to be toned down.

Like any other breed, the young Newfy must be trained gradually, in a series of short exercises based on his attention span. In addition, training should be administered at different times of the day and in different places, to prevent habits from forming.

THE NEWFY IN TRAINING

All training begins with a play session to allow the dog to let off steam and prepare for work. The actual training takes place both on land and in the water. It is always preceded by obedience lessons. From the time they are several months old, puppies are taught to heel, stay, and come when called. Later, the commands become more complicated (voice commands, gesture commands at a distance, etc.), and exercises are done on slippery or steep terrain similar to the conditions found in rescue situations. In addition to obedience training, puppies are socialized to the outside world: crowds, traffic noises, elevators, etc.

Training in the water is divided into two parts:

- The dog learns to retrieve objects and tow his handler, then strangers, and finally sailboards and boats; and

- The handler and the dog work as a team to build trust and develop cooperation. When the dog reaches fifteen months, true rescue training begins: Exercises become more difficult, the dog must climb to reach the water, he must tow heavier and heavier craft, and he may sometimes be submerged by large waves.

The frequency of training varies according to the dog's motivation and physical effort. However, basic obedience is reviewed every day.

The dog and handler must progress at the same pace. Establishing trust and cooperation between the two is fundamental. But this is possible only when the handler listens to his dog and can read him like an open book, to the point of anticipating his reactions.

The handler uses a different tone of voice, depending on whether he wants the dog to stop working or get back to work: The command to stop is issued in an abrupt, sharp voice. Encouragement to continue working is given in a lively, playful manner.

The most important thing to remember in training is that if a Newfoundland succeeds at an exercise, it is his own doing; if he fails, it is his handler's fault.

The Risks of Training

A dog may experience psychological and physiological problems during training. Overtraining (jumping, climbing, swimming, etc.) when puppies are too young can cause loose ligaments and aggravate existing dysplasia.

In addition, forcing a young dog to perform moves that frighten him can create permanent inhibitions. It would be unfortunate for a Newfy to fear water because he was forced to jump in as a puppy.

It might take several months to rebuild the confidence of a dog who has become discouraged during training. Through play, the handler can encourage the dog to perform an exercise he is refusing. Play helps eliminate a dog's timidity, reserve, apprehension, and fear. A dog can be raised to overcome the inhibitions related to his character, upbringing, or habits, and any genetic imbalance can be compensated.

Disaster Search and Rescue Dogs

A vital resource

Search dogs are used not only after major earthquakes. They may also be called to the scene of landslides; collapsed buildings, worksites, or mines; fires; train or airplane accidents; etc. Unfortunately, there is no shortage of such circumstances.

Dogs were first used to find people buried beneath wreckage after Great Britain was bombed during World War II.

As early as 1954, search dog training centers were established in the United States, Germany, and Switzerland. Swiss dogs were the first to gain international attention after the 1976 earthquake in Friuli, Italy, where twelve search dogs found forty-two survivors and 510 bodies. In 1977 in Romania, ten dogs found fifteen survivors and ninety-seven bodies.

In 1980, the first French search and rescue dogs were brought to El Asam, Algeria, where they found ten survivors and five hundred bodies. Today, search dogs are used after all major earthquakes (Iran, Mexico, Armenia). The dogs of the world were in the spotlight once again following the earthquakes in Turkey in 1999. Thanks to search and rescue dogs, several hundred buried victims were rescued.

Geophonic sensors that can detect very slight noises like heartbeats are also used to detect disaster victims. However, unlike dogs, these devices work only in complete silence, which is seldom possible in areas where wreckage is being cleared. A properly trained dog can work on any type of terrain—even in dark basements—together with human rescue workers, despite the noise of the machines used to clear wreckage (cranes, sledgehammers, bulldozers). Moreover, sensors cannot detect dead bodies, while dogs not only find bodies, they also have different ways of "marking" them, depending on whether they are dead or alive. This helps rescuers plan their response time. Professionals agree that rescue dogs are an indispensable aid in any kind of rescue work dealing with wreckage.

Teamwork

As in any work involving both dogs and humans, there must be deep trust and cooperation between the handler and his dog. The handler must know his dog thoroughly and be able to "read" him as he

Canine search-and-rescue team of the Fire Department of Paris searching through ruins.

works through the disaster area, anticipating his every move. Similarly, the dog must be able to trust his handler to follow him everywhere, regardless of the difficulties of the terrain.

This high degree of cooperation requires extensive training. After socialization and basic training (positions, heeling, etc.), the focus turns to actual search work. Various techniques are used. In general, the handler relies on the dog's attachment to him and to a particular play thing (a ball or chew toy). First the handler, then one, then several other people hide with the dog's toy. When the dog finds the victims, he "marks" them by barking and scratching at the ground. The dog's attachment to the toy helps develop this marking behavior, an essential skill for a good wreckage search dog.

When the dog is able to locate several victims who hide without him seeing, he is certified according to terms and conditions of the particular country. The handler and his dog are then registered at the national level as a civilian or military rescue team.

Canine Candidates

Good candidates for disaster search training have a keen sense of smell and are calm, poised, and energetic. They are also sociable, both toward humans and toward other dogs, since more than one dog may work in an area. In addition, playfulness is essential in training.

The most commonly used breeds are sheepdogs, particularly German Shepherds and Belgian Sheepdogs. The little Pyrenean Shepherd , the Doberman, and the Beauceron have also been trained as successful disaster search and rescue dogs.

Dogs for the Handicapped

Service Dogs for the Handicapped

For most of us, dogs are just pets. But for some people, dogs are constant companions who provide valuable help. These exceptional animals work as service dogs for the handicapped, the deaf or the hearing impaired and as guide dogs for the blind. They are trained thanks to private organizations established by dedicated, generous people.

The French organization ANECAH (Association nationale pour l'éducation des chiens d'assistance aux handicapés [National Association for the Training of Service Dogs for the Handicapped]) was established in 1989. It trains dogs used in rehabilitating people who have lost all or part of their mobility. Since its creation, ANECAH has trained more and more dogs each year, including about fifty in 1996. These dogs are either Labradors or Golden Retrievers, breeds known for their calmness, docility and ability to learn commands. Training is divided into several phases. First, puppies are placed in families who raise them. Then, dogs are trained by the association to respond to about fifty different commands.

The host family plays a vital role and influences the rest of the dog's training. As soon as puppies are three months old, they are "pretrained" or socialized, by the host family, who teaches them basic obedience. Every three weeks, the dogs and their temporary owners meet at a center where the puppies are monitored. The center staff may give advice on raising the puppy and, in some cases, decide to discharge dogs who show evidence of a character fault that disqualifies them from service work. This pretraining phase lasts until the dog is eighteen months old. Then he is trained specifically to help a person with restricted mobility. During this phase of approximately six months, he lives full-time at the center. In the last two weeks of training, dogs and potential owners are matched based on mutual affinity. Training is administered daily, with a trainer spending about a half hour with the dog each day. After twenty-four months, one-third of the dogs are discharged for behavioral or physical reasons (poor hip formation, etc.). The main goal is to find the perfect match between dog and owner, with a high degree of mutual understanding and a good use of the dog by the handicapped person. The potential owner participates in a relatively demanding, two-week program to learn how to care for his dog and give commands. He must take written and oral tests and complete a final exam. The complete training of one dog costs about 10,000 Euros. This limits the number of people able to take the program and especially the number of dogs who can be trained.

After this training period, dogs can respond to about fifty different commands. They can pick up fallen objects, fetch things (like the telephone), open and close doors, turn lights on and off, maneuver a wheelchair through tight spots, etc.

Service dogs perform many tasks that their owners cannot. But they also have a therapeutic effect on people—especially children—who suffer from various illnesses. In these cases, the dogs act almost like doctors. Apart from the tasks these dogs were trained to perform, they provide stimulation to handicapped children, who find comfort in their new friend, gain self-confidence andbecome more open toward others. They may even do things they never thought they could. The dog's help encourages them to test their limits. Research on the therapeutic effects of animals has been conducted, particularly in the field of autism, a disease with no known cause and no current treatment.

Service dogs also make it easier for people to approach the handicapped and develop a positive view toward them.

Guide Dogs for the Blind

Training schools for guide dogs for the blind have existed in France since 1952 and in England since 1930. These dogs receive roughly the same training as service dogs for the handicapped, but guide dog training is much more extensive, both in terms of the number of animals trained and the number of training schools.

One-third of the dogs used are German Shepherds and the remaining two-thirds are Golden Retrievers and Labradors. These breeds are chosen because of their obedience and learning ability. Puppies are bred specifically for guide dog training at a research center that supplies the schools. This research center focuses on genetic selection in dogs to eliminate character faults and bone and joint deformities (like hip dysplasia). The center staff are advised by veterinarians who teach at

national veterinary schools. As soon as the puppies are weaned, they are placed in host families who raise them, then distributed to the various training schools. Bitches return to the center regularly for whelping, so that the reproduction of breeding dogs may be monitored. The goal is to produce about twenty puppies per year, given that France currently has only about a thousand owner-guide dog teams.

Guide dog training occurs over four months divided into several periods during which dogs learn obedience first and foremost. Obedience training consists of simple exercises in which the dog must hold certain positions, retrieve objects, get used to wearing a harness and heel correctly. This phase lasts one week and is administered exclusively by a trainer. In the next phase, the dog learns to avoid all sorts of obstacles and indicate them to his owner. This is the pivotal point of the entire training program. The trainer is involved during the first month, then the dog is given to a blind person who must get used to the dog and let the dog guide him over various routes. At this point a close bond develops between dog and owner. The trainer serves as a link between the two and is also responsible for "training" the owner.

After four months at the guide dog school, the owner-guide dog team is ready to face daily life and work together for many years. The dog allows the blind person to re-enter society and pursue an occupation compatible with his handicap.

All over the world, similar guide dog training associations are being established to provide more handicapped and blind people with dogs who receive training of higher and higher quality.

Dogs Who Help the Deaf

In our society, being deaf or hearing impaired is a handicap that can quickly lead to isolation. Dogs are used to help remedy this problem.

A number of centers train so-called "hearing-ear" dogs worldwide, particularly in the United States, England and especially Holland (in France, such associations no longer exist). Established in 1984, the Soho Foundation near Nimegue in Herpen, Holland purchases dogs and trains them to help handicapped or deaf people. It works in cooperation with organizations in England, where most of its dogs are purchased. Most are Golden Retrievers, but some Welsh Corgis and Bearded Collies are also used.

From the age of eight weeks to one year, the dogs live with Dutch families, preferably with children, where they receive basic obedience training and learn to adapt to various surroundings (the city, the supermarket, the woods, etc.). Then they return to the foundation and begin real training for their future function. This is where the choice of breed becomes vital, since the dog's intelligence is truly put to the test: He must learn over seventy verbal commands and twenty gestures. Additional training is required because the voice of a deaf or hearing impaired person is quite different, both in terms of intonation and diction. And dogs who help deaf-mutes receive two years of training instead of one.

"Hearing-ear" dogs are trained above all to react to certain noises and communicate them to their owner. For example, the dog may jump onto the bed when the alarm goes off, tug on his owner's pant leg when someone knocks at the door or delicately take his owner's hand to alert him to an ill-timed visit. However, what owners appreciate most is that their new friend helps end their loneliness and isolation.

Statistically speaking, the training of one dog costs about 10,000 Euros. At the Dutch foundation mentioned above, 80% of the dogs successfully complete training. In 1987, Holland required forty-five service dogs, including fifteen for the deaf or hearing impaired.

Security Dogs

The role of security dogs has changed over the centuries with advances in weaponry and armies. They have served as canine soldiers dressed in lethal armor, as sentries, trackers, patrol dogs, message-carrying dogs and first aid dogs. Today, they play an important role in the detection of hydrocarbons, explosives and narcotics. In these new roles, their great loyalty, generosity and abilities still help ensure the security of men and society as a whole.

Dogs in the Army

Soldier Dogs

As early as the thirteenth century B.C., dogs served as full-fledged soldiers in the wars waged by humans. These mastiffs were fearsome weapons, subjugating the enemy with their vicious bites. They were of a breed originally from Asia and similar to today's Tibetan Mastiff but larger, standing 75 to 80 cm (29.5-31.5 in) tall at the withers, while today's dog measures 70 cm (27.5 in) at the withers. Fiercer than the sighthounds used in hunting by the pharaohs of Egypt, these mastiffs became popular in Egypt, then in Greece. They finally reached the Roman Empire after the Greek conquests. Meanwhile, the Gauls, Celts and Germans developed a breed derived from the Great Dane. In the first century B.C., soldier dogs were pitted against Roman and Gallic warriors in famous fights.

The training of soldier dogs was simple: Their role was to exterminate the men and horses of enemy armies. Over the centuries, these dogs were outfitted with spiked collars, armor with sharp spikes or blades on top and even leather coats covered with a highly flammable substance. Thus transformed into true war machines, dogs were sent in to scatter frightened or brutally wounded horses and foot soldiers. The use of such dogs ended in the nineteenth century, with the significant development of firearms.

Sentry Dogs

With their excellent sense of smell and instinctive tendency to defend and guard their owner, dogs were used as sentries at many forts, citadels, village squares and walled cities.

Plutarch told the story of the sentry dog Soter: Corinth was protected by a garrison aided by fifty mastiffs sleeping on the beach. One night, enemy armies arrived by sea. After a night of revelry, the Corinthian soldiers had become lax. But their dogs were not—they fought the enemy, though largely outnumbered. Forty-nine mastiffs were killed. Only one, Soter, was able to escape and sound the alert by barking. The Corinthian soldiers donned their arms and managed to ward off the assailants. To reward Soter for his courage, they gave him an elegant collar with the inscription, "To Soter, defender and savior of Corinth." Mastiffs like Soter were commonly used in the Middle Ages to defend vast expanses like Mont Saint Michel. Beginning in 1155, twenty-four English Mastiffs were released each night in the fortified city of Saint Malo to protect the ships from pirates. This practice ended in 1770, when the dogs attacked and devoured a young officer walking on the beach. Today, dogs still work as sentries in high-security facilities.

Tracking Dogs

Many dogs have been trained to follow the trail left by humans. When Christopher Columbus landed in North America, dogs were trained to find and kill Native Americans. At La Vega, thousands of Native Americans were put to flight by only 150 foot soldiers, thirty horsemen and some twenty soldier dogs. Later, Spanish plantation owners in South America used dogs to track runaway slaves. These dogs received minimal training: They were shown black mannequins stuffed with blood and entrails. Excited by the odor, the dogs quickly made the connection between these mannequins, given to them as food, and slaves. The slaves they found had little chance of escaping alive.

During the war in Algeria, tracking dogs were used to find enemy troops who had penetrated security points. One of these dogs was Gamin, a German Shepherd from the military kennel at Beni-Messous. When he first arrived in Algeria, he was so vicious that no one could get near him… no one except Gendarmerie Officer Gilbert Godefroid. On March 29, 1958, Officer Godefroid was awoken suddenly early in the morning when an estimated two hundred men broke through the electric fence at the Tunisian border. Gamin and his master were flown in by helicopter and immediately began a search, accompanied by the parachutists of the First Foreign Regiment. It was easy to find the fresh trail, but as soon as he released Gamin, Godefroid was hit by a barrage of automatic gunfire and fatally wounded. Though injured himself, Gamin lunged at the gunman and tore his throat.

Then he crawled back to his master and lay down on top of him to protect him. It took six men and a tent cloth to bring Gamin under control. He was brought back to the base camp and treated, but once again no one could approach him or give him commands. Military authorities decided to give Gamin a peaceful retirement at the gendarmerie's central kennel in Gramat, Lot where, according to the secretary's message, Gamin was to "receive attentive care until his death." But Gamin died of a broken heart only two weeks after his arrival. His ashes are still kept at the gendarmerie's National Training Center for Dog Handlers in Gramat and a monument was dedicated in his honor.

The Americans used tracking dogs in Vietnam. In this guerilla war, dogs were trained to silently follow the soldiers in order to locate and surround withdrawal zones and Viet Cong camps.

Message-carrying Dogs

Getting the latest news from advanced detachments and communicating with fixed points on the frontline is vital to executing or modifying military attack or defense strategies. Before the advent of telecommunications, dogs were widely used as messengers.

In ancient times, mastiffs were forced to swallow messages and were sacrificed upon arrival so that the precious documents could be recovered. This atrocious practice did not last long, not because of its cruelty, but because of the expense.

In the eighteenth century, Frederick II The Great of Prussia revived this practice for the delivery of inter-army mail in his kingdom. His message-carrying dogs were so popular during the Seven Years'War that an entire line of transmission and liaison dogs was developed.

Beginning in World War I, so-called "courier dogs" were developed. These dogs were selected based on very strict criteria: They had to stand 40 to 70 cm (15.5-27.5 in) tall at the withers; have a neutral-colored coat; be calm, intelligent, obedient and in perfect health; and have a keen sense of smell, eyesight and hearing. According to the Military Manual, these dogs also had to be between two and five years old, to ensure that they were at the height of their abilities and hardy enough to withstand bad weather, hardship and fatigue.

Their important role consisted of linking points several kilometers apart, often in difficult weather conditions. Courier dogs could reportedly cover five kilometers in twelve minutes during bombing. Paradoxically, the messages these dogs carried were clear and easily decipherable by enemy troops. But courier dogs were still very effective, since they were rarely captured.

Pack Dogs and Draft Dogs

Dogs can carry objects weighing up to 7 kilograms (15,5 lb). For this reason, they were commonly used in wars to carry munitions, supplies and even arms to the frontlines. During World War I, German dogs were captured carrying light machine guns. Two types of pack dogs were developed during this war: telegraph dogs and pigeon dogs. Telegraph dogs carried a spool of telephone wire that unrolled as they crossed a perilous route through trenches, amid gunfire, through barbed-wire fences, etc., in an effort to reestablish the lines of communication severed during combat. Pigeon dogs were trained to bring carrier pigeons to outposts.

The use of draft dogs dates to 1911, when the Belgians attached powerful dogs to machine guns on wheels. They used dogs instead of horses because dogs have greater stamina and can more easily follow men through the undergrowth. Dogs were also attached to supply carts and stretchers for transporting the wounded. The Germans even used dogs to pull sleds on the eastern front. Due to considerable debate over a dog's ability to pull an object on wheels, only the Belgian, German and Russian armies truly used draft dogs (the Germans for a limited time).

Patrol Dogs

With their highly developed protective and defensive instincts, dogs soon became popular in patrol work. Used to expel enemies hidden in the woods or in underbrush, they helped patrols upset ambushes and signaled the presence of enemy troops. Patrol dogs were also used to keep watch over prisoners on escort. Very few of these dogs made a name for themselves in history, but they helped many patrols clear out enemies and find their way.

First Aid Dogs

The Egyptians were the first to train dogs to find the wounded. After combat, dogs were released onto the battlefield to search for the injured, whom they licked and signaled to rescue workers.

First aid dogs next appeared in the late nineteenth century. They were trained to locate the wounded and indicate their presence by bringing back a personal object, often a soldier's helmet. After thus alerting the rescue workers, the dogs went back to search for more victims. First aid dogs were essential: The wounded could be transported only by dark, so the dogs helped guide the searches. The first Society of First Aid Dogs was founded in 1885 by Van de Putte from Belgium. This was followed by a German organization, founded by Bungartz, an animal painter. Not until 1908 did France begin using first aid dogs.

There are many stories of the activities of first aid dogs. A soldier from Le Mans, France injured on November 2, 1915 reported, "I had been hit in the arm by a shell and in the jaw by a bullet and a saber wound had detached part of my scalp. Half buried beneath the bodies of several mates, I felt someone caressing my forehead. It was a first aid dog licking my face. Despite my severe pain, I managed to hoist myself up a bit. I knew that dogs were trained to bring the caps of the wounded back to camp, but I had lost mine. The poor dog hesitated, so I told him, "Go on, boy, go back to the guys at camp". He understood me and crawled back to the camp. There he made such a fuss—barking, tugging on one person's cap and then another—that he attracted the attention of two stretcher-bearers. They followed him back to me and I was saved."

Dangerous Missions

Dogs have sometimes been used in difficult situations and in unusual conditions.

During the war in Indochina, the terrain and vegetation caused many problems for the French troops conducting operations there. In the first months of the campaign, they discovered the dangers that parachutists dropped in enemy territory might face. Only dogs could help speed the soldiers'-painstaking but necessary trench digging work. Dogs were therefore parachuted experimentally at the parachute school in Meucon on September 5 and 6, 1949.

The difficulties encountered during parachute training centered on the dog's jump from the plane and his landing. Lighter than humans, the dogs reached the ground far later and at a considerable distance from their handlers. This greatly increased the time necessary to find the dog and put him to work. Equipping the dogs with a lighter parachute solved this problem, ensuring that the dogs landed at the same time as their handler and in the same area.

Unfortunately, some dogs lost their lives in wars. With the German armies approaching, Soviet General Panfilon decided to have dogs trained to look for food beneath armored vehicles. The dogs were starved for one or two days before the attack, mines were attached to their back and they were released to run toward their horrible fate. Although terribly cruel, this practice did wreak havoc on the German troops.

First aid dogs. Petit Journal pictorial paper, April 18, 1915.

Stage One

The substance to which the dog should react is placed inside a PVC tube pierced with holes. It is too dangerous for a dog in training to be in direct contact with heroin or cocaine. For this reason, small rags that have touched these substances and absorbed their odor are used instead.

For several days, the trainer plays with the dog using the tube, until the tube becomes the dog's favorite toy. During this stage, the dog learns to associate his toy with the odor of the substance he smells through the holes in the tube.

Stage Two

When the trainer considers the dog sufficiently attached to the toy, he hides it in plain sight in an easily accessible place. The dog still must use his sense of smell to find it.

Then the trainer hides the tube in places that are more and more difficult to find, even impossible to reach.

During this stage, the dog also learns to scratch when the trainer buries the tube in sand. The loose ground incites the dog to dig for his toy.

Stage Three

The tube is hidden out of plain sight without the dog seeing. The trainer leads the dog into the room, briefly encourages him to find his toy and then releases him on the command "Search"! When the dog locates his unreachable toy, he must scratch to get the trainer to give it to him.

Stage Four

In the final stage, the trainer eliminates the tube so that the dog learns to search only for the drug, which he now associates with his toy.

Canine Activities Today

While dogs have always had the same aptitudes, over the years they have been trained to face conflicts in different places, using different techniques. Dogs have had a variety of functions over the centuries. First they were trained as parachutists and entrusted with carrier pigeons; later they learned to detect mines and gas, etc. Today, dogs are trained for other types of work: They are taught to detect explosives and narcotics, thereby helping humans face the increase in bomb threats and counter the spread of drugs.

All these dogs are trained at the Ring III level, since their handlers must be in complete control of their every move.

Drug Detection Dogs

The ideal drug detection dog is playful, energetic, medium-sized and flexible enough to squeeze through tight spaces and climb over or through obstacles. He also needs a great deal of stamina, since he may be required to conduct several searches in one day. Currently, Malinois Belgian Sheepdogs are the preferred breed because they are smaller and more lively than German Shepherds.

These dogs are also trained to attack, since in drug detection work handlers must sometimes search for dealers, who may aggressively resist arrest.

Drug detection work with dogs is conducted primarily inside buildings, where dogs are used to sniff out hidden drugs (heroin, cocaine, cannabis, marijuana, etc.) and thus speed the process when a meticulous search is necessary.

It is important to note that drug detection dogs are not drugged themselves. While dogs can suffer from withdrawal, this condition would not enable a dog to find hidden substances more quickly. On the contrary, dogs suffering from withdrawal would conduct disorderly, superficial searches and become aggressive toward people, even their handler.

Explosives Detection Dogs

Explosives detection dogs are chosen based on the same criteria as drug detection dogs. But dogs trained to detect explosives must be calmer and able to conduct searches without becoming excited.

The most popular breeds for explosives detection work are therefore Malinois Belgian Sheepdogs and German Shepherds.

Hydrocarbons Detection Dogs

This specialty exists chiefly in North America and is currently being developed in Europe. Dogs trained to recognize various hydrocarbons are brought to the scene of fires to detect the chemicals used by arsonists. They may also be used in preventing fires in forests at risk or after fires of criminal origin. Hydrocarbons detection dogs mark by scratching. Flammable chemicals are then removed from the site, or samples are taken from the places the dog scratches at the scene of a fire.

Hydrocarbons detection dogs work in conditions that put many demands on their sense of smell: They must cover areas that may people have passed through. In addition, fires destroy certain odors but release many others that may be toxic and are always unpleasant and accompanied by smoke.

A dog's willingness to search comes from his desire to find his toy and play with his handler. To the dog, drugs, explosives and hydrocarbons are only markers that he must discover to get to his favorite toy.

Guard Dogs and Patrol Dogs

A guard or patrol dog protects or follows a person indicated by his handler. In this line of work, the dog's vigilance and obedience are key. The dog must remain detached and show aggression only if the person begins to struggle. Guard and patrol dogs may also be entrusted with objects, such as cars.

TRAINING EXPLOSIVES DETECTION DOGS

The four stages of training are based on the same skills needed by drug detection dogs, but with several differences. Explosives searches are conducted both inside and outside for substances including dynamite, TNT, formex, nitrate, fuel oil, hexolite, tetryl, etc.

Explosives detection dogs mark by sitting or lying down, depending on the location of the substance. Sitting indicates high positions and lying down indicates substances that are on the ground or buried.

These dogs must show no aggression (such as barking or scratching), due to the highly sensitive mechanisms in the explosive systems used by terrorists (obviously, dogs practice and are trained only with the raw materials listed above).

In the first three stages of training, the dog learns to associate a toy with the explosive materials. The trainer places the toy first in plain sight, then in plain sight but in an unreachable location and finally in a completely hidden location. The toy is always accompanied by an explosive material.

In training, the dog's toy is hidden in "hot spots" corresponding to the possible hiding spots for explosives.

Dogs are never trained to bite, since the goal of explosives detection work is simply to pinpoint the location of charges (as a preventive measure or during a bomb alert). The dog and his handler work alone in the areas to be explored. Once a charge is detected, the area is evacuated and mine clearance teams take over.

DOGS IN FRANCE'S GENDARMERIE

France's Gendarmerie has used detection dogs since 1943. Currently, the organization has 388 dog-handler teams (one dog, one handler) trained in all areas of activity, including:

- manhunts (tracking) and defense = 209 teams, including twenty qualified for avalanche search;
- drug detection = 80 teams;
- explosives detection = 43 teams; and
- guard and patrol work = 36 teams.

These teams are spread over the country and based with gendarmerie units, forming a network to ensure rapid intervention in all regions.

Handlers are selected from among officers who volunteer.

The dogs, either German Shepherds or Malinois Belgian Sheepdogs, are purchased as adults (at about eighteen months old). They are assigned to a unit when they reach about two years old, after completing a training program with their handler at the Gendarmerie's National Dog Training Center in Gramat (Lot). When the dogs become too old to serve in the Gendarmerie (generally when they reach eight to ten years old, or after five to seven years of service), they are given to their handler free of charge. They can thus spend a well-deserved retirement with an old friend.

Gendarmerie dogs are trained daily.

Each year, they are involved in close to 40,000 cases, including about 1,500 manhunts, over 300 of which are successful.

That means that almost every day, someone is found by a dog or with a dog's help.

In the mountains, five to fifteen people are found in avalanches each year.

In France it has been said—and even written—that drug detection dogs are drugged themselves. This is completely false. If it were true, how would explosives detection dogs be made to do their job?

All work is based on the dog's attachment to his handler and on the reward. The dog is actually looking for his toy.

Both dog and handler are motivated by mutual respect and admiration. Their motto is "You and me for them".

General Jean-Louis Esquivié,
Commander of the Schools
of the National Gendarmerie.

Other Ways Dogs Help Humans

Dogs have always amazed us with the many qualities that make them so helpful. In the nineteenth century, they showed their acting skill in street shows and circuses. In the early twentieth century, dogs in the country still pulled small carts loaded with wood, bottles of milk, women, or children. Today, they use their sense of smell to help people find truffles, detect minerals, and, of course, hunt wild game.

Hunting Dogs

Hunting is a popular sport, a passion—an art for many—involving over a million dogs and their owners. Hunting is a sport for dog and owner alike, since it requires excellent physical condition to work long hours in all kinds of weather, as well as a strong character, determination and a keen eye. Of course, a good hunting dog must also have a superb sense of smell.

Hunting is strictly regulated. In France, for example, the season begins with waterfowl hunting in the second week of July, continues with pointers in September and ends with hounds and woodcock hunting in late February. Without the dog, a hunter's best friend, there is no hunt, since hunting is actually a sort of competition that the dog must win. Through instinct, knowledge of the territory and sheer cleverness, the hunted animal must beat its canine adversary, who has the advantages of intelligence, a keen sense of smell, poise, vigor and the skills specific to the particular type of hunt. Dogs specialize in hunting certain game—waterfowl, small and large mammals and birds—as well as in specific parts of the hunt, such as digging up foxholes. These specialized hunting dogs are classified in several of the groups established by the FCI.

Natural Skills and Training

All hunting dogs possess considerable natural skill as a result of careful selection by expert breeders over decades. Of all the characteristics required for hunting, intelligence is the most important. It is not enough for a dog to have a good nose, he must also know how to use it.

Training is necessary to make the most of this natural skill. It is a tricky job that takes patience and has no hard-and-fast rules, since techniques vary according to the dog, his reactions and, of course, the specific goal. Training is necessary, but it is also time-consuming and often does not progress as fast as one would like. Only an expert can train a dog well in two or three months. Usually, training requires six months of daily work.

Training must include obedience, retrieval and positions (like the famous "down"). The dog must also learn to use his nose. The sensitivity of an animal's sense of smell depends on species; in dogs it depends on breed. After a hunting dog has been trained, he must be able to sort through the scents carried by the wind to avoid making mistakes. Pointers must be able to search a particular area and remain motionless while marking, in order not to frighten off game. They must also retrieve dead game and bring it to the hunter. Hunting dogs must be taught all this with as little force as possible.

In principal and by nature, hunting dogs are not apartment animals or simple pets. If owners try to resist their dog's hunting instinct, it will come back to haunt them. Non-hunting owners of a hunting breed must be sure to give their dog daily opportunities to run and play. City life is often unsuitable for such dogs.

Pointing Dog Field Trial In U.S.A.

Field trials are a cult sport, pursued by a small fraterniy of fanatics. They started in England about 1850. The first American one was at Memphis in 1874 - that area is known as the Cradle of Field Trials, and the National Bird Dog Championship is held at Grand Junction each February.

A field trial is a contest for pointing dogs seeking upland game birds by scent quail in the South, pheasants in the Midwest, prairie chicken, sharp-tail grouse, Hungarian partridge on the prairies, ruffed grouse and woodcock in the Lake States, Pennsylvania and New England, chukar partridge in the Northwest. The sport is bloodless, fort the pointed birds are not shot. Field trialers are ardent conservationists.

A field trial is also a show a trial dog is a performer, and so is its handler. «Gun dog's a yeoman, trial dog's a showman», the saying goes.

As in baseball, there are levels of the game. The top trials are called the major circuit, about thirty trials held at the same time each year, starting in August on the Northern Prairies, then moving south, with quail trials in December and January in the Deep South, and the finale in mid-February the National Championship at Grand Junction, Tennessee.

The adult dogs on the major circuit are called all-age dogs. Like major-league baseball players, they are world-class athletes. Handled and watched from horseback, they can take your breath away with the speed and grace of their running, the statuesque majesty of their points (bird dogs instinctively freeze - become a statue - when they detect the scent of game birds. This instinctive reaction is called a «point».

Like racecars, all-age dogs perform on the edge - a hair's breadth from out of control, driven by a consuming instinct to find game. And like racecars, trial dogs often suffer «wrecks» when in their exuberance they forget their manners or get away from their handlers.

The dogs compete two at a time, drawn by lot as bracemates. They hunt a prescribed time (usually an hour) over a prescribed course. Huge grounds are required, for the bird dog can hunt through five miles of country in one hour. After all entries have run their braces, the judges declare the winners: a champion and sometimes a runner up-or first, second and third in nonchampionship stakes. Judging in field trials is entirely subjective. The dog that points the most birds is not necessarily named winner. The dog's hunting technique, rather than the quantity of its points, is key. The dog's perfomance is called his «race» - a race to find and point birds.

Before dogs reach full maturity at about age three, the compete in puppy and derby stakes. All stakes are open or amateur, depending on the handler's status (not the dog's - the same dog often runs its owner's direction and in open stakes with its professional handler in charge). Purses are modest - a few hundred to a few thousand dollars.

Clubs sponsor the trials, some as old as the sport. The grounds are quail plantations, state wildlife-management areas, western rangelands. The Northern Prairies are the training and testing ground for the dogs. From mid-July through mid-September, trainers from all over the country work their strings on native game birds in the plains country.

The Triple A league in field trials is called the shooting-dog major circuit. The dogs competing here don't range quite as far all-age dogs, but they are wide-going and splendid athletes too. They are also handled from horseback. Then come on-foot-handler trials, the fastest growing segment, including wild-bird trials in the North on grouse and woodcolk.

How does a dog win in field trial? It must hunt at extreme range with extreme speed, making bold, independent casts for far-off objectives or along edges on the course likely to hold to game birds. When the dog scents birds, it points with lofty

style and awaits discovery by its handler or his assistant, called the scout. The handler then flushes the quarry under scrutiny of mounted judges. As the bird flies to safety, the handler fires a blank.The dog must remain a statue. If the dog will do all this with aplomb, it is called «broke». Being «broke» is a great compliment to the dog, the big distinction between the field-trial dog and the ordinary hunting dog (Hunting dogs are usually just «country broke» - that is, they remain staunch untill the birds fly, but then they chase). Getting a dog «broke» and keeping it so is the daunting task of the handler. The dog points by instinct but it chases flying birds by instinct too. Teaching the dog to subdue the strong chasing instinct is a never-ending challenge.

Field-trial dogs guide the genetics of alle working bird dogs. As with racehorses, a few great sires dominate pointer and setter bloodlines. The lineage of all bird dogs goes back through field-trial winners to a handful of foundation sires from the turn of the last century.

A boy can save enough from a paper route to buy a weanling son or daughter of a National Champion, that makes the sport democratic, at least at the start. Campaigning on the major circuit is beyond the paperboy's reach, but many a great champion has been started by a farm boy. Fans follow the sport through a weekly journal, the American Field, founded in 1874, the oldest sporting magazine in America. The field also maintains the registry for working bird dogs and sanctions open stakes. An umbrella organization, the Amateur Field Trial Clubs of America, sanctions amateur championships and loosely regulates the sport. But the basic rules, set by tradition, have remained unchanged for a hundred twenty years.

The sport is intensely competitive, at alles levels. Participants, open or amateur, approach the games with deadly seriousness; all play to win. Their ultimate quest is the National

Truffle-hunting dogs Coll.Kharbine-Tapabor, Paris

Truffle-Hunting Dogs

The search for truffles—underground mushrooms so rare they are known to some as "black gold"—has traditionally been conducted using various animals with a keen sense of smell, including goats, sheep, pigs and, most recently, dogs, who are the easiest to train and transport. Any breed of dog can be used for this activity after receiving the training necessary for professional truffle hunting (in artificial truffle-beds) or amateur truffle hunting (in natural truffle-beds).

Raising a Truffle-Hunting Dog

In the traditional method of training a dog to hunt truffles, a litter of puppies is selected for this activity even before birth. As soon as they are born, the owner surrounds them with the odor of truffles by brushing truffle juice on the mother's teats and later adding truffle juice to their food at every meal. The dogs soon learn to associate the odor of truffles with eating and will systematically seek out this odor, especially when they have not eaten in some time. Owners must be careful not to add too much truffle juice because it can dull the appetite.

In the "treat" method, the dog is trained to hunt for a treat (such as Swiss cheese or ham) which is buried alongside the truffle. Soon, only the truffle is buried and the treat is given to the dog as a reward for discovering the truffle.

In the "play" method, specifically suited to puppies and young dogs, training is made into a game. A truffle is hidden in a sock or a plastic tube that the owner uses as a toy for his dog. After the dog has developed a strong attachment to the toy, the owner hides it and encourages the dog to find it. When dog discovers the object, thanks the odor of the truffle, he has also found his favorite toy. Soon, the truffle is hidden alone and the toy is given to the dog as a reward for discovering the truffle.

Circus Dogs (1870)
Coll. Kharbine-Tapabor, Paris

Hunting in Natural and Artificial Truffle-Beds

At first, the owner guides his dog on a leash to areas known to be rich in truffles. Soon the dog becomes accustomed to finding these areas himself, first on a leash and then without one.

Mineral Detection Dogs

Dogs were first involved in mineral detection work in 1962 in Finland, where they were used to find sulphurous rocks for prospecting. The same practice has been used successfully in Sweden, the former Soviet Union and Canada.

In other countries, dogs are now used to detect deposits of nickel and copper, even though these minerals are more difficult to find than sulphurous rocks, which emit a strong odor.

Mineral detection dogs are trained using play, the same technique used for training drug and explosives detection dogs. According to reports from eastern and Scandinavian countries, good mineral detection dogs can discover deposits up to fifteen meters underground. If this is true, perhaps dogs will soon be trained to detect gold or diamonds!

Circus Dogs

Nowadays, there are very few circuses and shows featuring dogs. However, this was not always the case, especially in the nineteenth century.

Canine actors made their debut in the streets of large cities, where they performed dressed as humans, standing on their hind legs. They later appeared with troupes of traveling acrobats who used primarily "mongrels", as these dogs were once called.

In 1896 at the Olympia in Paris, Miss Dore presented the first tightrope-walking Poodles. By 1850, people were being entertained by show dogs, including Munito, the famous Poodle who answered questions by choosing cards with letters on them!

From then on, progress was made very quickly and trainers realized that dogs had a lot more to offer in a trusting environment where they were rewarded, rather than frightened. They soon noticed that dogs learned to "ham it up" all by themselves during shows, that they adored applause and that they became sad and despondent when isolated.

Whatever the field, dogs learn well only if they are interested, can have fun and are allowed to work with their owner as a team.

November 3, 1957: preparation of the dog Laïka for the journey on board Sputnik II. She was the first animal in space.

As French author Alain Dupont mentions in his book about dogs, each trainer had his favorites: David Rosaire had his Pekingese, the Ybès had their Tenerife Dogs, Barbara Hochegger had her Borzois, Ewa Oppeltowa had Collies, Fredy Knie Jr. had Fox Terriers and Gabriella had a group of various breeds (Saint Bernards, Greyhounds, Pinschers, Papillons, Spitz, Afghans and Fox Terriers). The Fischers had a German Shepherd jockey, Lupescu Schoberto had soccer-playing dogs, Philippe Gruss had a canine tramp called Max, Old Regnas had acting dogs, the Palacys featured canine trapeze artists and Eric Baddington presented tightrope-walking dogs. Meanwhile, show dogs became increasingly popular. Most spectators were unaware that these dogs' mathematical skill and predictions were nothing but clever tricks.

It is important to realize that nineteenth-century dog "training" methods were rarely based on any knowledge of canine psychology and behavior. Cruel methods including force, brutality and even starvation were used to frighten poor animals into exhibiting a certain behavior.

In London in 1929, these conditions led to the establishment of the Jack London Club, which aimed to eliminate any show or exhibit using animals, especially dogs.

Bruxelles. — Laitières.

TEACH YOUR DOG TO COUNT!

Alain Dupont, a well-known French dog fancier, created this relatively simple method for training dogs to count.

Most importantly, you must be able to make your dog bark by making a specific gesture that looks insignificant but is actually a command to the dog. To do this, the next time you give your dog a treat or a meal, raise your hand while giving the command to bark. As soon as he barks, reward him and lower your hand, with your palm toward him, while giving the command to stop. Soon, you'll be able to make him bark by simply raising your arm (as when you fix his collar) and stop his barking by lowering your arm. Then, the next time you have company, you can casually ask them to give your dog a simple math problem (addition or subtraction). Ask the dog the question and discreetly raise your arm, causing him to bark. When he has barked a number of times equivalent to the answer to the problem, discreetly lower your arm to stop his barking. Now, all you have to do is reward him. Just remember that in order for this trick to work, you must know how to count!

TO COME

2002

Tome 2

Breeds : Group 3, 4 & 5

Group 3
Airedale Terrier
American Staffordshire Terrier
Australian Terrier
Bedlington Terrier
Border Terrier
Brazilian Terrier
Bull Terrier
Cairn Terrier
Czesky Terrier
Dandie Dinmont Terrier
Fox Terrier
German Hunt Terrier
Glen of Imaal Terrier
Irish Terrier
Jack Russell Terrier
Japanese Terrier
Kerry Blue Terrier
Lakeland Terrier

Manchester Terrier
Norfolk Terrier
Norwich Terrier
Scottish Terrier
Sealhyham Terrier
Silky Terrier
Skye Terrier
Soft-Coated Wheaten Terrier
Staffordshire Bull Terrier
Toy Manchester Terrier
Welsh Terrier
West Highland White Terrier

Group 4

Dachschund

Group 5

Ainu Dog
Akita
Alaskan Malamute
Basenji
Canaan Dog
Chow Chow
Eurasian
Finnish Lapphund
Finnish Spitz
German Spitz
Greenland Dog
Iceland Dog
Japanese Spitz
Kai Dog
Karelian Bear Dog
Kishu
Korean Jindo Dog

Laika
Lapland Reindeer Dog
Lundehund
Norbottenspets
Norwegian Buhund
Norwegian Elkhound
Samoyed
Shiba Inu
Siberian Husky
Swedish Elkhound
Swedish Lapphund
Swedish Vallhund
Volpino italiano

The Dog and His Owner

Dog Behavior and Training
Man - a Dog's Best Friend
Dogs in Everyday Life

Know Your Dog

Canine Morphology
Canine Physiology

Tome 3

Breeds : Group 6

Dogs in Sports and Recreation
Dog Shows, Sport and Leisure Competitions
Training Canine Athletes

The Stages of a Dog's Life
The Reproductive Stage
The Basics of Genetics
Whelping, Nursing, Weaning
Early Developmental Stages in the Puppy
The Growing Puppy
Maturity Comes Before Old Age

Dog's Nutrition
Basic Nutrition for Dogs
Basic Nutrition: The Maintenance Diet
Adapting Feeding to the Dog's Size and Age
Large Breeds: Nature has not kept up
with selection, so the Food must Compensate
The Eating Habits of Dogs
Mistaken Ideas About Feeding
Commercial or Homemade?

Tome 4

Breeds : Group 7, 8, 9 & 10

Canine Medicine
Preventive Medicine
Dog Diseases

The Setting of the Canine World
The Veterinarian and Related Professions
Raising Dogs
Tips for Outings, Transportingand Traveling with Your Dog
First Aid